JUSTICE FOR MY FATHER

JUSTICE FOR MY FATHER

AUSTIN STACK

eriu

First published in the UK by Eriu
An imprint of Bonnier Books UK

5th Floor, HYLO
103–105 Bunhill Row
London, EC1Y 8LZ

Owned by Bonnier Books
Sveavägen 56, Stockholm, Sweden

X – @eriu_books

⬚ – @eriubooks

Trade Paperback – 978-1-80418-977-1
Ebook – 978-1-80418-978-8

A CIP catalogue of this book is available from the British Library.

Typeset by IDSUK (Data Connection) Ltd
Printed and bound by Clays Ltd, Elcograf S.p.A

1 3 5 7 9 10 8 6 4 2

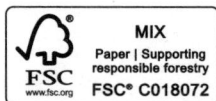

FSC
www.fsc.org

MIX
Paper | Supporting
responsible forestry
FSC® C018072

www.bonnierbooks.co.uk

*For my mother Sheila, and the other widows of the Irish security forces
that the IRA left behind, they suffered the most but gained the least
from the Irish Peace Process. They grieved for their husbands, raised
their families and watched the terrorists go free all at the same time.
These strong women are the real peacemakers in Ireland and
the country owes them a great debt.*

Foreword

by Paul Williams

In every respect of his short life, Brian Stack was a model citizen. He was primarily a devoted husband and the proud father of three young boys. He was also an avid and accomplished sporting enthusiast. In his spare time, he coached his boys and other children in boxing and football at the local clubs in Portlaoise. He was an international amateur boxing referee and a senior GAA referee at county level.

Brian Stack was also a patriotic public servant. In 1959, he joined the Irish Prison Service at a time when Ireland was practically a crime-free country. When the Troubles broke out in Northern Ireland a decade later and then spilled across the border, Brian Stack and his colleagues suddenly found themselves on the front line, alongside the Gardaí and defence forces, in a new war against terrorist-inspired subversion. Portlaoise Prison, where Brian served much of his career, became the State's main holding centre for the growing numbers of IRA and INLA subversives who were awaiting conviction. Following several dramatic escape attempts, the prison was transformed into one of the most secure in Europe – where armed soldiers equipped with anti-aircraft weapons patrolled the roof tops. These were extremely dangerous and challenging times for members of the security services.

Brian Stack loved his job and was highly regarded by everyone who worked with him. In 1983 that dedication was acknowledged by a promotion to the rank of chief prison officer overseeing the Republican prisoners. He had everything to live for. He had a happy family, loved his sports and had a solid career with good prospects for future promotion. On Friday 25th March 1983, Brian left his home with friends to attend the National Senior Boxing Finals in the National Boxing Stadium in Dublin. As the group returned to the car afterwards, Brian Stack was shot in the back of the head by an IRA gunman who was a pillion passenger on a motorbike. He suffered catastrophic injuries and was left paralyzed and brain damaged. He died from his injuries 18 months later, leaving his wife Sheila and their three young boys.

Brian Stack has the distinction of being the only member of the Irish Prison Service murdered in the line of duty during the Troubles. His name is etched beside the name of an Irish soldier, Paddy Kelly and nine members of An Garda Síochana who were also murdered by the Provos during their failed campaign to undermine the Irish State. In all these cases the IRA Army Council – the puppeteers of Sinn Féin – fought against admitting or apologizing for any of these crimes.

Republicans swat their scandals away by complaining that these cases are all in the past and that they should be forgotten. I got the same line countless times from the organised crime bosses I spent my life confronting; they moan about being the victims of a conspiracy by the media and the establishment. Republican terrorists share many characteristics with organized crime. In the cult-like universe where reality is reversed, everything the IRA did during the Troubles, no matter how heinous or savage, is justified by Provo apologists because the killers and maimers were 'fighting for the cause'.

This book reminds us why we must continue to call out the hypocrisy and mendacity of Sinn Féin which would prefer that this story was forgotten. It is worth remembering that the IRA were responsible for killing just over half of all those who died during the Troubles. Within that tragic body count are the names of all those like Brian Stack that the Provos want buried and forgotten.

Austin Stack was just fourteen when his father died. He later joined the prison service from which he retired as an assistant governor in 2024. He never allowed his father's murder to be forgotten. Over the decades, often to the chagrin of his employers in the Department of Justice and at much risk to his own psychological and physical wellbeing, Austin Stack relentlessly pursued the truth about his father's murder in a bid to bring the killers to justice.

This timely book tells the gripping inside story of that often perilous and lonely journey in pursuit of answers from the IRA and their political masters. Austin tells one particularly spine-tingling story of how he and his brother, accompanied by Gerry Adams, were taken in a van with blacked-out windows deep into South Armagh – IRA Bandit Country – to meet the Provos face-to-face. Austin later publicly confronted Adams at a press conference and accused him of reneging on promises to help the family get justice.

In many ways *Justice for My Father* provides a chilling insight into the Republican movement's collective cognitive dissonance and strictly imposed silence about past crimes because, one can reasonably assume, they are too ashamed and know it will never wash with a more discerning electorate. They will never give up the killers and psychopaths that the shadowy armchair generals sent out to do their dirty work. Denials, half-truths, obfuscation, diversionary tactics and whooping big lies are the key weapons deployed by the spin doctors of the Army Council when it wants to kill the truth.

The Republican movement specializes in smearing people's names, especially those of innocent victims, by posthumously accusing them of some perceived "crime". It is central to their damage limiting public relations modus operandi. Austin describes how Sinn Féin tried to thwart his campaign at every turn and even publicly smeared his father's name. His campaign means that he is constantly trolled by their army of anonymous online bots.

It is all part of a well-worn strategy to confuse, distract and draw attention to the next shiny object. Any self-respecting, 'normal' political party would never countenance such behaviour but Sinn Féin, as we have found out on innumerable occasions, are not a normal political party. In an authorized biography about convicted IRA gun smuggler and retired Sinn Féin TD Martin Ferris, it was effectively suggested that Brian Stack had been a bully in prison who got what was coming to him. Former Sinn Féin senator Maire Devine was suspended by the party in 2018 after re-tweeting a claim that he was a 'sadist'. In November 2024 Devine was elected a TD for the party who had clearly forgiven her.

However, some years ago Gerry Adams contradicted his comrades when he informed Austin that his father's work as a prison officer had never been mentioned or complained about in Provo circles. Which begs the question: if Adams knows so much why could he not at least explain the motive for the murder?

Though the IRA bear primary responsibility for the murder of Brian Stack, the State does not come out of this well either. A cold case review conducted because of Austin Stack's perseverance found major failings in the subsequent investigation of the murder. Key witnesses were not interviewed, material evidence went missing and critical intelligence was not acted upon which could have identified the gunman. In 2019, Garda Commissioner Drew Harris personally apologized to the Stack family for the "failings and shortcomings in the investigation".

The State has a duty to protect all its citizens but there is an added imperative when it comes to investigating the murder of a member of the security services in the street. This did not happen in this case. One of the many questions that this gripping book leaves the reader with is: why were senior officers so reluctant to investigate the murder properly? Why was it not given the priority that it deserved? After all, this was a cold-blooded attack on an unarmed off-duty member of the Irish security services and represented an attack on the State.

Brian Stack was murdered by self-styled Irish patriots who were nothing more than cowards. Their victim was the patriot – a servant of the public who was neither an oppressor nor an occupier. This book is a must read for anyone who has interest in Irish politics. It is a powerful account of a loving son's long quest for justice and his determination to put the record straight.

– Paul Williams

Prologue

The most important gift my dad ever gave me was his love. I felt it from the moment I was born in Portlaoise Hospital in August 1968. My 1970s childhood was full of love, with Dad ferrying me and my brothers to GAA (Gaelic Athletic Association) matches and boxing fights. He used every opportunity he could to teach us about life: about how to tell the difference between right and wrong; and about the importance of loyalty, decency, and pride of place.

My father's life, like so many lives during the Troubles, was cruelly cut short by an organisation which called themselves Irish patriots, but, in reality, they inflicted more pain and hurt on Irish families like my own than any other.

I want to set the record straight about him. I do so as every time I raise my dad's case in an attempt to get answers and justice for him, it is met with an onslaught of naked character assassination. This for the most part is carried out by anonymous trolls on social media who are supportive of Sinn Féin and the IRA. However, there are also instances where Sinn Féin members and public representatives have indulged in this behaviour. The tactic is a simple one: blacken the name of a man murdered by those they support in an attempt to justify the murder and to deflect attention away from the very real questions that I pose in relation to it. I know who my dad was, I know the values he held and I know what he stood for. I also know that there is not one single piece of evidence that supports these attempts at character assassination.

My father did his job in very tough and trying circumstances, at a time when Ireland required people like him to stand firm in the face of unrelenting terror. The Peace Process that emerged at the end of the Troubles left many cases unsolved. The victims and families of the bereaved were just expected to get on with life, not ask any questions and remain quietly in the background. Secret amnesties and on-the-run letters for IRA terrorists were insisted upon by Sinn Féin when negotiating the Good Friday Agreement. These were readily agreed to by both the Irish and British governments in their bid to deliver peace and end violence. Peace may have been delivered but justice and truth was ignored. My dad deserves better from the State he served so loyally.

PART 1:

BEFORE THE STORM

Chapter 1

Portlaoise was always known as the 'prison town'. You couldn't miss the hulking presence of Portlaoise Prison – it dominated the Dublin Road with its imposing walls and castle-like appearance. The British built the first prison in what was then known as Maryborough in Queen's County in 1830, following agrarian agitation.

Maryborough Gaol became Portlaoise Prison in 1929. It was the biggest employer in the town; lots of local businesses survived by providing services to the prison. Either you were a prison officer, you married a prison officer, you were the child of a prison officer, or you knew someone who worked there. The work of a prison officer could be tedious, with unsociable hours and, as my father found to his ultimate cost, dangerous. But it was also a job that was steady and pensionable, and it brought with it a certain status in our town.

Apart from being known for the prison, Portlaoise was the 'crossroads of Ireland'. Before the bypass was built in 1997 and the M7 motorway built, everybody travelling by road from Dublin to either Cork or Limerick drove through the town. Commercial travellers, farmers, showbands, GAA county supporters, passengers on the bus travelling from work in Dublin down home to the country at weekends all passed our doors.

My dad was born in Portlaoise on 18 October 1935 as the second youngest of 10 children and was christened Bernard after his father, who was Bernard (Barney) Stack. Barney Stack was born in Chicago, USA, but returned to Ireland as a very young boy with his mother, brother and sister following the death of his father. Barney was raised in Dundalk, Co. Louth, where his mother's people were well-known local business people. Coming from what would be described as a fairly comfortable background at the time, Barney, who was quite artistic, was able to study to become an architect.

In time he would marry my grandmother, Josephine Madden, a Tipperary woman from Mullinahone who came from a family steeped in Irish republicanism. She was related to Robert Emmet's fiancée, Sarah Curran, a tragic heroine in Irish history who stood by Emmet after he was executed for fomenting a doomed rebellion against the Crown in 1803.

My grandmother was born in 1889 and witnessed her family being evicted from their land during the Land Wars of that period. This left a huge mark on her and informed her political thinking thereafter. She and my grandfather settled in Portlaoise where he became the engineer to the Laois county board of health, a good job as he was the main inspector of public housing in the county. This was a job with a considerable amount of status in rural Ireland at the time.

Initially my grandparents were quite prosperous and lived in a large house in Togher, a which was just outside the town. They were one of only a handful of people in the area who owned a car. However, my grandparents' marriage broke down in the main due to Barney Stack's drinking, and he left the family home. My father was four at the time of the separation and it meant a huge change in circumstances for him and the rest of the family. The big house in the country went and the family moved into a smaller one owned by the Catholic Church on the Stradbally Road. My dad's older brothers, Jim and John, went to England to work and sent money home to help raise the younger family members.

My dad's eldest sister, Mary, also contributed. She cut a deal with the Medical Mission Sisters to train and work as a nurse until the younger children were finished school, when she would join the religious order as a nun.

Coming from a separated family in 1930s Ireland, where couples were expected to stay together for better or worse, involved a huge stigma – they had made their bed and were expected to lie in it. Having to rely on Church help for a home meant my dad didn't have a whole lot growing up, and he and his brother George encountered quite a bit of bullying.

This led the two Stack boys to the local Portlaoise Boxing Club, which was located in the Garda Barracks and run by a famous local garda sergeant called Billy Blackwell. The brothers became quite handy with their fists, especially George, and my dad was fond of telling stories about how they managed to keep the local bullies at bay with their new-found skills.

My dad carrying the name of his father was too painful for my grandmother, so she decided to abandon 'Bernard' and start calling him 'Brian'. My father attended St Mary's Christian Brothers for primary and secondary school, and once he did his Leaving Certificate he worked locally in one of many factories that had sprung up in Portlaoise during the 1950s. Then in August 1959, at 23 years of age, he joined the Prison Service.

At the time there was only a handful of prisons in Ireland, as these were the days before drugs and organised crime gangs, and the Troubles in Northern Ireland where still a decade away. Ireland was a relatively new State at the time, not yet 40 years in existence, and as they were expensive to run and housed few prisoners, there was a policy to close all the local county prisons. This left three prisons in Dublin and one each in Cork, Limerick and Portlaoise.

My dad was a very intelligent individual, but he missed out on the opportunity to attend third-level education, more than likely due to the poor financial circumstances of his family. Therefore, joining the Prison Service with its good pay, guaranteed pension and opportunities for promotion was probably the smartest move a young man like him from Portlaoise could make.

In those days, all young men who were accepted into the Prison Service had to report to Mountjoy Prison in Dublin, where they signed various documents such as the Official Secrets Acts, their acceptance of the terms and conditions of their employment, and the protocols involved in being an agent of the state. They would then have been brought to the officers' uniforms stores and issued with their first set uniform, which remarkably hadn't changed by the time I joined the service 32 years later.

Now having a uniform, the new officers would be assigned to Mountjoy Prison and they basically trained on the job. So, in August 1959, Dad left Portlaoise, left his friends and GAA colleagues for Dublin and Mountjoy Prison where he would spend the first few years of his service.

While I don't have much information on those few years he spent in Dublin, I do recall shortly after his death finding a Dublin Senior Hurling Championship medal, which I seem to remember was with a club called New Irelands that are now defunct. Whatever else he was going to do in Dublin, he certainly wasn't going to let his love of hurling lapse while he was there.

Returning to Portlaoise was always on the cards for Dad, and in 1961 he got a transfer back to Portlaoise Prison. At the time promotions in the Prison Service were few and far between, but my dad, being an ambitious man, always wanted to reach the top in the job.

For now he had to learn his craft, and in his free time he devoted most of his energies to his beloved GAA.

It was around this time that he started to mentor and train the juvenile teams in the Portlaoise GAA club and started to referee matches. Becoming a referee was something that suited him as he was very fair and was well able to control even the most challenging of games. He would become well known throughout the 1960s as an inter-county referee, and he took charge of many top-level games, including four Leinster Senior Championship Gaelic football finals. Those who knew him at the time will tell you that on his weekends off he was always travelling somewhere to referee a game. This became a bone of contention with my mother in their early married life, and he eventually chose to give it up and spend time with his young kids instead. I was probably about two years of age at this point, so I never actually got to see him referee a GAA match.

During this period, he was also to the fore in trying to re-establish the game of hurling within the town and in 1965 he was full-back on the Portlaoise team that captured the county junior championship. This was the first piece of hurling silverware that a Portlaoise hurling team had won in decades. While it would take another 16 years for Portlaoise to win a senior championship, he always believed that this was the foundation stone of that success and that it put hurling back on the map in the town.

It was about 1965 that Dad first met my mother, Sheila Donoghue, at a local dance. My mother's family ran Donoghue's, a well-known pub in Market Square in Portlaoise, where my grandfather, Danny, was an extremely well-liked host. He had taken over the bar in 1946 having served his apprenticeship as a grocer in the town. It was close to the Electricity Supply Board (ESB) district headquarters in Portlaoise, which was the other major employer in the town, and so it became known as the 'ESB pub'.

Due to its location and the popularity of my grandfather, the pub captured a lot of passing traffic, from GAA supporters travelling home from Dublin to bands such as the Dubliners (who never passed the door without calling in) and horse-racing enthusiasts and officials. Indeed, I remember one occasion when I was about four or five that the Dubliners called shortly after the pub opened, probably on their way home from a gig down the country. My grandfather was down in the store bringing up bottles to restock the shelves, and I wandered in behind the counter. I got an awful shock when Barney McKenna with a full beard and long hair peered over the counter and growled, 'Where's your grandad, sonny?'

My maternal grandfather Danny and my grandmother Margaret (née Phelan) had both come from the rural area just outside Portlaoise, and like my father's family they were strong de Valera supporters – these things mattered at the time. However, most of the farming people who would have gone into the pub when in town and particularly on Fair Day were not too keen to see my grandfather allowing his daughter go out with a lad from the town. Lads from the town were considered a bit rough around the edges by rural folk, and there was also the big GAA rivalry between the country and the town teams. But my grandfather got on really well with my dad and he loved the banter all that would have created. My mother was working as a secretary for a local Motor Factors, Bradshaw's, at the time and they became engaged.

Around this time Dad wanted to reach out to his father, whom he never knew. By this stage Barney Stack was living in a nursing home in Newry, Co. Down, and his family in Dundalk were looking after him. In an effort to get to know him and try to mend some bridges, Dad would travel to Newry once a week in the year before he got married to see his father. This also turned out to be the last year of Barney's life, and while Dad was glad that he had managed to take this step, he could never tell his mother that he was going up to Newry to see his father as it would have been seen as a betrayal. This showed the type of man Dad was: he was never afraid to make the first move or take the first step towards a reconciliation, even one as painful as this.

Dad and Mam got married in September 1967, at the ages of 31 and 23 respectively, and went on honeymoon in Jersey. When they came home, they moved into a new bungalow they had built on the Mountrath Road, which was on the outskirts of the town. This was a lovely three-bed house bult on half an acre, which they subsequently extended to six bedrooms so that my mother could run a bed and breakfast business. However, I know my mother found the initial transition from living over a busy pub to a quiet house difficult at first, especially when Dad was working nights and before I came along. It really was a huge change for her.

I was born in August 1968, Kieran in November 1969, and Oliver in January 1971, so the quiet life didn't last long for my mother, who by this stage had given up work outside the home in order to raise her young family. My dad was very proud of his family and the life he had created for all of us. He was, however, very much a man of his time, and he felt that it was his job to provide for the family, so every Thursday he handed over his pay cheque to my mother, who ran the family finances. She would give Dad pocket money, so to speak, which he would use to buy the daily newspaper and a few pints if he went to my grandfather's pub on a Saturday night. Dad was not somebody who drank much given his family history, usually two pints if he was out, but I can still see the pleasure he got from having a bottle of Guinness and a cigar if there was a big match on the TV.

In 1973 I was five and in my second year at primary school when Dad got his first promotion to Assistant Chief Officer. The ranking structure of the Prison Service then was broadly still the same as it is today: each prison would have had a Governor, Deputy Governor, Assistant Governor, Chief Officer 1 (larger prisons), Chief Officer 2, Assistant Chief Officer (there would have been a few in each prison) and Prison Officer. So Assistant Chief Officer would have been the first leg on the promotional ladder.

When this promotion was offered to him for Cork Prison, he didn't have much choice but to take it if he wanted to progress in the job. Not knowing how long it would take for him to get back to Portlaoise, my parents decided to move the family to Cork. Initially he would have stayed in staff accommodation while we tried to secure a house in the area.

My mother tells a great story from this time about taking me on the train to Cork to collect the family car after my dad had moved some of his personal belongings to Cork. Seemingly I was running up and down the train carriage as an excited five-year-old would do on his first train journey, when a man who was sitting opposite my mother stopped me and asked where I was going. My response left my mother mortified as I told the man that I was 'going to see my daddy in his new prison'. My mother says that for the rest of the journey she was getting sympathetic looks from the man.

Shortly after moving, my parents bought a house that was being built in a new estate in Cloghroe, which was near Blarney just outside Cork City. This was going to be a big change for myself and my brother Kieran, as we had already started school and had begun to make lots of friends in Portlaoise. We went from a large primary school in a town to a much smaller one in a country village where everybody saw us as outsiders, and they all spoke with heavy Cork accents, which took us a while to figure out.

It was while he was working in Cork that I became more aware of what Dad did for a living, and sometime around 1975, when I was seven years old, he brought myself and my brothers into the prison in Cork and showed us a prisoner's cell. I can remember seeing the prisoners playing football when I looked out the cell window.

I think he did that to take the mystery out of his job for us, but little did I know it would be another 16 years before I'd see the inside of a prisoner's cell again. We were to spend only three years in Cork, but in those few years my brothers and I were beginning to become more aware of the world around us, especially sport and politics thanks to the influence of Dad.

My dad was very heavily influenced by his mother, particularly in matters of politics and faith. During the War of Independence, she became one of Éamon de Valera's biggest supporters and followed him and the anti-Treaty side in the subsequent Civil War. When de Valera founded the political party Fianna Fáil, she became a diehard party member and indoctrinated my young dad in all things republican.

But my dad wasn't one to be easily led, and while my grandmother influenced his thinking, growing up I could clearly see that he had done his own research. Our house had a built-in book case that ran the length of the sitting room, and it was full of books on Wolfe Tone, Robert Emmet, the United Irishmen, de Valera, Michael Collins and many others. For an inquisitive young fella like me who loved history, this stuff was a treasure trove and I spent many hours going through those books, just like my dad had done. My parents, at the instigation of my Granny Stack, named me Austin after Austin Stack, a close comrade of Éamon de Valera and an All-Ireland winning captain.

When I was a young boy, my dad explained his thoughts and ideas around Irish politics and, in particular, republicanism. His views were very much based on pure republican values – he believed in democracy that derived from the people, and the will of the people was to be respected at all times. Fianna Fáil was founded out of the anti-Treaty split which followed the Civil War. It initially opposed the new State, but took its seats in Dáil Éireann in 1927 and entered government in 1932. Fianna Fáil sought to build up the State for the good of its people. The party believed in the unification of Ireland by peaceful means, as did my father. He never believed the Provisional IRA, nor its political surrogate Provisional Sinn Féin, had a mandate to do what they did during the Troubles.

He used to teach us about the founding of Irish republicanism, that most of the original founders were from the various Protestant faiths, and republicanism in Ireland was meant to be something that brought all faiths and classes of people together. He didn't just teach these things, he actually lived them as well – he was always trying to better the lives of young people in the community and those he worked with.

This real and genuine interest in his community led him to join the Fianna Fáil political party as a young man, as it was the party of Éamon de Valera, and he felt it was the one organisation that was best suited to representing people from all classes and creeds. He was very active in the late 1960s and early 1970s as the secretary of the James McIntosh Cumann (branch) in Portlaoise and as the local Director of Elections.

One of my earliest memories is of going into the Fianna Fáil election office in Portlaoise during the 1973 General Election to help pack envelopes with election material. Around this time, a political opponent of Fianna Fáil reported him to his work, as prison officers were not supposed to be actively involved in politics, so he had to take a step back shortly after the 1973 General Election.

Jack Lynch, who was a leader of Fianna Fáil, was from Cork. He had been Taoiseach until the 1973 General Election and he was still very popular, especially in his home county. Lynch used to regularly hold meetings outside the Church in Cloghroe after

Sunday Mass as a way of meeting the public. Dad used to wait with us for these meetings and tell us all about Lynch, whom he admired greatly: 'Jack Lynch won five All-Ireland Hurling Finals and one All-Ireland Football Final. Can you imagine? He did all that before becoming the Taoiseach! He's done great things for this country, lads.'

Jack Lynch was Taoiseach when the Troubles broke out in the North in August 1969. At the time there was a clamour to send Irish soldiers into the Bogside of Derry, where riots had broken out and local nationalists were being batoned off the street by the Royal Ulster Constabulary (RUC). It was a fraught time; emotions ran high. Many hoped Lynch would intervene, but the poorly equipped Irish Army would have been slaughtered. The rest of his two terms as Taoiseach would be dominated by the Troubles.

Dad really admired how Lynch had stayed calm in the face of pressure to send Irish troops into the North at the outbreak of the Troubles. In 1970 Lynch fired two cabinet ministers, Charles Haughey and Neil Blaney, under questionable circumstances as a result of the so-called Arms Trials and the alleged attempt by members of the cabinet to smuggle weaponry into Ireland to give to nationalists in the North.

Listening to Dad talking about Lynch both as a politician and a sports man in such glowing terms made me begin to take a keen interest in both. It was around this time that Dad would routinely come home from work, tog off into a jersey and shorts, and bring us all out the back to show us the skills of hurling. He would play for several hours with us in what was probably a release from work pressures, but also as a way of bonding with his sons.

By 1976, Dad had been acting as Chief Officer in Cork Prison for nearly a year and was enjoying the extra responsibility. But on Christmas Eve that year, the promotional panel came out and he didn't get the job. He always put this down to political interference as there had been a Fine Gael and Labour Party coalition government in power since 1973 and Dad was, of course, a Fianna Fáil man.

To make matters worse, he was also transferred to Limerick Prison. I can recall him being annoyed by what had happened, but he just had to keep his head down, work hard, and wait for the next promotional competition.

As Limerick was closer to Portlaoise, my parents made a decision to move the family back to the town and we returned to our former home. Dad spent that year living in the staff quarters in Limerick and travelling home at weekends. The one thing that always stays with me from that period is it was the first time Dad wasn't around for my birthday. He posted me a lovely card and a present of a leather belt, which I kept for years afterwards.

Dad always described Limerick Prison as a great place to work and he was fond of the staff there. He really enjoyed his time there but home was calling, so he got a transfer back to Portlaoise Prison in 1978.

We were really happy to have Dad home with us in Portlaoise. As young fellas who were sports mad, it was great having a dad who spent so much time bringing us to the games, and the bond created during those days was special. The '70s and '80s were great times if you were a supporter of Portlaoise GAA Club. The town won the Leinster Senior Football title in 1971 and again in 1976. So, on most Sundays during the club football season, we were put in the car and driven by Dad to wherever they were playing. He would get us close to the sideline and he would be nearly kicking every ball with the team and shouting encouragement.

In 1979, Portlaoise reached another Leinster Final and by this time Dad had gotten the club to make my brother Oliver the mascot. Everywhere the team went, we all went, but now we had great access to the changing rooms and players as Oliver had to tog off with the team.

The town lost the 1979 final narrowly to a Walsh Island team from Offaly, which included some of the famous Connor family. They came back in 1981 for another go at the Leinster title but again came up short in the final against Raheens from Kildare.

Dad still believed that this group of players would win the big one, and so in 1982 we set off again every Sunday – first around the football grounds in Laois. Then, after the county championship had been secured, we followed the team on their various stops en route to the Leinster Final in Croke Park where, finally, Portlaoise lifted their third Leinster crown by beating Ballymun Kickhams from Dublin.

The summer of 1982 was also special for me as I was starting on the Portlaoise U-14 team; the previous year I had been a panel member when we claimed the U-14 county title, and now I was a starter and Dad made sure never to miss a game. And, as a former inter-county referee, he was asked to officiate at some of our challenge games. As I was playing either as full-forward or corner-forward, he would often spend time in the back garden showing me how to play both positions and encouraging me to put what I had learned into practice.

In the spring of 1982, I began to have difficulties with my Irish teacher in school. He was one of these Irish zealots who thought that all the kids should have the same enthusiasm for the language as he did. I became the subject of this horrible behaviour when I couldn't memorise an Irish poem. One morning he brought me up to the front of the class to recite a poem called 'M'asal Beag Dubh' (My Little Black Donkey). I began, nervously, and within a couple of lines, I fluffed my words.

'Ah, Stack the fool is at it again,' the teacher mocked. 'As punishment, you are going to act out the role of the donkey. That way you'll remember your lines in future and never make this mistake again! Now, walk donkey, walk,' he laughed as he made me crawl around the classroom on all fours with the other kids' schoolbags tied to my back. 'Class, you have to play your part too. You must kick and push the donkey, like in the poem.' The other children did as ordered.

This was a traumatic experience and one I will never forget, but bad as it was, I didn't tell my parents. In those days, you didn't 'tattle' on your teacher, it just wasn't the done thing. About a month later, my dad was told about the incident by his sister, as my cousin was in the class and he had told my aunt what happened. When Dad questioned me about it, I told him everything and he couldn't believe it. He told me that I was not to act out any more roles in class and that he was going to speak to the teacher.

That evening, my dad came home from work early and let me know that the teacher was calling to the house on his way home. When he called, they went into our front room and were there for ages before I was called in. The teacher was sitting in an armchair opposite my dad with his legs crossed, smoking a pipe. My dad asked me to recount what had happened and as I was doing so, he just kept smiling and smoking his pipe. When I had finished, he took a long look at me, took a puff of his pipe and declared, 'That simply never happened.'

'Austin is telling the truth,' Dad barked at the teacher. 'I know he is telling the truth because I had to hear about this incident from another parent, before asking Austin what had happened. So he is telling the truth. Austin will not be acting out any more roles in your class. Now, please, leave my home.'

A few weeks passed without incident but then I was again asked to act out a role. 'No, you are aware of what my dad told me to do if you asked me to act,' I replied. 'Stack went home and told tales from this class,' he said menacingly to the other children. For my rebuttal, I was suspended for the last two weeks of the school year, so my parents decided to move myself and my brother Kieran to a different school.

The matter didn't end there though, as the boxing club had been using the hall in the Christian Brothers' school as its training premises. When the club held its AGM that summer, the head Christian Brothers sent word to the meeting that if my dad was involved with the club, they wouldn't be allowed to use the hall. My dad, being the type of man that he was, immediately resigned as he felt that the club was bigger than him and wanted it to succeed. The other committee members and coaches, apart from one man, also resigned in support of my dad. This was the esteem in which he was held by the others, and they formed a separate boxing club in the town. This new club became the dominant one and is now a renowned boxing academy.

This incident has stayed with me my whole life. My dad stood up for me and for what he believed was right, and he was prepared to sacrifice something that meant a lot to him to defend that. That's why I will never back away from defending what I believe is right, never allow myself to be bullied, and I will always fight for justice for my dad.

Chapter 2

During the early part of the Troubles, terrorists from the Provisional IRA split from the Official IRA, becoming the dominant version of the organisation, and concentrated their actions mostly within Northern Ireland. However, they slowly began using the Republic of Ireland as a base due to the border between Northern Ireland and the Republic offering a natural protection to them. On the southern side of the border, they found many sympathisers willing to offer a safe house in the immediate border counties, which were often used to launch attacks on isolated Protestant farmers who worked small holdings along the border. I had read that their idea was to 'ethnically cleanse' the border region of Protestant farmers by assassinating the sons of these farmers so the land could not be passed on. They wanted to create what they termed 'Green Zones' along the border.

There had been reports that the IRA had also moved into other criminal activity to fund their cause. Weapons and explosives were expensive, and while Irish Americans were often targeted as a means to fund these purchases in the Irish bars of Boston and New York, they needed a much more regular source of income and so they carried out bank robberies, took over dealing drugs in working-class areas, and operated protection rackets, especially in Dublin.

The number of armed robberies in the State spiked after the beginning of the Troubles, increasing from 17 in 1970 to 132 in 1972. The IRA never admitted to these robberies, but An Garda Síochána had no doubt who was responsible.

Initially, the Gardaí were ill-prepared and ill-equipped to deal with this new terror menace. After the Civil War ended in May 1923, Ireland became a relatively quiet country with low levels of crime. In fact, the State had closed many of the prisons that had been built by the British as we just didn't need them. While the vast majority of the Gardaí were committed to eradicating this new terror threat, they needed resources, equipment and training for this new type of policing.

The Irish government reintroduced the non-jury Special Criminal Court in 1972 to handle trials for those accused of Troubles-related offences to counteract the likelihood of witness intimidation in these cases. The IRA and other paramilitary groups were very good at getting to witnesses, and several cases collapsed due to the pressure that was being put on members of the public who were due to give evidence against the terrorists.

Another measure that the State took was to accept the word of a Garda Chief Superintendent that a person was a member of an illegal organisation. The only evidence required to convict a person of IRA membership was if a Garda Chief Superintendent gave sworn evidence in the Special Criminal Court that he/she believed that the accused was a member of the IRA. In these early stages, those convicted in the Special Criminal Court were mostly affiliated with the IRA and were sent to serve their time to Dublin's Mountjoy Prison, where they were housed on the D wing.

Following these measures, the State had some initial success against the IRA, and the D wing in Mountjoy was populated with some very senior figures within that organisation. Losing so many of those in leadership roles was causing a serious problem for the IRA, so they decided they needed to break some of them out of prison in order to maintain the momentum of their campaign. So, on October 31st, 1973, the IRA hijacked a helicopter at Dublin Airport and ordered the pilot to fly to Mountjoy Prison, where it landed in the D wing yard. IRA Chief of Staff, Séamus Twomey, and two other senior terrorists, Kevin Mallon and JB O'Hagan, boarded the helicopter and were lifted out of the prison in what became a major international embarrassment to the Irish government.

As a direct result of this dramatic escape, the Irish State decided it needed a more secure and dedicated prison to accommodate the increasing number of terrorists. They chose Portlaoise Prison. On November 9th, 1973 some 130 republican prisoners were transferred to Portlaoise and the ordinary prisoners in Portlaoise were transferred to Mountjoy. In doing so, they turned Portlaoise Prison into a maximum-security facility and into one of the most secure jails in Europe. There was a no-fly zone around the prison, barbed wire was used extensively, and Irish Army personnel were deployed around the perimeter. Gardaí were placed on segregated landings to deal with the prisoners.

This new security setting was not going to stop the IRA, and during 1974 and 1975 there were several escapes and attempted escapes. An attempt to dig a tunnel out of the prison was foiled in June 1974, but the most famous escape was that of 19 republican prisoners on August 18th, 1974. The prisoners escaped using gelignite, which blew holes in the walls and damaged a door of the prison. As a consequence of that breakout, food parcels to republican prisoners were banned, adding to tensions between prisoners and staff in the jail.

There were riots in Portlaoise town centre between Republicans and Gardaí. Many people in the town wanted an end to Portlaoise's status as the place where republican prisoners were housed, but the government wouldn't contemplate it.

The presence of so many republican prisoners in Portlaoise completely changed the dynamics there and made life very difficult for prison officers and their families.

Fourteen prison offers were taken hostage by Provisional Republicans in December 1974. Prisoners smashed down cell doors, chairs and tables, dismantled beds and barricaded the prison officers into cells on E Block. Six hundred gardaí and Irish soldiers surrounded the building, and they used rubber bullets to free the prison officers.

Prisoners and their families complained about being strip-searched, but there was no alternative. Eight prisoners went on hunger strike in January 1975, lasting for 44 days. In February 1975, a woman tried to smuggle explosives concealed in her vagina into the prison. A month later a number of prisoners tried to blast a hole through a door in the recreation room, which led to the prison yard. Soldiers stationed on the roof of the prison opened fire and IRA prisoner Tom Smith (27) was killed. Explosives were found in May 1975 concealed in the cavity of shoes that were brought into the prison by a visitor.

In June 1976, Gardaí foiled an attempt by the Provisional IRA to kill the then Governor of Portlaoise Prison, William Reilly, with a car bomb. Tensions began to escalate.

Twenty prisoners went on hunger strike in April 1977 over conditions in the jail, but it was called off 47 days later following the intervention of a Catholic bishop. The coalition government of that time made some concessions to restore the prisoners' special category status, but for pragmatic reasons only. Special category status meant that the IRA prisoners had enhanced conditions such as free association, longer unlock times and more visits. The government granted this to ease tensions within the prison.

The then Taoiseach Liam Cosgrave said some people regarded the Portlaoise prisoner officers as 'a lot of babysitters' but that the prisoners 'are in for the most heinous crimes against the people of this country not because they have no lights on their bikes'. They were the leading perpetrators of violence in a campaign in which 'almost 2,000 Irish people have been killed and nearly 10,000 injured'.

There were riots in Portlaoise during this period, which left many republican supporters and gardaí bleeding and unconscious, and people in the town hated the hassle and the unwanted publicity that came with it. Local poet, Pat Boran, wrote *The Invisible Prison*, a memoir of his time growing up in the town. He remembered his father giving a lift to somebody in the 1970s:

The stranger sits in.
'Where you headed?' he says.
My father looks him over again in the creative light.
'Portlaoise,' he says. 'Any good to you?'
'Ah,' says the stranger with the smile, 'where the prison is.'

Boran was right when he said that was all our town was known for when were children.

If you switch on almost any day and hear the name of the town mentioned, you can be sure you've tuned into yet another story of prisoner transfers, mass protests or, now and again, attempted or even successful escapes. As far as the world is concerned, the town and the prison, the prison and the town are one and the same. Portlaoise is where the prison is and little else.

Provisional Sinn Féin, as it was known at the time, used its newspaper, *An Phoblacht*, and a poster campaign to complain about conditions in the prison. My father and the other prison officers had to contend with republican propaganda, which did not take into account the fact that who he and his colleagues were dealing with were not ordinary criminals, but a determined bunch of ideologues who would stop at nothing to escape. Free association between prisoners had to be curtailed as it allowed for escape plans to be hatched. Prisoners complained that they couldn't use the craft workshop, but in reality they barred themselves from it by refusing to be strip-searched as they left.

The prison officers on the inside, including my father, knew they had the support of the majority of the people. Even Tom Barry, the legendary IRA commander responsible for inflicting the worst defeat on the British in the War of Independence, wouldn't support the Portlaoise hunger strikers. Barry's men killed 16 Auxiliaries at Kilmichael in November 1920, but he thought the relentless targeting of civilians by the Provos put them into a different category, saying they were 'losing support from all quarters and they had only themselves to blame'.

By the end of 1977, there were more than 130 republican prisoners in Portlaoise, 82 of whom were Provisional IRA and the rest were various splinter groups. The situation was always fraught. These terrorists considered themselves to be prisoners of war, and therefore believed they had a duty to escape. Some prisoners were serving time for particularly barbaric murders that happened in Northern Ireland and they were convicted under the Criminal Law Jurisdiction Act of 1976, which allowed them to be tried in the Special Criminal Court in Dublin.

There were a large number of these dedicated terrorists who had committed crimes in the Republic. The most infamous of these prisoners was Thomas McMahon, who was serving time for the 1979 assassination of Lord Mountbatten in Mullaghmore, Co. Sligo.

This was a particularly heinous crime in which the elderly royal, a very old lady and two teenage boys were blown up after McMahon had planted a bomb on their boat.

There were prisoners such as Peter Rogers, who had previously escaped from prison in Northern Ireland and fled south. In 1980, he murdered Detective Garda Seamus Quaid in Wexford. Quaid and a colleague had stopped the car in which Rogers was travelling and found explosives following a search. While attempting to detain Rogers he shot Detective Quaid and fled.

Also housed in Portlaoise Prison at this time were the IRA gang that had in 1974 committed the savage murder of Senator Billy Fox as he visited his fiancée. This murder was seen as sectarian, as Fox was a member of the Protestant Church of Ireland faith, as well as an attack on democracy, as he was also a prominent Fine Gael politician.

My father commented several times that the murder of Senator Fox was one of the most barbaric acts of the entire Troubles, and I think he felt that not only was the actual murder a particularly brutal one, but that it was an outrageous attack on democracy.

These republican prisoners were dedicated, ruthless, obsessed and most definitely indoctrinated terrorists. Today many would probably be described as 'radicalised'. They would murder or bomb their way out of the prison if that is what the Army Council of the IRA told them to do.

In the North, the Provisionals routinely killed prison officers. Between the ending of the special category status in 1976, after which republican prisoners were treated as common criminals by the British government, and the beginning of the second hunger strike in March 1981, republican paramilitaries killed 19 prison officers. The Provisional IRA had a rule that they would not attack members of the security forces south of the border, including prison officers, but we knew they would kill if necessary. Just outside Portlaoise in Garryhinch, they killed Garda Michael Clerkin and blinded another garda, Tom Peters, in a booby-trap explosion in October 1976.

By 1978, when Dad took up his tenure at the prison, he knew of the flight risk and the mentality of the prisoners held within its cells. The ever-present threat of a mass jail breakout continued. Relations between prison officers and inmates continued to deteriorate. A month before dad was shot, prison officers found explosives in the Irish National Liberation Army (INLA) section of Portlaoise, concealed behind some timber. Prisoners and their relatives complained about strip-searching, but without it prisoners and their relatives were more likely to smuggle guns, knives or explosives into the prison.

Tensions between staff and prisoners were running high, and this often resulted in the IRA prisoners deciding to riot. I remember one particular night while I was at the swimming pool with Dad and other prisoner officers and their children (prison staff had exclusive access to the swimming pool one night a week). We were all enjoying the evening when the main door of the building came crashing in. Initially everybody thought we were under attack, but a really large prison officer in uniform suddenly appeared at the edge of the pool, shouting that 'all hell has broken loose up there'. With that, all the officers, Dad included, jumped out of the pool and, without drying off, rushed to the prison. I was left sitting in Dad's car outside the prison for a few hours while he and the others restored order.

He was good at his job and I now wonder if that made him a threat. My father would find himself on the front line of the war between the Irish State and its biggest enemy, the Provisional IRA, and it would cost him his life.

Chapter 3

The prison my father returned to in 1978 had been transformed into a fortress. Large metal barriers were positioned outside the prison to prevent the approach of vehicles attempting to ram the walls, there was lots of barbed wire in place, search rooms had been built, and there was a police hut on the footpath outside the prison.

The new security measures also affected the town itself, with the new ESB offices being built with a flat roof in order to accommodate helicopters carrying Irish Army personnel from the Curragh Camp if needed. There was also lots of inconvenience as the Dublin Road would sometimes be blocked off when Sinn Féin organised protests outside the prison, which often turned violent.

In returning to Portlaoise as an Assistant Chief Officer I have been told by former colleagues who worked with Dad and whom I later worked with that he had two functions, one as the Assistant Chief Officer in E Block where the parliamentary prisoners were, and another as a liaison and mentor for new recruits who were sent to Portlaoise as soon as they joined.

When I was a young prison officer working in Saint Patricks Institution for young offenders in Dublin, a colleague who'd worked with Dad in Portlaoise told me: 'Your dad was ACO in the E block and he was on top of everything, he was so security conscious and double checked everything.' He went on to relay a story about why he needed to be so fixated on security:

> In Portlaoise in those days, you didn't know who was on 'our' side and who was on 'their' side. One time your dad as ACO went around and checked the master locks had been applied to the cell doors at final lock-up; he always did it after the officer detailed to master lock had done it. Then a few minutes after the master key had been returned to the key room, I was asked to go back with the master key and give a prisoner something. When I got to his cell, I found the cell door next to him open – this could only have been done by an officer after your dad checked that it had been master locked.

Later, when working in Mountjoy, a female colleague told me that she had been assigned to Portlaoise shortly after joining the job. She spoke of Dad as a caring and lovely man who went out of his way to help a new officer.

> He was the liaison ACO when I was sent to Portlaoise, he couldn't have been more helpful. It was winter and very cold but he made sure I had all my uniform, especially the over-coat, which was going to be needed. He then checked up on me every few days to make sure I was getting on OK and to see if I needed anything.

Both of these stories summed him up, as he was job-focused but also people-focused. Around this time, I recall my father having to work a lot of night duties, as the Assistant Chief Officer was in charge of the prison during the night. He would come home at lunch time and then sleep for the afternoon before going back into the prison.

My poor mother was always trying to keep us quiet, especially if we were playing football in the back garden, so that he would get a good sleep and be ready for night duty.

On December 12th, 1978, Dad was promoted to Chief Officer 2. This was his first step to the role of manager as opposed to supervisor. Having been back in Portlaoise for nearly a year, he had identified certain weaknesses in security and set about correcting the problems as he saw them. This interest in security improvements led to some tensions with his boss, the Chief Officer 1, Ned Harkin, who is reported to have said in response to a change in procedures that my dad had implemented: 'There is only one Chief Officer around here and I shaved him this morning.'

My father had suspicions, as did many in Portlaoise, about Harkin. Harkin was from Portlaoise and spent 40 years working in the prison. He became Governor of Portlaoise Prison after my father was murdered, from 1986 to 1988. Those suspicions surrounded the belief that he was a Provisional IRA sympathiser on the inside of the prison. This would become more apparent to me in the years after my father's death than it did at the time. His name would come up time and again in my later investigations. He passed away in 2010.

While he was dealing with tension and suspicions about the man who was directly above him in the chain of command, Dad was also acutely aware that all the prison officers working in Portlaoise faced similar tensions and suspicions around colleagues and, indeed, friends and neighbours.

Within 11 months, Dad was promoted, on November 6th 1979, to Chief Officer 1. This post was essentially head of security for one of Europe's most secure prisons. His job was to ensure that the hardened and dedicated terrorists did not escape, and he was good at it. He cultivated informants within the IRA and was always one step ahead of them when they were planning escapes. The pressure that he was under was so great that he would never take two weeks' holidays at a time, as he was afraid that the IRA would use his absence to effect an escape.

The prison also housed some ordinary prisoners who were sent to Portlaoise to carry out the degrading work of 'slopping out' the IRA prisoners' toilet waste. At the time there were no toilets in prison cells and a chamber pot was issued to each prisoner, which had to be cleaned out every morning. The IRA prisoners refused to do this, and so ordinary prisoners did this task for them and got 50 per cent remission off their sentences. During my own service I met several of those prisoners and every one of them told me how they had great time for Dad, as he always managed to look after them in one way or another. One prisoner recalled: 'Your dad used to get me out every year for the horse show.'

Dad knew that the job was having an impact on the mental health and home life of everybody who worked inside the walls of the jail. To combat this he encouraged staff to play sports, particularly hurling and Gaelic football, and if an officer wanted time off to play a match my dad would always find a way to accommodate it. In letting staff go off to play matches, he was encouraging physical fitness, but also giving them some much-needed breathing space from the job. Dad also organised quiz nights for the staff, along with starting what would later become a service-wide annual sports day for the prison officers and their families.

Dad had his own way of relieving stress: music. He loved traditional music and he had lots of tapes of the Dubliners, the Clancy Brothers, the Fureys, among others. On holidays in Ireland, those tapes would be loaded into the car cassette player and he would sing along to them as he drove us to our holiday destination. Dad would sing 'Seven Drunken Nights' by the Dubliners, waiting for us to join in from the back of the car.

While on holidays he just lost himself in the moment, and you could see he was a changed man when he got away from Portlaoise for a week. He would also do little things for us that meant a lot at the time, and thinking back on them today, they were thoughtful and special moments.

One of those moments was when he bought me and Oliver a tent. We had been looking for one for a while so we could put it up in the back garden and sleep out at night during the summer, as kids often did at the time. What we didn't know was that Dad had saved some of his 'pocket money' every week so he could buy us a tent. We were so thrilled the day he asked us to go to the shop with him to pick one out. Special things like this made him such a great dad.

Chapter 4

At home, as far back as I can remember, we always had boxing gloves, and Dad taught us how to box in the evenings when he came home from work. Indeed, on a Saturday night the kitchen would be transformed into a ring with chairs as the ropes, and I would spar with my brothers.

Sometime around 1978, a local boxing enthusiast called Peter Ryan decided to start up a new boxing club in the town, and my dad rowed in behind him and took on all the administration work as club secretary. Getting Portlaoise Boxing Club off the ground was difficult, as the club needed equipment and a permanent home. My dad knew that the previous club had been based in the local Garda Station and that there might be some equipment there. But most of it was damaged and beyond repair, except for the ring, which Dad felt could be used to fit the stage in the local Christian Brothers' school where we were training. This was the same club that he would eventually resign from after the incident involving the Irish teacher.

At work, Dad used to get the workshops in the prison to make other equipment, such as punchbags made of canvas and filled with sand, sawdust and old clothing mixed together. He was great at improvising like that to get things done, and while a lot of the established clubs had fancy punchbags bought from all the branded manufacturers, we had prison-made ones that would cut the knuckles off you.

While the GAA season was in the spring and summer, the boxing season was autumn and winter, so we literally went from one activity to the other. Dad took us boxing training on Tuesdays, Thursdays and Saturdays, and when there was a boxing tournament being hosted by another club or if the championships were on, the car would be packed with kids as we went to fight.

'It is so unfair,' complained Dad, as our packed car drove back from another tournament where we had lost a lot of fights. 'We're a new club and that's making us a target. All the established clubs have judges and referees themselves at these tournaments and they're favouring each other.'

'Is that's what's happening? That's so unfair. What will we do?' I asked.

'It'd be better if we had our own judges and referees,' he argued. 'Then we could balance everything out.'

And with that, Dad decided to do the relevant courses to become a boxing official; he became well known on the circuit as a fair referee at tournaments up and down the country. And, as he expected, the boxers in his own club began to get fairer outcomes from the other judges.

I often wondered why Dad became a referee in both boxing and Gaelic football. I believe it reflected his interest in fairness and fair play for all. With us he was always trying to find an angle or a way to improve our chances of success in the ring. My brother Kieran was about average size for his age, so in his weight class there would have been a lot of competition. To create an advantage for him, Dad trained him as a southpaw even though he was naturally right-handed. Southpaws are much more difficult to fight and, as a result, Kieran won the Laois/Kilkenny/Carlow County championships.

Oliver, on the other hand, was above average weight, but still not heavy enough to get into the next weight category where there wouldn't be as many competitors, so Dad came up with a plan to feed him Mars bars in the lead-up to the weigh-in so that he would weigh heavier. The plan worked and Oliver won the County and Leinster championships, and Kieran christened him the Mars Bar Kid.

Dad had a more difficult challenge with me, however, as I had developed a knack of losing split decisions to both good and bad boxers. I think I lost four Laois County championship finals due to split decisions. He was always trying to find the right opponent to fight me so that I could regain my confidence, and when he did eventually find such an opponent, the guy hit me below the belt and was disqualified. It was probably the only way I was going to break the unlucky streak.

On Friday, March 25th, 1983, the National Senior Boxing Finals were being held in the National Boxing Stadium in Dublin. This was the highlight of the year for the amateur boxing calendar, where reputations were made and broken. The arena hummed with activity as the fights took place, starting with the light flyweight contest and ending with the heavyweight contest. It had become a given in our house that Dad would be attending, but Kieran, Oliver and I thought we'd be tagging along too.

'What do you mean we're not going?' Oliver cried. 'Dad, I just won the Leinster title last week, surely it's important that I go!'

'Exactly. And us too. It's a Friday night, so we've no school in the morning,' I argued. 'And we go every year, Dad, why not this year?' Kieran backed us up.

'I'm sorry, lads, it's not my turn to drive, so I don't get a say.' Dad explained how the Boxing Club's committee rotated the drivers to big tournaments in Dublin. 'There's no room in the car. Joe Ging is doing the driving, he's bringing his son Christy, and

Jimmy Sullivan, Tom Timmons and Seamus Fitzgerald. We'll be packed in like sardines!'

That made six in a car built for five. We, as were so many children in the 1970s to 1980s, were used to piling into a car, sitting on each other's knees without seatbelts, and bouncing along potholed roads. Health and Safety wasn't the concern it would later become, but even then there were limits. There obviously wasn't room to take us with them, but that didn't stop us pestering my dad about it all day.

'But Daaaddd!' we complained together.

My mother had already organised for us all to go on a shopping trip to Northern Ireland the following day. At the time there was a huge advantage in going across the border shopping, especially for electrical goods and alcohol. This was due to the advantageous currency exchange rates. On a trip to Newry a few months previous, Granny Donoghue and my mother had bought video recorders, which were only coming onto the market at the time. They told us that the customs officers just walked up and down inside the bus when they were doing a check, but never took anything from people.

'If you don't stop pestering your Dad right now, I'm cancelling the shopping trip,' Mam urged. 'You'll be going to bed early too, so I don't want to hear any more whinging out of the three of you tonight!' When my mother dropped Dad down to Joe Ging's house that evening, we were still annoyed. We weren't going with him and we couldn't do anything about it.

Chapter 5

As I wasn't in the National Boxing Stadium that fateful night, I have pieced together the events using witness statements from the Coroner's Court, media reports and the recollections of Dad's friends.

All the accounts of my dad's movements while he was inside the National Stadium that night suggested a happy man among people he knew, talking about the sport he loved. He spent a large part of the evening walking around talking to other referees, coaches and club officials. It was his way of networking to arrange fights in future tournaments for boxers from Portlaoise. My dad was admired by his fellow boxing officials as many of them respected his ability as an organiser and administrator in his role as secretary of the Portlaoise Boxing Club, and also for his fairness in his role as a judge and referee.

He had never disclosed his job in Portlaoise Prison to fellow boxing administrators, and many commented afterwards that they would never have guessed. He very much kept his work life separate from his home life. That was both a security measure – in early 1980s Ireland you never knew who you were talking to – and a way for him to cut the cord once he left work in the evening. Among his own tribe, he was a boxing referee, a judge and an administrator, not a prison officer.

He had a keen interest in the heavyweight final that night as a boxer called Noel Guiry from Mullinahone in Co. Tipperary was fighting. My grandmother hailed from this part of the country, and my father probably took Noel Guiry under his wing because of this. Guiry had won the Junior National Championship a year previous. Not long before the national finals, Guiry won his first international cap for Ireland and Dad had played a big part in persuading the selectors to pick him for that bout against England.

I can still remember how excited he was that somebody whom he had shown a great interest in and whom he had mentored was on the verge of winning the senior heavyweight title. The heavyweight final was traditionally the last fight of the night at the senior finals. Guiry was fighting against a brilliant young boxer from Enfield in Meath named Seamus McDonagh. It was a close contest. Three of the judges voted for Guiry and two for the Meath man.

When Guiry's hand was raised in victory by the referee, my dad was reportedly delighted and felt vindicated that he had backed him. So, while the rest of the travelling party from Portlaoise went back to the car which Joe Ging had parked on Washington Street, just off the South Circular Road and opposite the National Stadium, my dad decided to go into the dressing room to congratulate Noel Guiry on his victory.

Five minutes of celebrations and back slaps later, Dad rushed onto the South Circular Road, heading for Joe Ging's parked car, where his friends no doubt had much to say about the close fight. There would be more discussion. Waiting eagerly in the car, Joe checked his watch: 10.49 p.m. – they still had time to dine at Joe Wong's before the long drive home. Joe Wong's was on the Naas Road and was one of the best-known Chinese restaurants in Dublin at the time. It was a place we knew well from our visits to Dublin and a treat to stop at on our way back to Portlaoise.

Many heading south from the boxing championships would have the same idea and they would meet there for a thorough review of the night's fights. Failing that, they would stop off at the Talk of the Town chipper in Newbridge – we always looked forward to a bag of chips as a treat and seeing the other boxers there. These stops were the essence of camaraderie in the boxing community and were part and parcel of the day out.

There were several eyewitnesses as to what happened next. One was Corporal Joseph O'Brien, a soldier on sentry duty at the Griffith Army Barracks next to the Boxing Stadium. At approximately 10.30 p.m., he noticed a man standing beside a motor bike between parked cars. The man seemed agitated. Corporal O'Brien thought he might be trying to break into a car. He spoke to another soldier in the vicinity, Trooper Paschal O'Connor, and suggested that the fellow with the white helmet was going to break into a car across the road. When nothing happened, he returned to sentry duty. He would later recall:

At about 10.49 p.m. I heard a sound like a backfire. I was outside my hut near the guardroom and inside the main gate. There was a flash in the darkness. I ran to the gate and I saw a man who appeared to be dressed in completely dark clothes run from Washington Street towards South Circular Road. At the same time I noticed that the motor cycle with the white tank had been driven by the man with the white helmet to the mouth of Washington Street, and this man who was running jumped onto the pillion seat and it sped off towards Leonard's Corner. When I first noticed the man at the motor bike, he was leaning up against a blue car, which was on the footpath. As the bike drove off I got a whiff of cordite. It is the distinct smell which follows the firing of a firearm.

Corporal O'Brien started looking around straight away to see what had happened and he saw my dad lying on the ground. He immediately ran into the guardroom and made an emergency call. He got the switch operator to telephone the Gardaí and told him about a shooting opposite Griffith Barracks on South Circular Road.

Meanwhile, a crowd of startled onlookers emerged when they heard the shots and saw Dad lying on the ground. Three of those where doctors from Belfast who had been on duty at the boxing finals that night. They were brothers John and Martin Donnelly and their friend Eugene Maguire. Being from Belfast, when they heard the sound of gunfire, they knew something bad had happened and immediately ran to assist my dad.

Having initially assessed his injuries, they found the bullet entry wound at the base of Dad's spine. They attempted to get a pulse and heartbeat without success. Dad had gone into cardiac arrest and needed to be resuscitated quickly. They immediately realised the seriousness of the situation and performed an emergency tracheotomy on my dad as he lay on the street. This procedure is a field hospital technique that these doctors would have been familiar with, whereby a hole was cut in the windpipe at the front of my dad's neck to allow the doctor to insert a tube to get air into his lungs.

Their quick action on the street saved my dad's life, and they had managed to get a pulse and heartbeat before an ambulance from the Dublin Fire Brigade arrived at 11.10 p.m. He was taken by the ambulance to Dublin's Meath Hospital which was close by.

Four men who didn't know my dad when the night began had saved him by the end of it. The following day, despite the pain we were going through, I was grateful to hear that strangers had been fighting for him.

PART 2:
PURGATORY

Chapter 6

I was in bed well before the boxing had finished. I had my own room at the front of our house, the driveway running directly towards my bedroom window. The house was built on half an acre and, over the years, Dad and Mam had extended it to have six bedrooms so that my mother could run a B&B business for extra income. On that night, we had no guests.

For some reason, I had an uneasy feeling and I couldn't get to sleep. It was like a sixth sense – I just knew that something wasn't right, but I didn't know what. I spent the first part of the night tossing and turning, and I eventually drifted off to sleep.

It must have been sometime around midnight when all the activity started. I could see cars coming into the driveway, their headlights shining directly into my room. When I sat up in the bed, I could hear people talking in the kitchen. I knew that this was unusual, so I got out of bed and went towards the noise to see what was going on.

When I walked through the kitchen door, the first thing I noticed was a man in a trench coat with his back to me. He was on the telephone in the corner of the kitchen. At first, I didn't recognise him, so I was frightened. It was then that I heard Granny Donoghue speaking; she was talking to me but I had been concentrating on what I thought was a strange man in the corner of the kitchen.

'Austin! Are you listening to me?' Granny whispered, as if not to upset my mother. Granny was a hard-working woman and a real lady. As the eldest grandchild, I always had a very special bond with her and everybody used to comment that I was her favourite. When I was small she revelled in the role of grandmother and used to put myself and my brothers in the car and take off for the day. She'd take us to places such as Newgrange or to visit her relations in the countryside.

After I got my bearings, I saw my granny sitting on the couch beside my mother, who looked distraught. 'Your father is in hospital. He's been hit by a motorbike while crossing the road after the boxing,' she gently explained. 'Your uncle Seamus is on the phone trying to find out more information.'

I couldn't really hear what she was saying until I realised that the man in the trench coat was my uncle. When I looked around, I saw my mother's other brother, Sean, was also in the room, and I instantly knew that this was more serious than Dad being hit by a motorbike.

Even so, I was 14 at the time, and at that age you don't question all the important adults in your life when they tell you what's wrong and insist you go back to bed. So, I went back to my room and experienced one of the longest nights of my life, wondering what had really happened and sensing that it definitely wasn't a motorbike accident. Various things were going through my mind and one of those things was the potential that Dad may have been attacked.

A few months earlier, a retired Chief Officer from Mountjoy Prison, Mick Weldon, had been attacked and beaten up in his bedroom at home by a group called the Prisoners Revenge Group (PRG). The PRG were a group of mostly hardened Dublin-based criminals, and while some of these would have had links to the IRA, they were essentially ordinary criminals with a grudge. After that Dad started to lock his bedroom door at night.

In Ireland at the time, we had two TV stations, RTÉ One and RTÉ Two, and two radio stations, RTÉ Radio 1 and RTÉ Radio 2, and the one place you could be sure of getting information was the hourly news bulletins on the radio. I knew that the radio news bulletins would report an incident like a motorbike knocking down a pedestrian, particularly if it was on a Dublin street, so I automatically turned on my radio, but I was too late. Both radio stations went off air at midnight, so by the time I tuned in they were closed for the night and I had no way of getting any information. It crossed my mind that if Dad had been attacked, the BBC or Radio Luxembourg might carry it on their news bulletins due to the potential connection with Northern Ireland. Having tried both and still not getting any information, I was becoming more and more restless. I just couldn't go to sleep not knowing what really happened, so I stayed awake all night waiting for RTÉ Radio 1 to come back on air.

Even though I had factored in the possibility of an attack on Dad, I wasn't prepared for what I heard when the newscaster read the 7 a.m. news bulletin: 'In breaking news, a man is in critical condition in the Meath Hospital after being shot last night outside the National Boxing Stadium on the South Circular Road in Dublin. Brian Stack, who is the Chief Prison Officer of Portlaoise Prison, was shot by a masked gunman who fled the scene on the back of a motorbike, driven by an accomplice. Gardaí are asking for any witnesses to contact them at Kevin Street Garda Station.'

I was completely shocked, and I froze for a few minutes trying to take it all in. We had become accustomed to hearing daily reports about attacks of this nature in Belfast or Derry, but not in Dublin, and certainly not involving somebody so close to us. My first thoughts were, 'Is Dad OK?' and 'Is he going to survive?' I didn't know what the term 'critical condition' meant, but I knew it wasn't good. By now I was sitting up in bed trying to make sense of it all, I even waited for the next news bulletin at 8 a.m. to be sure that I had heard it properly the first time.

Then I somehow went into autopilot, or maybe it was just adrenaline kicking in, and I quickly started to process things. I think I must have assumed that my mother had gone to Dublin to the hospital, but I didn't know for sure, as nobody had told me – I had been left 'sleeping' all night. Straight away I thought that someone had to tell my two brothers before they heard it on the radio. At the time all teenagers had 'gettoblasters'. These radios, which had good FM stereo and long-wave frequencies, were how we listened to our music, and I knew the first thing my brothers would do when they woke up was turn on the radio. I got up and went down the hallway to the twin bedroom they were sharing, and they were both sound asleep.

I went over to Kieran, who was a year younger than me, and woke him up before getting into the bed beside him. He wanted to know what I was up to, so I asked him had they heard people coming and going the night before or had they turned on the radio. When he told me that they hadn't heard a thing and had been asleep all night, I knew I was going to have to tell them, something no 14-year-old should have to do.

By this time, Oliver had woken in the bed opposite and I called him over to our bed, saying I needed to tell them something. Sitting in the bed between my two brothers, I put my arms around them and began by telling them about the car headlights waking me, the commotion in the kitchen, and finding Mam, Granny, Uncle Seamus and Sean there when I went to investigate.

'Granny told me that Dad had been hit by a motorbike crossing the road and was in hospital.' I paused, taking a deep breath. 'Granny told me to go back to bed, but something didn't feel right, and I couldn't sleep. I knew the report would be on the news, so I listened to the radio first thing and I just heard what actually happened.'

I started to get emotional. It felt like I was telling a story, something that wasn't real. I didn't feel like I was in my body or that these words were coming out of my mouth, but I continued.

'The news report said that Dad was shot last night.' I paused, looking at their faces, which didn't shift. 'He's in critical condition at the Meath Hospital in Dublin. The man who shot him got away on the back of a motorbike and the guards are looking for witnesses.'

'Ha ha ha, very funny, Austin,' Oliver replied.

Kieran reprimanded me: 'That's not even funny, Austin.'

'It's true. I'm not joking. Dad's been shot. We can turn on the radio and listen to the next update so you can hear it for yourself,' I said gently.

It seemed like an eternity until the next news bulletin came on, and I felt that they were both getting more anxious as we all waited. I was also getting anxious as I began to doubt myself and wonder if I had dreamt the whole thing, then I began to think, 'What if Dad has passed away and they announce that on the news?'

When the news finally came on the radio, Dad's attack was the lead story and we listened without saying a word to each other. When the report had finished, I remember putting my arms back around my brothers, they both cuddled into me and we all sat there silently, not knowing what to say. While I had the benefit of hearing it twice already that morning, it was still so difficult to hear, so difficult to process, and then I had to comfort my brothers who were both in shock.

A few minutes later, while we were still coming to terms with things, the bedroom door opened and my granny, whom I didn't know had stayed the night to look after us, came into the room.

I can still see her face as she looked at us and then looked at the radio. She instantly knew that we had heard the terrible news about Dad, and for a moment she didn't know what to say, but then she said, 'I hoped that you wouldn't hear it on the radio' and came over to hug us.

* * *

Granny was old school and a bit of a soldier with a stiff upper lip, but also someone who would go out of her way to protect you. She was brought up on a farm in Raheen in rural County Laois in the 1920s and 1930s. Her mother had died when she was very young, leaving a large family to bring themselves up while their father worked the farm. Straight away she knew she had to protect us by not letting us know how serious my dad's condition was; she was probably fearing the worst but was never going to tell us that. She just told us that Mam had gone to Dublin and that she would try to find out more and let us know how Dad was when my mother made contact.

Granny was also a very religious lady who had found great comfort in the Church after my grandad passed away. So she decided the best thing that we could all do at this point was to get dressed, have breakfast, and go to 10 a.m. Mass in Portlaoise to pray for my dad. Going to Mass was the last thing I wanted to do and I could tell that my brothers felt the same way, so we got dressed slower than we normally would and all played with our food, not really eating it.

When Granny pulled her car into the church carpark, I was getting more and more nervous as I didn't know what to expect, but I also knew that I'd have to stay strong for my brothers, figuring that if I was feeling nervous then they would be too. We were lucky that by the time we got to the church most people had gone inside, so we made it in the front door without meeting anybody, and we were just in time as Mass was about to start. Granny started walking up the side aisle, with us behind her, until we found a seat halfway up the church. I could see people staring at us and whispering to each other as we passed and I felt so uncomfortable. Then, during Mass, the priest made a point of praying for my dad, and again people turned around to look at us. Some gave this pitiful look, others just stared, and more nodded to say 'we are praying for him'. The minute Mass was finished people started coming over to us and saying how sorry they were to hear the news; they were looking for an update on his condition and generally just trying to show support.

They were all so genuine and meant well, but neither my brothers nor I were in any way ready for this type of situation. I just wanted to scream 'get me out of here' or shout at them to leave us alone, but I just stayed silent and kept my head down hoping they would all go sooner rather than later.

Granny got us out of there within minutes, but the shock of all that attention made me aware of just how public the news of Dad's shooting was going to be.

Chapter 7

My mam was brought up in Market Square in Portlaoise, where her parents had run the well-known pub, Donoghues, since the 1940s. After my grandad Danny passed away, Granny had moved into a house opposite the pub, which was now being run by my uncle. In the immediate aftermath of the shooting, the pub became a focus for the media who were constantly ringing it looking for updates. My parents' phone number was not in the telephone directory and neither was my granny's, so the public phone box in the pub became the only way journalists could try to contact our family.

The calls began early that morning and didn't stop. I quickly became aware of just how intrusive and upsetting 'getting the story' was for the family who *were* the story. When we went to Granny's house that morning, hours after hearing that news bulletin, me, Kieran and Oliver just sat in silence. It was like we were all trying to deal with things in our own way. Then at some stage during the morning, Granny brought us back to our own house to get some things to keep us busy, so I got a book to read. We had a VHS video recorder at home and were always recording Gaelic football and soccer matches and watching them on repeat. So we each grabbed a VHS tape with our favourite matches and brought them back to Granny's house.

While I was trying to keep my mind occupied watching the videos, I was also half listening to the radio that Granny had in the kitchen, trying to pick up any small bit of information. One report was playing on repeat: 'Reports have come in that IRA prisoners at Portlaoise began cheering and banging on their cell doors, celebrating the news of Brian Stack's shooting. They are also believed to have taunted other prison officers, threatening that they would be next.'

When I heard this for the first time, I was really angry and all sorts of questions started going through my head:

'How could the prison officers let all the prisoners do this?'

'Why is it specifically the IRA prisoners celebrating?'

'Why hasn't anyone come forward to claim responsibility for the attack? Don't the IRA normally do that?'

Over the course of the day, we were constantly asking Granny if there were any updates from the hospital on my dad's condition. She probably knew the truth, which was that he wasn't expected to survive as some of his major organs, particularly his kidneys, had started to fail, but she couldn't tell us that, we were just told that he is 'still the same'.

By this time, unbeknownst to us, the team in the Meath Hospital had removed the bullet from the base of Dad's neck. This bullet had severed his spine and the doctors knew that he would be left paralysed in some way. Mam was initially told that he might lose the power in one of his arms and that he might also have some brain damage, but they just couldn't assess that at the time. The reality, however, became much bleaker as the night dragged on, and it became obvious that he would be paralysed from the neck down and that the brain damage could potentially be worse than first thought. As you can imagine, this was not news that Granny was eager to impart to us, and she did a good job of shielding us from the realities of the situation in those first days.

That evening, I waited patiently for the *Six O'Clock News* to come on TV. If I couldn't get an update on Dad's health, I wanted one on the shooting. I was really anxious for answers and any bit of information on who did it, why they did it, and why this was happening to us.

The TV report said that the leading terrorist prisoner groups in Portlaoise Prison at the time, the IRA and the INLA, had both issued statements denying responsibility for the attack. The Prisoners Revenge Group, who had been responsible for some recent attacks on off-duty prison officers, such as the one on retired Chief Officer Mick Weldon, also told the media that they had nothing to do with the shooting. This left the media speculating that maybe some new splinter terrorist group or a disaffected former prisoner holding a grudge might be responsible.

Even at 14 and with everything that was going on that first day after my dad had been shot, I just didn't believe that it was credible for the media or the police to take the statements from the IRA and INLA at face value, but this is what appeared to be happening. The media reports were focusing on the 'splinter group' theory, but in my heart I knew who was responsible and I knew that it had to be the IRA. 'The IRA prisoners were the ones who cheered, why would they have done that if the group hadn't ordered the shooting?' I thought. It didn't make sense. With all my interest in politics, I was aware that the IRA had a rule book, known as the 'Green Book'. I knew the rules forbade them from taking action against gardaí, army personnel or prison officers in the Republic of Ireland. This rule was Standing Order No. 8 and read, 'Volunteers are strictly forbidden to take any military action against twenty-six county forces under any circumstances.' I was also aware that they had already breached this rule several times and to cover it up they would issue denials of responsibility.

Chapter 8

The first few weeks after the shooting went by in a blur.

My mother was spending most of her time in Dublin at my father's bedside in the Meath Hospital. By this stage my dad's brother, George, had arrived home from England, and his older sister, Bernadette, who was a nun in New York, had also made the journey to Ireland to be with us. My dad's younger sister, Carmel, and other older sisters, Theresa and Mary, were also with us.

Uncle George was particularly close to Dad, and he told Mam, 'The morning after Brian was shot, I was listening to the radio while driving into work in London. A news bulletin on BBC radio reported that an Irish prison officer had been shot. They didn't say his name or where he was from, but I just knew straight away it was Brian. I don't know how I knew, I just did. I didn't know what to do with myself, so I just drove and drove and ended up miles away from the office.'

Sister Bernadette was one of the older members of Dad's family and she had been a nun since she was 16. She immediately got a flight home from America on hearing the news and hadn't even arranged for somebody to collect her at the airport. As she was travelling across the Atlantic Ocean, the man sitting beside her gave her his newspaper and commented, 'That's a terrible thing that's happened,' as he pointed to the story about Dad. 'That's my brother,' she replied. 'I'm on my way home to be with our family.' The man she was talking to transpired to be Ireland's Minister for Agriculture, John Deasy, who was returning from business in the USA, and he offered to give my aunt a lift to Portlaoise in the State car that was collecting him.

As we weren't allowed to go see Dad, me and my brothers spent those early days in Granny's house, where we'd try to entertain ourselves as best as we could by playing football on the street or watching TV. We couldn't stay in the house all day, but if we went outside there would always be somebody asking how Dad was. It was so difficult coming to terms with what had happened and we were all trying to deal with it, and then suddenly we were thrust into this spotlight where people were coming over to us on the street and enquiring about Dad. I know most of them meant well, but at 14 I wasn't ready for all the attention, especially as I had no news to share. Sometimes I felt that I was being rude to them by just giving a short 'he's still the same' reply.

Then there were people who were trying to show support but went about it in different ways. There was the local parish priest, Fr Gregory Brophy, who was a former army chaplain and was very direct. He told us to pray over the Easter and that Dad would improve 'as great things happen at Easter'. Then there were three older ladies who were sisters and would go everywhere together, and one of them lived around the corner from my granny. When they would see us out playing football one of them would get worked up and launch into a tirade about what had happened, and she would always finish her outburst with the line: 'If I ever get my hands on those bastards . . .'

When you're put in a situation like that you just want to with-draw from the world and go into your own space. This horrible thing had just happened and everybody wanted a piece of you. I stopped going to football, hurling and boxing training, and instead found the peace and quiet of listening to music in my bedroom the best way to cope.

After three weeks in the Meath Hospital, the doctors decided to move Dad to the National Rehabilitation Centre in Dún Laoghaire. They had stabilised him but he was still in a coma, and they knew at this stage that there would be paralysis due to the bullet severing his spine. The National Rehabilitation Centre was a centre of excellence for paralysis cases, so it seemed like the best fit for him.

In 1983 there were no motorways in Ireland, so to get to Dún Laoghaire you had to travel through every town en route to Dublin and then navigate your way through the south side of the city until you got to the hospital. This was a long trek for my mother to do every day, and with the trauma of seeing my dad the way he was, she just wasn't fit for much when she got home each evening. In order to help her, the Governor of the prison, Bill Reilly, looked for volunteers from the officers to drive my mother to the hospital each day. Ten of Dad's colleagues offered to do this and created a rota, which took the pressure off my mother and made that daily trip a little less stressful.

After the Easter break, we went back to school. Oliver was in his last year of primary school, while Kieran and I had moved to the Salesian College in Ballinakill after the falling-out we had with the Irish teacher and the local Christian Brothers at St Mary's CBS. The Salesian College was about 20 miles from Portlaoise and was built on the site of the old Heywood House, which had previously been an aristocratic demesne set out in lovely gardens and woodland. The boys' school accepted boarders and day pupils, and my parents planned for us to attend that first year of 1982/3 as day pupils and then start boarding the following year. My brothers and I had been made aware of this plan, and I certainly didn't mind as the boarding was for five days only and you got to go home at the weekends. But for that first year, my dad had arranged for us to take a lift every day to school with one of the teachers, Mr Joe Lynch, who lived in Portlaoise and drove to Ballinakill.

I didn't know what to expect that first morning when I got back to school after the Easter break, but I knew everybody would be looking at us differently. Every morning on our drive, our teacher would ask how Dad was doing, then as soon as we'd arrive at school, our friends would ask the same thing. I could tell that certain teachers were tiptoeing around me and you could feel there was a sense of compassion there, but I didn't know how to handle it all. I felt trapped, like I was now labelled as 'the kid whose dad was shot'.

Nobody teaches you how to deal with this sort of thing; there was no counselling in those days and we were generally left to find our own way to deal with the situation. We would go back to Granny's house every evening after school until Mam came home from Dublin. Granny tried her best to make sure our day went well and I know if I was going to confide in anyone at that time it would have been her. She was so good to us and really stepped up to the plate to help my mother.

The summer holidays came very quickly that year but it was a much different summer than we'd ever experienced. There would be no following Portlaoise or Laois GAA teams around Leinster and there was no Dad to offer encouragement at football or hurling training. I tried to train with the U-16 footballers and hurlers, but my heart just wasn't in it, so I gave up after a few sessions. The manager of both teams was a great friend of Dad and I knew that if I was picked for the team, the other kids would say that I was getting the sympathy vote. It was the same with the boxing: if I now started to win some of those split decisions that always went against me, the other lads would suggest that the judges were looking after me.

Really all my brothers and I wanted was to see Dad. We were constantly asking Mam to bring us to Dublin with her, but her standard answer was that the doctors wouldn't allow it. I know that both her and the doctors were trying to shield us from the reality of Dad's situation, but it got to the point where they couldn't really say no any longer.

* * *

'Boys, I have some news,' Mam said, after calling us three together. 'This Sunday, after you head to Croke Park, Uncle Des is going to bring you to Dún Laoghaire to visit Dad.'

Finally, we were going to visit Dad. Mam tried to prepare us for what we would see.

'Your Dad is still in a coma. He has a ventilator machine helping him to breathe and he's still in the Intensive Care Unit, so you might get a shock when you see him,' she explained, knowing no matter how well she prepared us it wouldn't be enough.

On June 5th, 1983, two months and 11 days after we said goodbye to Dad as he left for Dublin, Kieran, Oliver and I headed up to see Laois play Louth in the Leinster Football Championship with Uncle Des. Laois lost the game, but that didn't dampen our spirits, because we were more excited about seeing Dad than anything else.

After the game, Des brought us to Dún Laoghaire where my mother was waiting with one of the consultants, Dr Patrick Murray. We were brought into what looked like some sort of waiting room and Dr Murray sat opposite us. He was nice and calm, and he explained to us what we would see when we went into the room where my dad was. He told us what Dad would be like and not to be alarmed by the sound of the ventilator or all the machines in the room. He also told us to talk to Dad because, even though he was in a coma, he could still hear what we were saying.

We then set off nervously towards the Intensive Care Unit, having tried to take in everything we were told. When we got to the room, I saw two armed gardaí posted outside to protect Dad, which straight away brought home the fact that whoever had tried to kill him might make a second attempt. This was really scary and made me wonder if we were all in danger, especially my mother.

When we got inside, the nurses took over. I can still remember how kind they were as they brought us in. The room was a lot smaller than I had envisioned and the first thing that hit me was the sound of the ventilator – it made this really loud, deep breathing noise, going in and out over and over again. If you have ever heard a ventilator in the 1980s, you will know this sound – it's not something that you forget and it will stay with me forever.

As the room was small, the nurses guided me to one side and my brothers to the other, while my mother stayed at the end of the bed. When I looked at Dad, the first thing I noticed was that his eyes were open. I thought that he had woken up and I got a bit of a shock.

'Oh no, darling,' said the nurse, quickly noticing my shock. 'I'm sorry, we should have told you that his eyes would be open. He's still in a coma, he hasn't woken up yet.'

I hadn't been expecting that, I just assumed that if you were in a coma your eyes would be closed. The last time we had seen Dad was when he set off for the boxing match on that fateful night over two months previous. What we knew as a fit, strong and active man was now lying paralysed, in a coma, breathing with the aid of a ventilator and had various tubes and wires attached to him. This was not the Dad we knew, yet it *was* our Dad.

The nurses who had been preparing for our visit knew that we had been to the football match in Croke Park and one of them asked me if I had the match programme. Initially I thought that maybe she was interested in the match, but when I said that I had the programme, she told me to hold it in front of Dad's eyes and to talk through the team for him, starting with the goalkeeper. I started naming the team and telling him how each player had played and I wasn't getting any reaction, but the nurse kept reassuring me by saying, 'He can hear you.'

Then an extraordinary thing happened. When I got to the eighth player, who was a famous Laois midfield star of the time, Big John Costello, Dad's face took on this curious look. John Costello had worked in Portlaoise Prison but had given up the job and football a few months previous to go find his fortune in the USA. Dad knew this and the look I was getting was one that seemed to say, 'What's he doing playing? I thought he was in America.' I couldn't believe that I'd gotten a reaction from him and straightaway the nurse told me to keep going and keep him engaged. When I had finished talking about the team, she then told me to talk him through the match as he appeared to still be listening.

We were allowed to spend about 20 minutes with Dad and we all took turns telling him about school and what we were doing. I didn't get another reaction like the one when I mentioned John Costello, but I was so happy knowing that he knew we were all there with him.

Years later, when I was reading through the coroner's inquest file, I noticed Dr Murray's statement that made reference to our first visit to see Dad. He told the inquest: 'He remembers the day of the accident and remembers talking to an official. His next memory is in the month of June when his wife and three boys visited him in the ward of this hospital.' It was amazing to read that this visit had such an impact and was his first memory after being shot, even though he was still in a coma.

* * *

At the end of the summer, Kieran and I went back to school in Ballinakill, this time as boarders, and were joined by Oliver. The first-year students started a day after the rest of the school and I can still see him in his first ever school uniform. He looked so grown up but also so sad. Oliver took the transition to boarding school very badly and he was on the phone to Mam nearly every night asking to come home. As the youngest in the family, he was close to my mother, so leaving her and his friends so soon after Dad had been shot was a big shock to his system.

On top of homesickness, Oliver started to get bullied by a group in his class who saw that he was uncomfortable in the school. It was classic bully boy stuff to pick on a kid who was vulnerable. They would never dare take on Oliver one on one as he would have sorted them out, so they bullied him in a pack.

As any big brother would, I started to watch out for Oliver and I quickly noticed the bullying. I decided that I had to do something to stop it as these things only get worse if they are not addressed. I came up with a plan that following breakfast as boarders were leaving the canteen: I would wait in the parlour where the priests saw visitors, which was just at the end of the corridor leading to the canteen. I would have a friend stand at the door of the parlour and as each of the individuals involved in the bullying passed, he'd open the door and invite them to step in. Then I would pounce. The door would be closed and my friend would stand guard as I had a robust chat with each of the bullies.

It worked as planned, but while I was interrogating the last lad, the school principal, Fr John Horan, pushed past my lookout and came into the room. As he entered, I was holding the lad by the scruff of the neck against the wall and basically telling him that if he didn't leave Oliver alone, he would have me to answer to. Fr Horan took a look at the scene and said to me, 'Stack, is this some sort of inquisition?' to which I replied, 'Yes, Father.' He then turned on his heels and as he left the room said, 'Well, carry on then.' He obviously knew about the bullying and had decided to let me deal with it.

After this incident, the bullying stopped and Oliver began to settle in to Ballinakill, but he still to this day feels a little resentful about being sent to boarding school. While boarding in Ballinakill was always part of the plan, Kieran and I had a year as day boys to find our feet in the school, but Oliver was thrown in at the deep end only a few short months after the shooting. My mother always felt that she was following the plan and that with everything that had happened, boarding was the best option as she would have to spend every day in Dublin at Dad's beside.

*　*　*

While all this was going on at school, my dad was making some progress and in early September he woke up from his coma. The day he woke up my mother was there with her sister, Catherine, who had been a great support to her, and he immediately recognised Catherine but not my mother. He actually asked Catherine, 'Who is that with you?' This left my mother gutted and she often said that it was very hard to take.

After he woke up, Dad was able to breathe independently so he was moved from the ICU to a regular ward, and it wasn't long before we were brought to Dún Laoghaire to see him awake for the first time. That first visit was a tough day for all of us and while we had been prepared for what to expect by my mother, the unexpected always happens.

After coming out of the coma, Dad's speech was very poor and he had to have speech therapy to help with that. We had been told this before we went for the visit, so we weren't expecting there to be great communication. His bed was the last one on the right-hand side of the ward and, as we were walking down towards him, we could see that he was sitting up in a wheelchair. As we got near to him he saw Oliver and called out to him, saying, 'Booby', the pet name my dad had called Oliver when he was younger. Oliver got upset and ran from the ward crying, but he quickly came back – it was such a shock to him and to the rest of us that he remembered that pet name and had actually said it.

Sitting in the wheelchair, Dad looked gaunt and frail, like a really shrivelled-up old man. We all did our best to talk to him, to tell him what was going on around the town and at school, but you could tell that his attention span was short and he was also quite deaf – we had to speak up so he could hear. It was also quite frustrating because he had practically no short-term memory, so we'd have to repeat things to him.

As well as being paralysed from the chest down, Dad had also suffered a lot of brain damage due to the lack of oxygen going to his brain on the night of the shooting. The doctors didn't know what the extent of that would be until he woke up. The poor speech and lack of short-term memory were two of the effects, but he also got very frustrated and cranky – he was like a four-year-old child.

Seeing Dad like this was so difficult for us as he was a man who had such presence before the shooting, and I found it hard just to be natural around him as things were so different. I think that being in a ward with others and having armed gardaí sitting opposite us didn't help; I really would've preferred to be alone with him and have some privacy so we could both deal with the reality of what was facing us.

I don't have too many good memories of the time he spent in the ward after waking up, but one memory stands out – we all watched the 1983 All-Ireland Football Final on the TV, which was on a stand at the end of the ward beside my dad's bed. Dublin were playing Galway and there were still a few of the famous players from the Dublin team of the 1970s in action, and Dad knew I'd be supporting Dublin, just as I had when we went to the finals in the 1970s. The game was one of the weirdest finals of all time with Dublin having three players sent off and Galway losing one player the same way, but the 12 men held out to win and Dad was so happy for me that Dublin had won. The problem was that five minutes later, he wouldn't have known that Dublin won unless you told him.

For the next six months, we would spend our weekends home from boarding school on the road to Dún Laoghaire to visit Dad. While it was tough seeing him the way he was, I knew that he enjoyed the visits so much.

As well as the speech therapy, the hospital did a lot of rehabilitative work with him in the first few months after he woke up, hoping that he might recover a little movement in one or both arms. But it got to the point where they couldn't do much more for him in Dún Laoghaire and he was essentially holding down a bed. The hospital management were trying to get Mam to think about taking him home. I also think the hospital didn't like the fact that there were two armed gardaí in the ward all the time. The security around Dad had not been lifted and there was still a real fear that those who had shot him would at some stage attempt to finish the job.

My mother tried to keep the visits just to family as Dad would get tired very quickly, but also because of the security concern. The armed gardaí who were stationed in the ward opposite his bed would be on the lookout for strangers approaching, and when we were there one Saturday a man came towards the bed whom the gardaí had never seen visiting before and whom my mother didn't know. As he approached the bed, the gardaí intercepted him and he was brought to a Garda station and questioned at length. It transpired that the man had been at the boxing on the night Dad was shot and was one of the first people on the scene. He had placed his coat under Dad's head while he was lying on the ground. The man was a good Samaritan and his motives were entirely innocent, but it showed how vulnerable he was to a repeat attack while in the hospital.

With a lot of encouragement from the hospital, arrangements were put in place for Dad to make a day trip home for Christmas Day. He hadn't been outside of a hospital since the shooting and this was going to be a big undertaking.

First, there were the political and security considerations. The Don Tidey kidnapping had taken place a few weeks prior to this and in the rescue of Mr Tidey on December 16th, Private Paddy Kelly and recruit Garda Gary Sheehan were murdered by the kidnap gang.

Then there was the pressure that my mother must have been under that day, which doesn't bear thinking about: she had to drive to Dún Laoghaire, collect Dad, put him in the car, drive home and then get him into the house from the car. She then had to cook dinner and, finally, return Dad to Dún Laoghaire that evening. While it was great to have him home for Christmas Day and as kids we enjoyed having him back in the house, it was not in any way like previous Christmas celebrations. Instead of the happy, loving dad who got great joy in watching us open presents, we had a man who because of his brain injuries was cranky, demanding and needed my mother's full attention. I think the whole experience was too much for both him and my poor mother.

* * *

I was now in third year in school and studying for my Intermediate Certificate. I was beginning to really feel the pressure on three fronts: first, I was worrying about Dad and what happened; second, I was studying; and third, I was trying to be seen as 'just me' and not somebody to be pitied or the 'guy whose dad was shot'. I couldn't concentrate on study at all and I really started to act up in school. I tried to create an alternative Austin, the class clown, so I could be recognised for something different. I remember one time jumping in and out of a window in French class as a way of trying to confuse the poor teacher. She would turn away and I'd jump out the window. I could see her looking at my desk and thinking to herself, 'He was there a minute ago', and when she'd turn away again, I would simply jump back in and be sitting at the desk when she looked back. I was gaining a reputation as a joker and prankster.

It all culminated in me joining two other lads on a mission to break out of the boarding school for a night and visit the local village. In the evening time after school, there would be training for the various sports teams and also study for those not playing sports. After these activities were finished, we used to go to the canteen for supper and then back to study for another few hours. Study took place in a large common area and was supervised by a member of staff. We were all supposed to attend but there was never a roll call taken, so there was an opportunity to abscond for a few hours.

'Lads, I have an idea,' whispered one of my friends. 'Why don't we head up to the village tonight?' A few of us nodded with excitement. 'We can jump out the window from my room and leave it open so we can get back in later.'

'This will be great craic. We'll never get caught,' said one of the boys, whom none of us trusted.

'Sorry, John, you're not coming. We can't go in too big a group,' I replied, hoping that'd be the end of it.

As it was dark, we were able to leave the school grounds without being seen, and we walked the two miles to the village on a country laneway. When we got to the village, we didn't know what to do next. It dawned on us that we had made this impulsive decision that was more to do with bragging rights and being seen as pranksters than anything else. We called into a small village pub that was run by the father of one of the day pupils and we asked to see him. We were chatting to him when he noticed that two of the teachers who lived in the village had driven by and were heading back towards the school – someone had clearly ratted us out. We knew at that stage that we were rumbled, so we decided to try sneak back into the school. We managed to avoid the search party and get back without being seen.

When we got to the school grounds, we hid in the bicycle shed until we thought the coast was clear and then went back to the school building, the idea being that if we got caught in the school, we could say that we just bunked off study, which wouldn't be as serious an offence as going to the local village. We were only in the school building when we met the principal, who was raging with anger. He told us that he knew where we had been as he had been told by the lad who we wouldn't bring. The game was up and we were all suspended for a week.

The following day was Friday and we were going home for the weekend, and before I left I was given the suspension letter to give to my mother. Up until Dad was shot, I had been a quiet person in school and probably bordered on being shy, and now I was going home with a suspension letter. My mother was furious when I gave her the letter – I went straight to my bedroom when I gave it to her as I knew I'd be confined to the room for the week I was suspended. She was so embarrassed that she couldn't tell my granny what had happened, so when she left for Dublin each day I was left in the house on my own. When I went back to school it's safe to say that I had learned my lesson and while I participated in the odd prank, I didn't have to do anything that would draw attention to myself as my reputation was already secure.

In 1983 there was no counselling of any sort and we were essentially left to get on with things in our own way, and this ultimately led to me acting up in school. Eventually I would figure things out for myself, but it took many years – counselling would have been so beneficial to me, but these things were not deemed important back then.

Chapter 9

In March 1984, 12 months after the attack, Dad came home. The hospital had been very keen to move him on, especially after Christmas, but my mother couldn't just take Dad home that easily. The house needed to be adapted.

Dad required a special bed and a specially adapted car. In preparation for him coming home, my mother had to convert a large bedroom into a space that was essentially a hospital room. She also had to get planning permission to build an extension to that room, which would serve as a large wheelchair-friendly bathroom. The hospital advised on the purchase of a large rotary bed for Dad, which rotated from side to side and was designed for patients who were completely paralysed so that they wouldn't get bed sores.

A tracking system was installed on the ceiling after the building work was completed to accommodate a hoist to lift Dad out of the bed. The sides and ends of a net sheet were attached to the hoist which was installed on the tracks, so when Dad was being taken for a shower, the hoist moved him along the track into the bathroom. Likewise, if he was getting out of bed, the hoist could lift him from the bed into the wheelchair.

In order to be able to bring Dad on little trips out of the house, we needed a suitable car, so my mother had to purchase a Nissan

Prairie – a boxy 1980s-style SUV. The car had to be adapted so that the front passenger seat could be removed to allow Dad's wheelchair to be lifted into this space, again by a hoist, which was built into the car.

Unsurprisingly, there was a lot of pressure on Mam to get these things done before Dad came home, and they all cost money, which she just didn't have. By this stage Dad had been pensioned off, so her weekly income had been halved.

Dad would have been on full pay for the first six months after the shooting and then he would have gone to half pay for another six months. When this period was up, Mam got a visit from the prison Governor, Bill Reilly, and an official from the Department of Justice. 'Mrs Stack, we don't have great news,' Bill Reilly began. 'Brian will have to be signed off from the Service and go onto a pension. But this is problematic, I'm not sure if you know about that.' Mam nodded her head. The civil service pension scheme became available to prison officers just after Dad and Mam had married, and to get into the scheme officers had to pay back money to cover their service up to that point. In Dad's case, this was £500, which was a lot of money in 1967, especially for a newly married couple.

'As you know, Brian, like a lot of others, never paid into the pension scheme, so he is going to be left without a pension unless we do something,' Reilly explained. 'That's why my colleague from the Department of Justice is here. The Department are prepared to reopen the scheme for a short period for everybody. This will mean that Brian can get a pension, and you can pay the pension contributions that are due from his lump sum gratuity.'

While there wasn't a lot left from the lump sum to pay for the work to the house and the car, Mam always said it was the best decision she made as it guaranteed her an income for life. Mam was forced into making decisions on her own while under enormous stress, but she did the right thing and got a loan from the bank to cover the works to the house and the car, knowing that a claim to the Criminal Injuries Tribunal was in motion. In the meantime, however, the loan had to be paid back, we had to be schooled, and food had to be put on the table.

When Dad came home, Mam also had to pay for carers to come to help her with him. Initially, she had two retired psychiatric nurses helping out for a few hours each day. The work was tough as there was a lot of lifting and pulling involved and the two retired men just couldn't cope with the physicality of it, so they left after a few months. My mother then enlisted the help of her sister, Catherine, who was a trained nurse. Together they did the daily routine of showering Dad, dressing him, and getting him into the wheelchair.

This wasn't an easy time for Mam. Apart from the physical part of the caring, which would take its toll on anybody, she also had to deal with Dad's mental state. He could best be described at this stage as being like a big, frustrated child. He kept asking the same questions over and over, as he couldn't remember the answers. He would go through a whole range of emotions in the space of five minutes – he would get angry and shout, he might then become sad and cry, and he might have a happy phase for a few minutes. Mam wasn't getting any sleep either, as he would regularly call out at night looking for her to do something simple such as scratch his nose. Even though she would be tired, she would make the effort to bring him somewhere for a drive at the weekends when we were at home.

My brothers and I tried our best to help at weekends and during the summer of 1984 when we were around all the time. I had done the Intermediate Certificate exams in June and knew that I probably hadn't done too well, but at the same time I was hoping not to let Dad and Mam down. I used to enjoy doing little things for Dad like reading the newspaper with him – as a Fianna Fáil household, the newspaper was always the *Irish Press*. I would put his reading glasses on for him and hold the newspaper, he would ask me about the various stories and I would help him choose which ones to read. I knew that the sports and political stories were his favourites, so they would always be read first, and then if there was anything else he had an interest in I would show it to him.

Mam had also bought Dad an electric razor as it was much easier to shave him using it, and I loved doing that job as it meant I got time alone with him. I always hoped he would be having one of his better days when I'd be shaving him so I could have a conversation with him.

On one such morning, after I had finished reading the news-paper with him and then started to shave him, he welled up and started to cry. He had been fine up to that point, but it all got too much for him – here he was lying in a bed, paralysed, and his 15-year-old son was shaving him. He was very much a tradi-tionalist and would have seen it as his job to show his son how to shave, but now the roles were reversed and I was shaving my dad. I could see that this was hurting him and even though there were no words spoken by him, I knew why he was upset and I started to cry myself.

Shortly after this, he got it into his head that he needed to do something that a dad should do with his son, so one afternoon my mother was going into town on an errand and he told her to take Kieran and Oliver with her because he wanted to talk to me. When they were leaving, my mother told me that Dad wanted me, so I went into the front room of the house where he was sitting in the wheelchair looking out at the road. He asked me to pull up a chair and I thought maybe he wanted me to read him one of the many books that were in the front room.

'Austin, I think it's time we have the talk,' he began, as I squirmed knowing what was coming. 'How much do you know about relationships and sex?' I shrugged, and he proceeded to tell me everything he believed I needed to know at that point. Because of his condition and brain damage, the talk was frustrating for him as I knew the things that he wanted to say or express but wasn't able to. I certainly hadn't been expecting this and he caught me off guard, but while I was embarrassed, I had to show interest as I knew that he was trying to do the right thing as a dad. He just wanted to be able to still do dad stuff with his son.

While Mam tried to get Dad out in the car at weekends, there was still a security concern around him and she would let the local Gardaí know if we were planning a trip. While there was no full-time protection on Dad since he came home from hospital, gardaí would randomly call to the house and walk around the perimeter. Because of the security threat to Dad and also because of his condition, Mam had to make sure that she knew everybody who called to visit Dad during his time at home. She was particularly wary of the media, especially newspaper reporters, due to the various methods they employed to make contact after Dad was shot.

Most people who would visit would call in the evening time, and they would usually be friends from the world of GAA, boxing, politics and work. Dad really enjoyed the chats with them and after somebody visited once or twice, they got to realise that they had to keep repeating things due to his short-term memory loss, and that he may not even remember that they had called previously. During those chats with visitors, I used to love listening to him tell stories about GAA matches or boxing tournaments from the 1940s and 1950s; he had no problem recalling things from when he was younger and I had never heard a lot of those stories before. It gave me a real insight into some of the characters around the town from when he was growing up, most of whom would now be adults I respected and looked up to. Sometimes he would be asleep when people called and Mam would just make the visitor a cup of tea and have a chat to them herself. Other times Dad got cranky or frustrated when there was a visitor but, in fairness, they all understood the situation and knew it wasn't the old Brian that they were dealing with.

The local priests were also regular visitors to the house. Dad was quite religious, which he got from his mother, and many of the nuns and priests in the town would have remembered her as being particularly devout. But Dad was popular with them too, not only through his work with the GAA and boxing clubs, but also from his interactions with them when they came to the prison. When a prison chaplain comes into a prison, they see a person not a prisoner – their job is pastoral and spiritual care. For many prison officers, this is difficult to understand, especially as the chaplain may not always put security first and would forget that they were in a prison. From what he used to say, I think that Dad got what they were about and this led to him having a great relationship with them.

I remember when my brother Kieran was making his confirmation, a prisoner was also in the church that day to be confirmed. The prisoner was accompanied by a prison officer who brought him to and from the ceremony. I can still see this small elderly nun approaching my dad outside the church afterwards and thanking him for all he did to ensure that the day went well for the prisoner, and also thanking him for laying on a few cakes and treats as a celebration for him when he would go back to the prison.

The one group of people who stayed well clear and never visited Dad were politicians. In fact, the only politicians to call on Dad from what I can recall were the local county councillors, and I think Michael Woods, who was the Fianna Fáil Justice spokesperson, called to see him while he was in Dún Laoghaire.

* * *

That summer of 1984, the Portlaoise GAA club were doing well on all fronts and a historic quadruple of minor and senior titles in both Gaelic football and hurling was on the cards. Dad was anxious to try to attend a game, especially if his beloved Town got to a final. The problem was that it would be impossible to get him into a match, as at the time wheelchair access and security were not really a priority for the local GAA. Also, most matches would normally be played in the county grounds of O'Moore Park, but as it had undergone some renovation work, with a new terrace replacing the old grass bank and the pitch being re-laid, all the games that summer had been played in other much smaller grounds around the county. However, O'Moore Park was going to be ready for the county finals with the hurling taking place on Sunday, September 9th and the football taking place on Sunday, September 16th. The senior and minor finals in both codes are always played on the one day, with the minor match acting as a curtain raiser. As expected, Portlaoise reached all four finals, so there was great excitement around the town. Dad was so proud that the club he loved and had given so much time to was on the verge of achieving something special.

On the week leading up to the hurling final, anybody who called to the house couldn't avoid getting into a conversation with him about the match and how hurling had finally gotten a foothold in Portlaoise. What Dad didn't know was that he would be going to the game. With the development of the new concrete terraces at O'Moore Park, a car could now be brought into the grounds and parked in front of the stand. Dad's friends in the GAA club, knowing how excited he was about the matches, arranged for him to be able to attend.

So, after dinner on Sunday, September 9th, we got Dad ready and brought him out to the car for the short journey to O'Moore Park. When we got to the grounds we were waved in like royalty and directed to the space in front of the stand, which provided a great vantage point from which to watch the match. Before the matches started, there was curiosity from the supporters in the grounds as to who was in the car, but when people realised who it was there was a procession of well-wishers coming over to chat to Dad, many of whom were old GAA acquaintances who were delighted that he could attend.

The minor match between Portlaoise and Borris-in-Ossory was up first. The minor grade at the time was U-18 and I had played U-14 hurling with quite a few of the Portlaoise team, so this game was one that I was looking forward to. Portlaoise came out on top by a score of 2-10 to 1-05, winning the first leg of the quadruple, and after the presentation of the cup to the Portlaoise captain, David Coughlan, he did a very special thing. David was a neighbour from the Mountrath Road and Bill Phelan, the team manager who was a long-time friend of Dad's, asked him to bring the cup over to Dad in the car. David got the whole team to come with him and they surrounded the car. I can still see the smile on his face as David put the cup through the car window for him to see.

The senior final that followed was a close affair which ended in a draw, Portlaoise 1-08 and the Harps 2-05. That evening, Dad was talking about the games and looking forward to the replay, which had been pencilled in for Sunday, September 30th. He was also eagerly waiting for the two football finals, which were to be played the following Sunday, September 16th.

We didn't know it at the time, but that county minor hurling title would be the last time Dad saw his beloved town win a match. He wouldn't be around for the completion of the famous quadruple.

Chapter 10

When we got home after the county hurling final, Dad still couldn't believe that the victorious minor team had brought the cup over to the car, and it took a while for the excitement to wear off. Once he had some food and was back in his bed, we had to get ready to go back to boarding school. We normally had two bags when going back to school for the week, one with schoolbooks and the other with clothes, sports gear and food. My mother also packed a few treats for us and, before we left, Granny and Aunty Catherine also arrived with treats.

After we packed the car for the short 20-minute drive to Ballinakill, we went into the bedroom to say goodbye to Dad. He was still in good form and gave us his usual speech about working hard and staying out of trouble. We lined up in turn to give him a hug, before heading off.

When we got back to school, it was still early in the new term, and I was getting used to my new surroundings in the senior living quarters. We older students had our own rooms as opposed to the large dormitory for those in the junior cycle. This was a huge level of freedom compared to a dormitory, as I had my own space and could now read and listen to music until whatever time I wanted. However, this meant that I would see less of my brothers, but I still made it my business to check in on Oliver in the evenings.

On the evening of Tuesday, September 11th, less than 48 hours after we'd arrived, I was getting ready to spend a few hours relaxing with my friends before bedtime. We'd normally play pool and watch TV in the seniors' common room or just listen to music in one of the student's rooms. That night, I was with two friends and we were on our way back to the common room when the school principal, Fr Horan, approached me and asked to see me privately. It was strange to see Fr Horan at this time of day, and when he asked to see me, I began to wonder if I had done something wrong. As we stepped into an empty room off the corridor, I still had no idea what he was about to tell me.

'Austin, I'm very sorry to have to deliver this news,' Fr Horan gently said as he stood facing me, 'but your father took ill earlier today and has been taken back to hospital. I don't have any other information right now, but you should pack your bags. Your aunt will be here to pick you up in the morning.'

To me this sounded ominous, and I immediately knew that something serious had happened and that Dad was in a bad way.

'Would you like to tell Kieran and Oliver or would you like me to do it?' Fr Horan asked.

'Can you do it, please? But wait until the morning so that they can get a good night's sleep,' I replied. Having been the one who broke the news to them about the shooting, I really didn't want to be the one giving my brothers more bad news.

'Very well. Try to get some rest yourself,' Fr Horan said as he patted me on the shoulder and headed down the hall.

I went back to find my friends who were in one of the student bedrooms at this stage. The second I walked into the room they started to quiz me on what the principal had wanted. I sat on the edge of the bed and told them what he had said, and that I would be going home in the morning. A lot of the time young fellas wouldn't know how to react if their friend's got news like this, but in this case they just sort of flew into action and came down to my room to help me pack and stayed with me to make sure that I was alright.

That night was again one of those restless nights where I didn't get much sleep. I didn't know what had happened to Dad, I didn't know if he was conscious or unconscious, and I didn't even know which hospital they had taken him to. When something like this happens, your mind starts working overtime, especially during the night.

The following morning, I asked my friends not to say anything to anybody else until I had spoken to my brothers. The last thing I wanted was them hearing the news about Dad before Fr Horan had spoken to them. After breakfast I waited outside the canteen for Kieran and Oliver, and when they came out, I asked them had Fr Horan spoken to them and they said that he had.

They both looked at me seeking answers, but this time I didn't have any and was as much in the dark as they were. I tried my best to put their minds at ease by saying it might only be something minor, even though I knew this probably wasn't true, and I said to them that the sooner we got home the better, as we would know more then.

I went with them to the junior dormitory to help them pack their bags and carry them downstairs to the front of the school building where we were to be collected at 9 a.m.

When I returned inside to collect my own belongings, the whole building had gone quiet all of a sudden and there was nobody around. Classes had obviously just started, but it felt really eerie, and when I returned to my brothers, the three of us sat in silence on the steps outside the school waiting to be collected.

We weren't waiting long when my uncle Sean's wife, Ann, arrived to bring us home. 'Boys, I'm so sorry,' she said, hugging us as she helped us into the car. 'Your dad was taken to Portlaoise

Hospital yesterday, but the doctors decided to move him to the Meath Hospital in Dublin, so he's on his way there. I'm to take you home to Portlaoise now.'

She didn't have much more information, but straightaway I began to think that Dad's kidneys had failed again – this happened to him after the shooting and he had been lucky that he was brought initially to the Meath Hospital as it was a centre of excellence for dealing with urology issues. My thought process was that if they are bringing him there, then it is nothing more serious than a kidney problem. That gave me a sense of relief.

When we got back to Portlaoise, we were taken to my granny's house and it was there that we learned the truth about what had happened.

'Boys, I'm very sorry to say that your dad's situation doesn't look good,' Granny explained. 'He collapsed yesterday morning and has been unconscious since. We need to pray for him.'

I was shocked and trying hard to take in what she was saying. I just kept going back to how he was the Sunday after the hurling finals. He was in such good spirits. The turn of events in a few short days was difficult to understand. I had just started to think that maybe his mind and moods were getting better and then out of the blue things just went downhill.

My mother had had a stressful few days by this stage, and she was in Dublin at Dad's bedside. On Monday he had been tired after the day out at the county finals, but she still got him up and the day went well with no sign of problems. On the Tuesday morning, she managed to get him dressed and into the wheelchair and, having had his breakfast, he was sitting in the kitchen as she went about the household chores. Then at some stage in the middle of the morning Dad just slumped in the wheelchair. Mam immediately saw what had happened and ran over to him. She saw that he was unconscious and tried to wake him, but with no success. She started to panic as she was on her own, so she ran out the front door and rushed to a neighbour who lived a few doors up and who she knew was a nurse.

The neighbour, Theresa, came back down to the house with Mam and they got Dad into the recovery position. Theresa started doing mouth-to-mouth resuscitation to try to bring Dad back. She told Mam to call for an ambulance as she continued giving Dad first aid. The ambulance came very quickly and Dad was taken straight to the Emergency Department in Portlaoise Hospital. Once he was stabilised there, they took a decision to send him back to the Meath Hospital in Dublin as his organs were starting to fail. Mam often talks about why she didn't ring for the ambulance straight away instead of running up the road to get a neighbour, but she also says that she didn't know what to do. None of us knows how we'd react in similar circumstances, but the one thing that I do know is that calm rational thinking goes out the window, especially when you are faced with such a situation and you are on your own.

After the doctors in the Meath Hospital did an initial assessment of Dad, they told my mother that he wouldn't be waking up this time and that she needed to prepare for the worst. Most of his internal organs had gone into failure and he now had severe respiratory issues as well. The toll of everything that his body had been through finally caught up with him. Eighteen days later, on Saturday, September 29th, 1984, my brothers and I had just finished breakfast when the phone rang. We were in the front room watching a Saturday morning sports programme and I could hear my granny answer the phone but she didn't seem to be doing much talking. After she put the phone down, she came into the front room and just looked at us and said, 'Boys, I'm so sorry, your daddy has passed away.'

When we got the news, Oliver was really upset and started to cry, while Kieran and I sat there in silence. While I was upset and really hurting, it had been 18 days since he slipped back into a coma and I knew that he was unlikely to come out of it, even though this had never been said to me. Similar to the night when Dad had been shot, I went into autopilot and just tried to make sure my brothers were alright.

When my mother had called Granny, she told her that the doctors had said it would be good for us to go to Dublin to see my dad laid out in the hospital, as this would be nice and private. They knew what was coming down the line – a big State funeral – and they wanted us to have this moment with Dad.

I have no recollection at all of this visit and I have gone over things a hundred times, but it is the one part of that few days that I just don't seem to be able to recall. My mother told me that her sister Catherine had gotten her husband, Des, to drive us to the hospital in Dublin. Oliver remembered the visit very clearly and said that when we went into the ward, Dad was in a bed, laid out perfectly, and that we had some time there with him.

Over the day, relatives started to gather in Portlaoise and questions about the funeral began. Initially, we didn't know when the funeral would take place as a post-mortem would have to be carried out. Mam was anxious about that, because she didn't want Dad's body going through that after all that had happened. She just wanted his remains to be treated with dignity and for him to be brought home for the funeral as would normally happen.

The Gardaí, however, told Mam that she didn't have any say in the matter as legally there had to be certain steps that were followed. The first of these legal steps was formal identification of my dad's remains to the Gardaí, so at 4 p.m. on the Saturday, my Uncle Sean officially identified Dad.

As it was the weekend and there was only one State Pathologist at the time, my mother was informed that the post-mortem would probably be carried out on the Monday, and after this my dad's remains would be returned to the family.

Mam, with the help of some of my relatives, began to plan the funeral. She was very particular about the priest she wanted to perform the ceremony and she knew that the Parish Priest, Fr Gregory Brophy, wouldn't be happy with one of his curates being asked to say the funeral Mass. When she had picked out scripture readings for the Mass, Mam asked Kieran and me if we would read these as part of the ceremony.

'Mam, I can't,' I said, suddenly welling up with tears. 'Can Kieran and Oliver do them instead?' For some reason I just didn't feel like I could do this. Maybe everything from the previous 18 months just caught up with me and I wanted to be left alone and not have to perform in front of what was going to be a packed church.

'Can I accept the State Flag and Dad's hat as my part of the ceremony?' I asked, to which she replied, 'Of course.'

Kieran and Oliver agreed to deliver the readings, and my mother's sister Mary drilled them over the next few days. They rehearsed and rehearsed those readings making sure they got them spot on.

Practical and simple things also needed to be taken care of, such as getting jackets, shirts and ties for my brothers and me. This was done by arranging for a local menswear business to have one of their employees go with us to the shop on Sunday when it was closed.

Once we were suited and booted on that Sunday, we did what many thought was a peculiar thing. The replay of the County Senior Hurling Final between Portlaoise and the Harps was being played that afternoon, and the drawn game three weeks previous had been the last time Dad had seen the Town play. Dad's brother George had arrived from England and, like Dad, he was a huge hurling fan. He wanted to go to the game and asked myself and my brothers to go with him. Mam thought that going to the game would take our minds off things for a few hours and she encouraged us to go. For my part, I wanted to go to that game for Dad. The drawn game was like unfinished business and I wanted to make sure Portlaoise won by bringing a piece of Dad to that game.

If I thought that we could go to that game and just remain anonymous spectators on the terrace, I was sadly mistaken. When we got to O'Moore Park and found a good spot on the terrace to watch the game, I noticed that quite a lot of the other hurling fans had seen us and many came over to offer their sympathy. I particularly remember a school friend coming over to sympathise and then asking what on earth was I doing there.

After the teams had warmed up and the national anthem had been played, the stadium announcer made an unusual request.

'It is with great sadness that we learned of the passing of Brian Stack yesterday. Let us honour him now for all he did for Laois and Portlaoise GAA with a minute's silence.'

This was something that I probably should have expected, but when it happened it caught me completely unaware, and seeing thousands of people standing in silence to remember my dad made me very emotional and I started to cry. That was such a special moment as it showed the respect that the GAA people in County Laois had for Dad and even though I knew people were watching us, I cried but stood tall.

On Monday, October 1st, Dad's remains were taken to the Dublin City Morgue where a post-mortem was to be carried out by Dr John Harbison, the State Pathologist. During a post-mortem, there is always a garda present while the pathologist is doing their work. They ensure that the doctor is not disturbed while working on the remains and make sure that nothing unusual happens. There would also normally be gardaí from the Garda Technical Bureau present, who would obtain any forensic evidence and take the deceased person's fingerprints.

In this instance, what is very unusual is that nobody from the Technical Bureau attended and the only gardaí present for the post-mortem were very senior: Detective Superintendent John Reynolds and Detective Inspector Michael Connolly, both from Kevin Street Garda Station, which was the station responsible for the investigation into Dad's shooting.

* * *

Months later, on December 7th, in his evidence to the Coroner's inquest, which we as a family were not privy to, Dr Harbison relayed the details of the post-mortem.

He first spoke about Dad's lungs: 'Lung sections differ from one side to another. Most show patchy acute bronchopneumonia, accompanied by areas of intra alveolar haemorrhage. One section shows an area of unresolved pneumonia.'

He then spoke about his examination of Dad 's brain: 'On 28 November 1984, at my laboratory, I examined the brain. It weighed 1,508 grams. It was externally normal. On section, apart from some prominence of the small blood vessels in the white matter, it was also normal.'

Finally, he relayed his finding in relation to Dad's spine. He spoke at great length and in a lot of detail about the damage that had been done to it from the gunshot. He described the 'dark staining over the ligaments, almost certainly a residue of extra-dural bleeding' and 'the fragment of metal, apparently lead, wedged between the spinal cord and the pedicle and left transverse process of the fifth cervical vertebra'.

In his summary, Dr Harbison stated: 'The deceased man, Chief Officer Brian Stack, in my opinion, died of bronchopneumonia, due to partial respiratory paralysis, due to a bullet wound in the neck.'

Having delivered his summary, Dr Harbison then concluded that this was the cause of death.

The inquest jury, having listened to Dr Harbison's evidence and the evidence of eyewitnesses at the scene of the shooting, delivered the following verdict as the cause of death:

'Brian Stack died on 29 September 1984 at the Meath Hospital, Dublin 8, from bronchopneumonia, partial respiratory paralysis, bullet injury to the cervical spinal cord, injuries received when he was shot at Washington Street, Dublin 8, on 25 March 1983, by a person who is yet unknown.'

This verdict by the inquest jury was crucial as it clearly linked Dad's death to the shooting and if at some stage the Gardaí were in a position to charge somebody with the shooting, that person would now face a murder charge.

*   *   *

Once Dr Harbison had finished with the post-mortem, Dad's body was officially handed over to Mam, and while she had made some initial arrangement, she could now start to plan properly for the funeral.

The prison Governor, Bill Reilly, and a Department of Justice official had already visited Mam and told her that the Government would like to give my dad a full State funeral, and now it had to be worked out which parts of the funeral would be family-based and which would be carried out by the State.

It was decided that the removal would take place on Tuesday, October 2nd and that Dad would be waked in the City Morgue in Dublin before being brought back to Portlaoise. This was to be a private affair for family and friends as much as it could be, as the funeral itself would be far more public with a lot of media attention.

I have vivid memories of that Tuesday going to the City Morgue in Dublin for the removal. I can still remember getting out of the car when we got to the morgue and people swarming around us to sympathise. It's funny the things that you remember, but I know the first person to reach me and offer his hand was the man who visited Dad while he was in Dún Laoghaire, the one who had put a coat under Dad's head as he lay on Washington Street after the shooting. He just stood out from the rest of them and if he walked into the room now, I'd still recognise him.

Once we got past all those who wanted to sympathise with us, we were led into the morgue itself where Dad was laid out in a coffin. At first, we had some time alone as a family with Dad before those waiting outside were allowed in. We were told that this would be our last chance to see Dad privately and to say our goodbyes to him before the coffin was closed.

I was a bit nervous as I approached the coffin, as I wasn't used to seeing dead people, let alone somebody so close to me like my dad. When I got to the coffin I was overcome with grief and just wanted to hug Dad – he looked so well. He was dressed in a smart navy pinstripe suit and he just looked like the Dad I remembered. He always took pride in his appearance and now, for the first time in a long time, he was looking like he had that night 18 months before when he left for the boxing.

I leaned over the coffin and decided that I would kiss Dad on the head, but as I bent down and was about to kiss him, I was suddenly pulled back and I didn't know what was going on. When I turned around to see who had pulled me back, I realised that it was my aunt Catherine. Catherine just looked at me and said, 'Austin, please, you can't touch him anywhere on the head.' She was a nurse and knew what would have been done at a post-mortem. She gave me a little hug and explained that I couldn't kiss

Dad on the head after a post-mortem as I might disturb some of the stiches in his scalp.

While this might seem like a weird conversation to have at your Dad's removal, Catherine was being practical and trying to ensure that our grief was not compounded by something unexpected happening. She also knew that my two brothers were behind me waiting to kiss Dad as well. She was protecting us and did it in such a nice way. I always trusted Catherine, she was my godmother and we were always close, so I knew when she told me this was for the best that she was right. So, I decided then to kiss Dad on his hands, which had been joined together and had rosary beads around them. My brothers then followed and kissed Dad the same way.

Not being able to say goodbye to Dad properly by kissing him on the head is something that will always stay with me, and it makes me angry that the IRA took that from me. I'm not bitter by any means, but what they did to Dad meant that there had to be a post-mortem which violated Dad's remains in such a way that I couldn't kiss him as he lay in the coffin. This might seem like a small thing to some people, but it was important to me and it still hurts that I couldn't do it.

After the wake, when the coffin had been closed, Dad's remains were taken to a hearse for the journey back to Portlaoise. At the time none of the towns along the route to Dublin had been bypassed, so we had to go through each of them. We were in the car behind the hearse and it seemed to take forever to get to Portlaoise, as traffic in all the towns along the way was terrible. When we arrived in Portlaoise, the hearse went around to the side of the church where there is a smaller entrance that is used for funerals. This entrance leads to a small oratory where the coffin is kept overnight following the removal service.

Once we got out of the car at the church, we were again greeted by sympathisers while the undertaker prepared to bring Dad inside.

Once you go through the small oratory in the church in Port-laoise, you then come into the main foyer. As Dad's coffin was wheeled up the centre aisle, I was totally shocked by the number of people who were there – the church was full to capacity, which was unheard of for a removal. It took me a while to get over the size of the crowd that had turned up, and I kept looking around to make sure I wasn't imagining things. As the priests came out on the altar to receive Dad's remains, I noticed that the Bishop was there. Dr Patrick Lennon had been Bishop for some time in our diocese and he had confirmed my brothers and me. Dad would have been impressed that the Bishop had turned up to perform the removal service.

Traditionally in Ireland, after the removal service is finished, the family of the deceased stay seated in the front pew of the church and all those in attendance will queue up to walk past the remains and sympathise with each family member by shaking their hands and offering words of comfort. There were so many people there that night that it took forever for them all to line up and get to us. I even remember a girl who I had fancied for some time coming up to me, smiling, and saying how sorry she was, and I just wasn't able to engage with her as I was too weary from the day.

We were so tired that night when we got home, but Aunty Mary still put Kieran and Oliver through their paces with the scripture readings one last time. By this stage, I was so glad that I had passed on the opportunity to do one of them as the pressure they were under must have been immense. We all went to bed early as we knew the following day was going to be huge, but I don't think any of us slept. I know I certainly didn't and I can only imagine what was going through my mother's mind as she tried to sleep that night.

On Wednesday, October 3rd, we were all up early in the house and while we were very anxious, we got ready and went down to Granny's house. My mother wanted to keep our house private and on the morning of a funeral there are always people who will call to the house, so Granny offered to let people come to her place if they wanted a few minutes with my mother. When we got there, Granny brought myself and my brothers over to the kitchen of the pub, which was directly across from her front door, and told us to wait there while people called to the house.

Shortly after this the first people started to arrive and as I looked out the window, I saw PJ McEvoy, who was General Secretary of the Prison Officers Association (POA), leading a deputation into Granny's house. I was surprised at this, as Dad had a rocky relationship with the Association. The POA had been trying to gain full trade union status for some time and there had been a lot of industrial unrest in Portlaoise because of this. At one point about a year before Dad was shot, they staged a walk-out, and because Dad and other managers didn't go out, they were expelled from the POA. PJ was a controversial figure even to his colleagues in the trade union movement, and he had been involved in several internal upheavals, but on this occasion, he did the right thing and had brought a group of prison officers from Northern Ireland to Portlaoise to show their support for my family.

These officers from Northern Ireland had been through some very tough times themselves, having seen 19 of their colleagues murdered in the previous few years. They also witnessed a colleague murdered in the escape from the HM Prison Maze on September 25th, 1983. It has been alleged that some of those escapees immediately returned to active service with the IRA and were allegedly involved in the Don Tidey kidnapping.

Once the people who wanted a few minutes with Mam had left, it was time to go to the church. As we pulled into the carpark the first thing that I noticed was all the uniforms of the different branches of service in the Irish State. As I would have expected, there were lots of prison officers in uniform, but there were also so many gardaí and army personnel there as well.

When we parked the car and got out, we were surrounded by people trying to sympathise with us, and it was all getting a bit too much for me. That's when I was rescued. Tony Flanagan was an army man who had served on peace-keeping duty in the Lebanon and was heavily involved with my dad in the local boxing club. He had been standing to one side of the crowd looking immaculate in his dress uniform and saw that I was struggling a bit, so he pulled me to one side for a short but sharp pep talk.

He looked me in the eye and said: 'Austin, you are not to cry in here, do you hear me? You are to keep it together for your Dad, he was a great man. Now go in there and do him proud.'

With that he straightened my jacket and sent me back into the fray; it was like he was sending me into battle. All these years later, I still remember his words and how it got me to keep it together inside the church. As much as I wanted to cry that day, and I welled up inside several times, I didn't cry because of what Tony had said to me outside.

I saw all the media and the dignitaries for the first time when we went around to the front of the church before going inside. The large black State cars that are used to drive ministers around were parked in the small parking area in front of the church. Politicians were all standing around chatting to each other on the steps leading up to the front door. I recall immediately recognising Tánaiste Dick Spring of the Labour Party and Minister for Communications Jim Mitchell of Fine Gael. Mitchell would have known Dad from his time as Minister for Justice as in those days they had a more hands-on role in dealing with prisons, especially Portlaoise Prison which he would have frequently visited.

As we got to the top of the steps, the Taoiseach Garret FitzGerald approached my mother to offer his sympathies and in turn spoke briefly to the rest of us. After he had spoken with us, the rest of the government ministers there did likewise. As well as Spring and Mitchell, the Minister for Justice Michael Noonan had also travelled to the funeral, as did the opposition Spokesperson for Justice Michael Woods of Fianna Fáil. President Patrick Hillery was out of the country and was represented by his aide-de-camp Commandant Joe Campbell, while the Garda Commissioner Laurence Wren was also present.

I was very conscious of the media who were gathered around the front of the church trying to grab photos of us, but I did my best to ignore them and just wanted to get inside. I think for the remainder of the day I didn't notice them at all, as I was in a world of my own thinking about Dad and grieving in a quiet and personal way.

When we got inside the church, a guard of honour consisting of chief prison officers had placed the Irish tricolour flag and Dad's hat on the coffin, and they then carried Dad to the top of the church where the altar was. We followed them through the packed church, where there was only standing room, until we got to our seats at the front.

When we took our seats and were ready for the funeral Mass to start, a large group of men suddenly walked out onto the altar and began to sing in a way that took us all by surprise. This was the Prison Officers Male Voice Choir, who were based in the Dublin prisons. I hadn't heard of them before and, while they were singing, I didn't know who they were, but they delivered the most beautiful repertoire of songs that I'd ever heard at a funeral and they made the day so special for us.

When the choir finished singing their opening song, the priests who were celebrating the Mass came onto the altar, led by Fr PJ McDonald. Mam had asked him to be the lead celebrant as she felt that he was a down-to-earth man who would best represent what my dad was all about. I think she also knew that he would deliver a strong homily, which he did by condemning those responsible for the attack on Dad. He said: 'They were acting against God's Commandants and against the wishes of right-minded people in this country . . . They should realise that they were guilty of what was wrong and evil, and public representatives should ensure that the law is carried out to the full in an effort to bring such people to justice. I say their ways and means are wrong.'

When it was time for my brothers to do the scripture readings, I was so nervous for both of them, but they were brilliant and they read with such faultlessness that so many people commented on it afterwards. They did Dad proud and the work that they put into practising those readings with my Aunt Mary really paid off.

Once the funeral Mass was over, the prison officers' guard of honour carried Dad's coffin out of the church and placed it in the hearse for the short journey to the local cemetery, which was on the Stradbally Road. My dad was going to his final resting place on the same road where he grew up.

As the hearse left the grounds of the church, two rows of prison officers lined up alongside and behind it, and they marched as we walked behind them. The road outside the church was lined with people who knew Dad from his activities in the GAA, boxing club and Fianna Fáil. They wanted to form their own guard of honour and did so in a silent and dignified way as we left the church grounds.

I can't remember much else about the short walk to the grave-yard, but when we arrived, I can still see this vast wall of blue as hundreds of prison officers lined the road for the last few hundred yards of the journey.

Once we arrived, the prison officers' guard of honour took over again and carried Dad to the graveside, which was just inside the cemetery. When my father's mother passed away in 1974, the family had purchased a large plot in the graveyard so that the extended family could all be buried together. The plot directly beside it was where my grandad Donoghue was buried, so all the family were as close together in death as they were when alive.

There were so many people at the graveside that I didn't see the guard of honour take the flag and hat off the coffin, and I had to be pushed forward through a group of mourners to be presented with them by the prison Governor, Bill Reilly. When Governor Reilly gave me the hat and flag, I could feel a lump in my throat and I was about to get emotional and cry, but I remembered what Tony Flanagan had said to me and I kept it together, even though at this point I knew that this was it and Dad was never coming home again.

It was strange standing there holding his hat and the national flag, knowing how much both emblems meant to Dad, but also knowing that he would never have wanted me to be holding them standing by his graveside at such a young age.

Once Fr McDonald had said the final prayers, the guard of honour lowered Dad into the grave. As you can imagine, this was the saddest thing that a young boy can experience, and at that moment I was feeling all sorts of different emotions: I was angry at those who had taken Dad away from us, I was bitter because I didn't get to say a proper goodbye to him or kiss him on the head in the morgue, I was proud of him and what he had achieved in his life, but I also knew that things were going to be very difficult going forward as there were so many unanswered questions.

In the days and weeks following the funeral, people were again so good calling up to see us and making sure we were OK. But, as Mam often said afterwards, while people are very good at the time, they all have their own lives to live and eventually you are left on your own to deal with the sadness and the emptiness.

Chapter 11

Exactly one year after my dad was buried, I began my final year in secondary school. That first year went by in a complete haze. I couldn't concentrate on anything and wasn't sleeping. I would lock myself away with a good book or listen to my favourite music to take my mind off things. Bands such as Thin Lizzy and AC/DC got me through some tough days and nights. By the age of 17, most kids normally have a good idea what they want to do in life, but I wasn't a normal kid and had no real plan for my future studies.

I didn't see much point in studying subjects that bored me, but I was sucked in by history and loved studying it, along with geography, which had political elements to it. Politics was what motivated me and I knew that's all I wanted to do. Dad knew this and that is why he had taken so much time to educate me in the ways of Fianna Fáil and true republicanism, and why he took me along to political meetings at such a young age.

My confidence had also been given a huge boost when my school took a group of us to a seminar on emigration that was held in the Killeshin Hotel in Portlaoise one evening. During the 1980s, Ireland was not in a good place economically and many young people did as previous generations had and emigrated after school in order to find a better life for themselves. The seminar had a few keynote speakers, some of whom were politicians, and after they delivered their presentations there was a questions and answers session.

Most of those in attendance were young people and they were rather shy about asking questions at the start. I was sitting there and had noticed an inaccuracy in something one of the speakers said and I felt that it needed to be corrected or an explanation given. So, when no other person raised their hand to speak, I did and made my point. When the speaker couldn't explain himself, it looked like he had misinformed the attendees during his presentation and I was congratulated for my contribution by some of the politicians present.

After this confidence boost, I developed a real passion for making an argument, particularly if it was something that I believed in, and I was soon involved in the school debating team and public-speaking competitions. But these things weren't going to get me a university course or a good job, so I had to decide what course I wanted to try and get into after I did my Leaving Certificate. I found that the only degree course that in any way interested me was a political studies degree in Limerick, but I knew that I would struggle to get the points for entry as it was a much sought-after course.

That summer of 1986, while I was awaiting my Leaving Certificate results, I worked in a menswear clothes shop and also re-joined the local Fianna Fáil Cumann. It was the first time that I went to a political meeting without Dad and I was delighted when they put me on the officer board as the Youth Officer.

When the exam results came out, I hadn't done as well as I expected and I decided to repeat some of the subjects the following year in the hope of getting onto the political studies course in Limerick. I repeated these subjects in Ballyfin College, just outside Portlaoise, and again found myself deeply involved with the debating team, which had a great reputation throughout the Leinster region. It was here that I encountered probably the best teacher I had ever come across.

Jack Carter was the History and English teacher and he had a unique way of teaching, which I totally bought into. He would get us to read a chapter from the textbook and then, in every class for the rest of the week, we would have a class discussion or debate on what we had read. Then on Friday he would ask us to write the answer to an exam-style question over the weekend.

As I had read so many books outside the textbook and had so much knowledge of history, the class sometimes descended into a debate between myself and Mr Carter. Several times during a class he would remark, 'Stack, tell them' after a tricky question would be posed. He pulled me aside one day after I had submitted answers to a few of the written questions and told me, 'You know all this stuff, you have a fantastic knowledge of history, but you just have a difficulty in framing your answer properly.' He then smirked at me and, rubbing his chin, said, 'But we are going to sort that out for you.'

He certainly did this and while my results went up in the subjects that I repeated, I still didn't get enough points for the course in Limerick and had to settle for a business studies course in Athlone Regional Technical College.

I started in Athlone in September 1987 and soon found that I was at a major disadvantage on the course as I had not previously studied accountancy. While the other subjects such as law, economics and business administration didn't pose any problems for me, I just couldn't get my head around trial balances and the whole accountancy methodology.

Just like when I was in secondary school, if a subject didn't interest me, I switched off and concentrated on the things that I was good at – and in Athlone that was law and business administration. I again found my way to the debating society and had some great nights debating some unusual topics. I also founded a Fianna Fáil Society in the college and started to take a keen interest in student union affairs.

In October 1987, Fianna Fáil held its annual youth (Ógra) conference in Galway, and the Laois organisation decided to send a delegation even though we had no formal youth structure in the county. I was asked to be part of the Laois delegation and I contributed to several debates, and I really got bitten by the politics bug.

When we returned, we decided to set up an Ógra wing of the party in Laois and I was elected as its chairperson. I threw myself into the role as we organised seminars and took part in campaigns such as the 'Buy Irish' one.

The local media seemed to be very interested in what we were doing and they covered all our events. This led to a big uptake in youth membership of the party and very soon people had started to call me 'Mr Ógra', a name that some still use for me today.

Meanwhile, back in Athlone, the old guard of the student's union were retiring and some friends, seeing my organisational ability, asked me to consider running for one of the permanent full-time positions. 'I'm only a first year, so I really can't run for president,' I replied to their suggestions. However, they wore me down and I told them, 'I guess, though, it'd be OK for me to run as vice-president, so you can put me forward for that.'

When nominations closed, there was only one other candidate in the field for vice-president and I thought that I could win that election. However, there was a problem with the nomination process and they had to reopen it for a few more days.

'Did you know that there was only one candidate for president when the ballot closed?' asked one of my friends. 'Seriously, Austin, you'd be a shoo-in. Go for it!'

So, I withdrew from the race I probably would have won and entered the election for president. Unfortunately, another candidate had the same idea, and I lost out by 20 votes in a three-way contest.

When the time came that summer to do my exams, I completed them all but wasn't confident about the accountancy one. Once they were finished, I headed off to London with some friends from college to work for the summer and kept my fingers crossed while awaiting the results.

*   *   *

The summer of 1988 was a great summer to be in London, especially after Ireland beat England in the Euro '88 football tournament. Every Irishman in London had bragging rights for months after that.

In order to get work in London, I went along to the local job centre and filled out forms giving details of the type of work I was interested in. I had always been able to cook and I enjoyed it, so while many of my friends went to building sites, I got a job working for a catering company who had a contract at London Transport's Leytonstone depot.

I was initially taken on as a part-time worker for 20 hours a week, but shortly after I arrived the company sacked a worker for theft and I was asked to cover their full-time role. I was doing that for months and enjoying the work and banter with the bus drivers when a new area manager was appointed and, unknown to me, advertised for the full-time role without asking if I was interested. One morning when he called to the depot, he told me that I would be reverting to part-time hours the following week. The message was delivered in a way that left me in no doubt that the area manager had a problem with Irish people and he told me if I didn't want to revert to part-time work then 'you know where the door is, Paddy'. It was the first time I had experienced obvious, straight-up prejudice against my Irish background and I was shocked.

As luck would have it, that same evening when I was in the local pub having a pint, a new landlady who had just been appointed asked me if I knew anyone who would be interested in the job of bar cellarman. They'd be in charge of ensuring that there was always enough stock, making orders, and restocking the shelves in the bar, as well as serving the customers in the pub. When I told her that I had helped my grandad in the store of his pub in Portlaoise from a very young age, she asked if I wanted the job. I had no experience working behind a bar but I'm the type of person who picks things up quickly and very soon I was indispensable to the landlady as I ran a tight ship in the cellar.

In October 1988, I went home to do an aptitude test for the Gardaí, which I had applied for a few months earlier. While I was at home, I applied for a chef course with the training body CERT and secured a place to start in January 1989.

Meanwhile, I took up a job doing part-time chef work locally for the few months and was hoping to pass the exam for the Gardaí. I had never done one of those timed aptitude tests before and I wasn't really prepared for it. Needless to say I didn't score high enough to be called for interview. After that I resolved to train myself for those tests if I ever got called for one again. After I completed the chef course, I was placed with the Great Northern Hotel in Bundoran to finish my training as a commis chef.

Just before I left for Bundoran, the Prison Service advertised and my mother got the application form and gave it to me. I was really surprised that she wanted me to go into the Prison Service, but she said to me, 'You need a proper job', and told me to fill out the form and send it off. I had no intention of filling out that form as the Prison Service was the last job in Ireland I wanted; there was no way on earth that I was going to go into a job that had seen my dad murdered. So, when I got to Bundoran, I threw the application form away and told my mother that I had sent it off.

'Well?'

'Hi, Mam,' I replied, having answered her fifth call that week.

'Well? Have you heard from the Prison Service yet?' she pestered.

'No, nothing yet,' I lied.

'I can't understand it. You should have heard by now. I was thinking, do you think your application could have been lost in the post?' she asked.

'Maybe, that's a possibility,' I lied again.

Mam started to enlist the help of politicians to see if there was anything that could be done to get me another chance to apply. They couldn't do anything and told her that it might be advertised again soon and to make sure that the next time I sent the application by registered post. I couldn't say that I had thrown it away as by this stage I was too embarrassed, especially after Mam had made all those representations for me.

My illusions of grandeur about life as a chef soon came crashing down as I found myself regularly working 80 or 90 hours a week for very poor pay and having to put up with cranky chefs whose default reaction to everything was to throw the biggest pot they could find at you. I thought to myself, 'What am I doing here?' But I knew I had to stick with it until something better came along.

Luckily for me, a few months later when I was at home in Portlaoise one weekend, I heard that the owner of a local menswear shop was enquiring about me. Jimmy Lewis was a talented footballer who was well known locally and his dad would have played football with mine. Jimmy was six or seven years older than me and had started a menswear business that was going well for him, and I had worked for him over the busy Christmas period on a few occasions. He usually employed one full-time staff member and that guy had given in his notice, so Jimmy needed somebody reliable to help him. When I heard that Jimmy was enquiring about me, I called around to the shop to see him and he offered me the job straight away. I would be earning nearly twice what I was getting in the Great Northern Hotel, I would have guaranteed regular hours, and I was at home in Portlaoise. For a young fella, this was a no brainer, so I ditched the chef career to sell men's clothes.

I spent a great two years working for Jimmy and I found that it was something I really liked and was good at. Being back home, I threw myself into local politics and was elected secretary of both the Portlaoise town Cumann and the wider electoral area for Fianna Fáil. At a national level, I had been elected to Fianna Fáil's National Youth Committee and was also the youth representative for Leinster on the party's ruling National Executive. I found that I was getting noticed for my organisational ability and I enjoyed politics, so I was soon spending most of my free time doing party work.

As a 20-year-old, I was attending meetings, conferences and dinners with government ministers and parliamentarians, and to be fair I never once felt out of place. Fianna Fáil really was an organisation where anybody could make it, no matter what you did for a living. Apart from travelling to Dublin for organisation meetings and conferences, I was also travelling around Leinster helping other counties to set up their youth wings. This was the part I really enjoyed as I got to meet loads of enthusiastic young people like myself and watch them build something in their own area with my help.

In those years after school, I was essentially trying to find myself. Being known as Brian Stack's son was both a help and a hindrance.

Within Fianna Fáil, the local party initially put me in several positions of trust because of who I was. The upside of which was that I was able to display my organisational abilities and move up the ladder within the party, something that wouldn't have happened if I wasn't Brian Stack's son. On the other side of the coin, I enjoyed my time in London as nobody knew who I was, whereas in Portlaoise I had a label and it was very hard for me to be my own person rather than being 'the son of Brian Stack'.

In 1990, the Prison Service job was advertised again and this time my mother was making sure that the application got to the Civil Service Commission on time. She got the form and after I filled it out, she took it from me and posted it by registered post. Even though the form had been sent off, I still had no intention of joining the Prison Service, but things were changing at the shop. I could see that Jimmy was running down the stock and I knew that he wanted to pursue a different career, so I was contemplating putting a package together to see if I could buy him out of the menswear business. I felt that if I could do that then I would have my own career and not have to go into the Prison Service.

But the menswear business was not to be, as things progressed very quickly with the Prison Service competition. I scored very high on the aptitude test, having done some training for it, and was called for interview in October 1990. There was great excitement around the town among young people of my age about this competition as the country was still in a recession and this was our way of securing a good paying job with a great pension.

When I was notified of the interview date, my mother turned into the typical Irish Mammy and went into action, leaving no stone unturned in her quest to get me into the Service. She rang one of the governors in the prison and asked him to call up to see her on his way home that evening. When he called, I had just come in from work, and Mam was explaining to him that I had been called for interview and my date was at the end of the following week. He told her he knew the governor who was doing the interviews and asked Mam if he could make a call from the phone in the hall. I could overhear him speaking and he told the other governor that 'Brian Stack's son Austin is up for interview next week, he's a good lad and works locally here in town'. He wasn't telling the other governor to put me through, but he was giving him some information as to who I was. It was a crafty way of letting him know I'd applied without making an inappropriate approach.

Even though I knew more about prisons than many of those going for interview, I still spent the following week doing my research and making sure that I was as prepared as I could be. When the day of the interview came, I polished my shoes, put on my best suit, and Mam dropped me down to the train station. I had given myself plenty of time when I got to Dublin, as I knew I had to get the bus to the Civil Service Commission offices on Grand Canal Street. This wasn't a problem for me as I was familiar with Dublin and was well able to navigate my way around the city using the bus system. When I arrived in Grand Canal Street, I had an hour to spare, so I was able to go in, relax and gather my thoughts while the board interviewed the person ahead of me.

I had never been called to a proper formal interview before and I knew from others around the town that there were four people on the interview panel, so I was fairly nervous by the time the chairperson of the board came out and brought me into the interview room.

The interview was in a conference room that had a very large table in the middle, where the four interviewers sat waiting to interrogate me. As well as the chairperson who was from the Civil Service Commission, there were two Prison Service governors and the Prison Service psychologist. Facing off against these four men across the large conference table was a completely different experience to anything I had done before, and I was wishing the whole thing was over before it even started.

As the interview progressed, I grew more confident and felt that I was performing well, and I was beginning to wonder why some of those I had talked to around Portlaoise were saying that the interview was so tough and they were left drained after it. But I was being led into a false sense of security, and out of the blue I was hit with a bombshell question. One of the governors sat upright in his chair, looked me in the eye, and asked, 'Austin, what would you do if you met the man who murdered your dad on a landing in the prison and he was taunting you about it?' This question rooted me to my seat and I was shocked that they thought it was appropriate to ask me, but I gathered my thoughts quickly and said, 'I would tell the Assistant Chief Officer on the landing.' Assistant Chief Officers are the supervisors on prison wings and they are in charge of the day-to-day running of those wings. I knew this and knew that they were the first line in the chain of command and that they would have to report it upwards.

It was a safe answer, but also the correct answer to a very unfair question. As Dad had been an Officer, Assistant Chief Officer, Chief Officer Class 2 and Chief Officer Class 1, I was straight away able to tell them about those grades and also that the Assistant Governor was at the time equal in grade to a Chief Officer Class 1. I also knew that the Deputy Governor and Governor were the two most senior grades and so I was able to say that without too much thought, and it refocused me after the previous question. When the interview finished I was really happy with my performance, but I was wondering if the question they put to me about meeting Dad's murderer was asked as they didn't want to give me the job, and

I started to think maybe I shouldn't have applied or gone for the interview. It now became a waiting game and I'd find out soon enough if they were going to let me through.

While I was awaiting the outcome of the interview, I went back to work and was still hoping that Jimmy would show his hand in relation to the menswear business. He was still running down the stock but not by enough to make it look like he was going to sell up. I really didn't want to join the Prison Service, but as the months dragged on it was becoming more evident that I would be left with no other choice.

Then one day in November when I went home for lunch, there was a letter on the hall table addressed to me with the State harp on the envelope. I knew that this was the letter that would decide my fate, and I didn't know if I should open it or not. Mam also knew what this letter was. She looked at me and said, 'Well, are you going to open it?' So I took a knife and used it to open the envelope. She was standing over me as I read the contents of the letter, which informed me that I had passed the interview and was now being called for a medical examination which would take place in early December.

'Ah, Austin, that is brilliant news,' Mam said as she gave me a big hug. 'You'll be set for life now!' I wasn't so sure.

The following Saturday night when I was in the Welcome Inn pub, which was the most popular bar in the town at the time, people started coming up to me and congratulating me on getting through the interview stage. Everybody knew that once you were called for the medical examination you were in, unless the doctor discovered something unusual.

'Austin Stack, how are ya?' asked Noel, whom I knew from around the town. 'I hear you've passed the interview for the Service. Fair play!'

'Thanks, Noel,' I replied. 'Yes, I just have the medical to pass now.'

'Well, let me tell you about that,' he jumped in. 'I failed the medical exam when I did it two years ago, all down to my eyesight. The doctor they use for that exam is really strict and he failed me. So, I went and got laser treatment done on my eyes. I'm now waiting for a second chance at that medical, same as you. So, fingers crossed.'

Hearing about the strictness of the doctor regarding the eyesight part of the test had me worried in one respect, but on the other hand I thought that this might be my way out. I had worn glasses for distance since I was about 15, but my eyesight wasn't so bad that I needed them all the time so I only used to wear them when driving.

Again, Mam swung into action and suggested that I get contact lenses. I was open to the idea of trying them out as I played junior football for Portlaoise that summer and was finding it difficult to see the action when the ball was at the other end of the field. I was thinking that the lenses would come in handy for something if the Prison Service didn't work out.

I went along to a local optician and she did all the examinations. Contact lenses were still relatively new at the time and she told me that I had a choice of a soft lens that you changed every month or a hard lens that you changed yearly. I tried both and thought the hard lenses were horrible and couldn't understand how anybody could wear them. So we settled on the softer lens which had to be ordered in due to the shape of my eyes.

As the medical examination date came closer, I began to feel more confident about going into the Service as I felt I had no other options. But with a few days to go until the examination, I still hadn't received the contact lenses, despite the optician making several calls to the supplier. Desperation took over at that stage and I came up with a plan. I knew that I could read the big letter at the top of an eye test chart so I asked the optician how many different charts there were in circulation. She told me that there were three different ones and they all had a different big letter at the top. My plan was simple, really: buy the three different charts and learn them off by heart. And that is exactly what I did. I spent three or four days memorising each line on the eye charts and once I knew the top letter, I would be able to call out any line on that chart that the doctor asked me to. Then on the morning of the medical examination I got a call from the optician to say that my contact lenses had arrived. I remember being so relieved and rushing down to collect them.

When I arrived at the examination, I was full of confidence as my sight was the only thing I had been worried about. The exam itself was a totally standard medical and I had no problems with anything. Then the time came and I was asked by the doctor to stand at a line on the floor, which was placed a little distance away from the eye chart. I straight away saw that I could read the big letter at the top which was 'Q', and I knew that if all else failed and the lenses didn't do their job that I would be able to call back any line on the chart to him. But when I looked down the chart even as far as the tiny letters on the bottom line, I was amazed that I could read them all and breathed a huge sigh of relief, especially after the doctor asked me to call out the letters on the second-last line of the chart and I was able to do so without any difficulty. With the medical over it was now a case of waiting to get called into training.

It was towards the end of January 1991 that I took a phone call from a woman in the Civil Service Commission to say that I had been successful in my application and that I would be shortly receiving a letter confirming my start date. She told me that I would also receive a letter asking me to give an undertaking to lose some weight before I started. I had always carried a little weight as it was just my natural body shape, and when I was boxing, I was always in the heavier weight classes for my age, but I wasn't in any way unfit and if I had been asked to do a physical or fitness test, I knew I would have passed easily.

When I asked the woman how much weight they wanted me to lose and was there a time frame for losing it, she just told me that I would be asked to give an undertaking to lose weight. I thought that the whole conversation was a bit pointless and was beginning to think that maybe it was a prank call, so I said to her, 'If I sign the letter and lose one pound before I start then I have kept my undertaking.' She confirmed that this was the case and within days I got an envelope with two letters in it. The first letter was my invitation to start training on July 22nd and it outlined the things that I would need to bring with me, such as a tracksuit, shorts, runners and a black belt. The second letter was the weight-loss undertaking, which I duly signed and returned to the Civil Service Commission.

I threw myself into a fitness drive to lose some weight even though there was no specific amount to lose – I just didn't want to give them an opportunity to say I hadn't kept my promise. I went back playing Gaelic Football, which I hadn't played since rupturing the anterior cruciate ligament in my right knee when I was 18. The surgery for that was pioneering at the time and the recovery was nearly a whole year, so I hadn't really felt comfortable playing since then. I decided that I would give playing junior football a go that year and we started training for the winter league in January. I trained with both the junior and senior team from January to July in order to lose the weight and enjoyed being back out on the pitch playing again. That six months of training four nights a week really stood to me once I went into the Prison Service college.

I had told Jimmy I was leaving as soon as I got my start date so that he could prepare a replacement for me in the menswear shop. I had planned on taking a break for a few weeks before I reported to the Prison Service, so I booked my holiday time for the first few weeks in July and I would then be officially finished in the shop after my holidays. However, my plan for a break between jobs didn't work out as at the start of my last week in the shop I got another phone call from the Civil Service Commission. I was told that two people who were attached to the Customs Service were due to start training in the group on July 1st, but they had decided to remain in their current jobs. I was asked if I would be available to start training the following Monday instead of July 22nd. The phone call caught me by surprise and I agreed to report for training the following Monday. Within days I got the amended letter to report to Mountjoy Prison on Monday, July 1st, 1991.

* * *

I remember that Monday so well as my mother drove me to Dublin. Mountjoy is known in the Prison Service as 'The Mothership', and up to very recently all new recruits had to report there. In my case, this seemed a bit silly as I knew that we would be put on a bus and brought back to the Prison Service Training College, which was located in Portlaoise.

When we got to Mountjoy, Mam pulled up the car and she gave me a hug. Then she looked at me and said, 'You'll never be a millionaire but you will always have a good standard of living and a guaranteed pension.' She then wished me the best of luck, and I nervously got out of the car with my bag and started to walk down the long avenue towards the imposing main gate of Mountjoy, knowing that my dad had made a similar walk nearly 32 years previous.

As I approached the main gate, my heart started to beat faster, and I was proud but emotional as I rang the bell on the gate and waited to be admitted. As with all older prison gates, the main gate was a huge double gate that, when opened, allowed vehicles to enter. Built into one of the gates is a smaller pedestrian gate or 'wicket gate', as it is known in prison speak. Within a minute of ringing the bell, the wicket gate was half opened by a prison officer who was wearing his full uniform with tunic and hat. The officer looked me up and down and before he could say anything I gave him my name and told him that I was reporting for training.

On hearing this he opened the gate fully and directed me towards another officer who was holding a clipboard. I knew instantly that this guy was going to be like an army drill sergeant; he stood there in an immaculate uniform that had the sharpest creases ironed into the shirt sleeves and trousers that I'd ever seen. His hat was unusual as he had splashed the peak to make it sit flat on his forehead, and his shoes were boots that were so shiny they could have been used as a mirror. This was Officer Willie 'Boots' Connolly and I could tell that he revelled in the role he was undertaking.

As I approached Connolly, he barked at me: 'Name?' When I told him who I was he again barked at me: 'Have you a letter for me?' When I handed the letter from the Civil Service Commission to him, he pointed to a set of steps in the gatehouse and barked at me for a third time: 'Up there and wait.' As I turned to walk up the steps, I could see the officers who were coming on duty looking at this scene and smirking to themselves, and I knew that it was all part and parcel of the game.

I pushed open the door at the top of the steps and found about a dozen other lads, all in civilian clothes, looking sheepish and nervous. They were all sitting on a bench that was fixed to the wall and ran around the room in a U-shape. I could see that they were all silent and nobody was talking, so I looked around and found a space to sit.

Being the outgoing type of person that I am, I looked at the lad who was sitting to my right and I introduced myself to him. He told me that his name was Paul Moore from Athy and we began chatting. This broke the ice and everybody started to introduce themselves, and as more and more people entered the room, they were asked who they were and where they had travelled from. One of the last to arrive was Noel from Portlaoise who had warned me about the doctor and the eye test; he was the only familiar face in the all-male group of 25. Usually there would have been a few more people from Portlaoise in a group as nearly everybody in the town would apply to join. Having a prison in the town and having so many people working in it meant that locals were drawn towards the Service more than people in other towns. The other striking thing about our group was the lack of women in it. In the previous three or four years, the Service began to allow female officers to work in male prisons and recruitment of female staff had taken off, with most groups having up to five women in them.

Once everybody had arrived and we were waiting for 'Boots' Connolly to come up to us, a female officer on her way into work took the time to look into the room and wish us all luck. It was something that I will never forget as to me it summed up the camaraderie and friendliness that I would experience throughout my career, but especially during my time in Mountjoy Prison.

After she left, Connolly appeared and frog-marched us across to the conference room, which was located behind the general office. Once there, a clerical officer arrived and went through numerous forms that we had to sign. As he put it, 'This is where you sign your lives away.' Forms such as the Official Secrets Act, Acceptance of Pay and Conditions, and Deduction of Unions Fees were all put in front of us.

Once we had completed the necessary paperwork, we were then brought over to the stores building to be kitted out with uniforms.

This wasn't the exact science that I was used to from the menswear shop, as the clerical officer in the stores just looked you up and down to decide what size trousers, shirt, tunic, overcoat, shoes and hat to give you. I was lucky in that I knew all my sizes and, unlike some of my colleagues who ended up in ill-fitting uniforms that were usually too big for them, I at least had a head start when it came to looking the part. After getting kitted out, Connolly led us out to a waiting bus and we were brought on the hour-long journey to the Prison Service Training College in Portlaoise.

When we got there, we were all allocated our own room, each of which had an ensuite toilet and shower facilities. Once I had found my room and left my bags there, I went back to the assembly area for our first meeting with Eamon Kavanagh, who was the Chief of Training. He outlined the eight-week programme to us and said that after three weeks we would be sent to Mountjoy and Wheatfield prisons to spend a week in each for on-the-job experience.

As another group would start training while we were out in the prisons, we would have to do week six of our training in the old training centre at Everton House in Dublin, so we had to arrange our own accommodation for those three weeks in Dublin. Then we would complete our final two weeks of training back in Portlaoise.

The training was fairly basic at the time and consisted of daily classroom sessions on the prison rules, warrants, courts, role plays on different situations, self-defence, drill instructions and fitness. At the end of each week, there was a written exam on the theory we had learned that week and there was also a physical fitness exam that had to be passed. We also had a room inspection on a Friday to ensure that we were keeping our rooms clean. After 5 p.m. each evening, we had free time and were told that we could go into Portlaoise and socialise if we wanted, but the doors of the training college would be shut and locked at 10.30 p.m. and everybody had to be in their rooms by 11 p.m.

Training went really well in the first few weeks, and I was scoring highly on the weekly exams. I hadn't told any of the others in the group about my dad and what had happened to him, and I was unsure if Noel even knew as he wasn't originally from Portlaoise.

At some stage during the third week, we were doing a classroom session that 'Boots' Connolly was delivering when he touched on the topic of personal security and the dangers of the job. Without warning, he looked at me and said, 'Austin can tell you first-hand about what happened to his dad', and then he proceeded to use my dad's murder as an example of why we needed to be careful and stressed that this was how dangerous our job could be.

As soon as he had finished, everybody was staring at me and I didn't know which way to look. I knew that they hadn't a clue about what had happened to Dad and I hadn't mentioned it as I wanted to be taken on my own merits within the group. Most of them would have been like me 14 or 15 when Dad was shot and none of them were from Portlaoise, so I knew that they wouldn't have known. Connolly had caught me completely by surprise and I was shocked that he hadn't given me a heads-up about what he was going to say. I was so annoyed but I couldn't say anything as I didn't want to cause myself problems with Connolly or the other training instructors. After my experience at the interview, I felt that there was a lack of compassion in their way of dealing with me and what I was going through, and there appeared to be no thought given to how tough joining the service was for me.

In fairness, a few of my colleagues in the group came to see me privately after and told me that they felt really bad about how the situation had been dealt with and asked if I was OK. Nearly every

Left: Letter of appointment to the Prisons Service, 1959.

Below: Dad and Mam at a dinner dance, 1966.

Family photo in the front garden, September 1971.

Tramore beach, summer 1972.

Left: With Dad on my First Communion, May 1975.

Below: Hurling in the garden, May 1976.

Dad, Mam and my dad's sister Bernadette, October 1981.

Family fun at Christmas, 1981.

Left: Dad with the Laois, Kilkenny and Carlow boxing champions, 1982.

Below: Dad with trophies for boxing tournaments, 1982.

Above: Dad and Mam with friends on the Laois GAA trip to USA, October 1982.

Right: At home on Christmas Day, 1983.

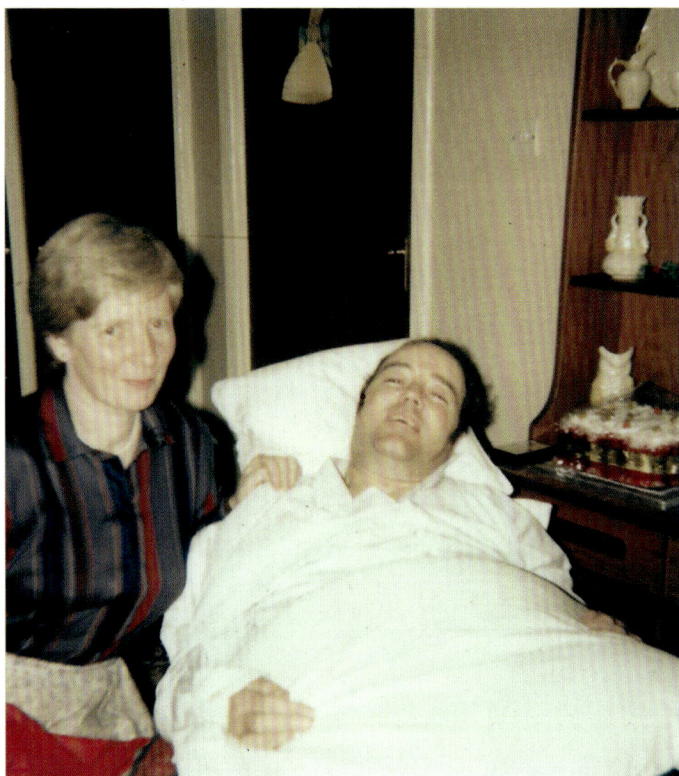

Day out with Dad, summer 1984.

Colleagues bring Dad's coffin into the church at his funeral, October 1984.

Right: Me with Dad's hat and flag at his funeral, October 1984.

Below: Unveiling of a bronze bust of Dad, with Mam and my brothers Kieran & Oliver, in the Prison Service College, May 2013.

one of them told me that if they were in my shoes, the Prison Service was the last job they would do.

For the three weeks that I would be in Dublin while training, I stayed on the couch in my brother Kieran's flat in Harold's Cross. For the first week of job experience I was sent to Mountjoy, where they buddied us up with an experienced officer and we got to cover all the important posts such as the main gate, reception, and landing duties. We stood out from the rest of the officers in our new uniforms and spit-polished shoes, and the prisoners were quick to rib us about being new recruits. One of the lines they used to frequently throw at us was 'I've done more jail time than you.'

The second week we were sent to Wheatfield Prison in west Dublin, which was a new prison that had opened only two years previous. Wheatfield was the first prison built by the Irish State; all the other prisons were built by the British in Victorian times. This prison was laid out differently to the other prisons and was very American in design, with small units and doors being opened electronically rather than by keys. We were sent there to see a different style of jail but the work was essentially the same and prisoners, no matter where they are, will behave the same way.

During that week in Wheatfield, I really got to know one of my colleagues from the group, Eddie Mullins, as we went for walks around the outside of the prison every lunch time. That week was the start of a friendship that saw us work together in many different prisons during our career, and at various times we have been there to offer each other advice and support. In a job in the Prison Service, you always need somebody like Eddie who you can call if you need a chat, and that has worked both ways for us through the years.

For the third week in Dublin, we were sent to Everton House and our training there mostly consisted of learning about the new control and restraint techniques that the Service was trying to roll out. At that stage there was no formal policy on these things and they were just showing us various ways of grabbing and subduing prisoners. I remember at one stage during a role play not being able to put a hold on the colleague who was playing the role of the prisoner, so I just caught him and flipped him over my shoulder using brute strength. Connolly was instructing the session and he was the person in the service who was trying to pioneer these new techniques, and he looked at me and shook his head in disbelief.

For our last two weeks of training, we were back in the training college in Portlaoise. The mood within the group had definitely changed after spending three weeks away and everybody was a bit braver and cockier. On the Thursday night of that first week back in Portlaoise, I went football training with the Portlaoise Juniors and afterwards I went to meet the lads from the group in the Welcome Inn. By the time I got to the pub, the group had taken over a corner at the end of the bar and some were already getting boisterous. The owner of the pub, Aidan Delaney, actually asked me when I arrived if I would have a word with them, as he felt some of the women in the bar didn't feel comfortable going past the group as they went to the toilets. After I spoke to the lads, I went and took a seat with some locals at the counter and had four or five pints there before joining the rest of the group for the walk back to the college.

We were all in good spirits and we made it back to the college before the doors were locked. When we returned, we made a small presentation to 'Boots' Connolly as he was going on holidays the following morning and he wouldn't be with us for our last week. There was a real party atmosphere in the place and after Connolly left us, we had a chat about going up to the local night club. We decided to get out of the windows in some of the ground floor bedrooms and leave them open so that we could get back in. I knew from living in Portlaoise that this had been done regularly by trainees in the college and there were never any problems. So that night, 15 of us left through the windows and walked up to the Killeshin Hotel where the night club was located.

When we got inside, I spent most of the evening chatting to some girls I knew and I was hoping to catch the eye of one of them in particular. They were from Mountrath, which was a town near Portlaoise, and I knew them from school debates and had also gone out with one of their friends for a short period. During those days, the DJ would play two slow sets of romantic songs towards the end of the night and at that stage lads would usually ask a girl to dance, and if she said yes, you knew that she liked you and things went from there. I was doing my best to impress this particular girl and was waiting for the slow set to ask her for a dance when one of the lads from the training group, Tom, came over and asked me where the toilets were. Thinking that the slow set was still a bit away, I decided to show Tom where they were as I needed them myself.

When we were in the toilets, I got chatting to one of the lads I played football with and Tom stayed with me as we chatted. As we left the toilets, Danny, who was a prison officer from Portlaoise and was in the job about two years, approached us and told us that there had been trouble on the dance floor. He said, 'Some of the lads you are training with were in a fight and you'd better get back to the training centre.'

Tom and I decided to go back to the college and we left the night club by going up the steep stairs to the ground-floor street exit. When we got there, we could see that some sort of a fight had taken place and I saw a group of fellas giving the last few kicks to one of my colleagues, who was lying on the ground. I shouted at them to leave him and as they were running away one of them pushed me back down the steep stairs that I had just come up. Tom helped me back up and at that point some of my colleagues started to appear and one in particular needed medical attention for cuts to his eye and lip. Two of the group decided to bring him to the hospital and the rest of us went back to the training college.

Once we got back in through the windows and found our own rooms, I don't think anybody realised the storm that was about to hit us. The following morning our injured colleague didn't make the morning parade and the training tutor went to see him in his room, where he told the tutor that he had fallen down the stairs in the pub. The tutor was satisfied with the explanation and the rest of the day passed off normally, so we all went home for the weekend.

When I was out in Portlaoise that weekend, I began to hear stories about the fight and over the course of Saturday and Sunday these stories grew legs and became more exaggerated every time I heard them. This made me feel a bit uneasy as I knew word would get back to the Prison Service. And it did, because on Monday morning we were all told that a complaint had been made and they wanted a statement from each of us.

I gave my statement telling the truth and thought nothing could really happen to me as I had just gone for a few drinks and hadn't been involved in the fight. Once they had received all our statements, the 15 of us who went out to the nightclub were suspended. I was so embarrassed and didn't know how I was going to tell my poor mother about what had happened. I was also only too aware that she was going to be so ashamed walking down the town because by this stage the whole town was talking about what had happened.

The following day I had two visits to the house. The first was from the Gardaí, who had decided to investigate the incident. I gave them a statement but couldn't be of much help as I had only come upon the very end of the fight. Shortly after that, two officials from the Prison Officers Association (POA) arrived to chat to me. They had phoned ahead to say that they were coming and had met a group of my colleagues in the Green Isle Hotel in Dublin earlier that morning.

When the POA officials arrived I was shocked at what they had to say to me.

'Austin, we have reason to believe that you were the one who started the fight,' one of them said.

'Me? What?' I replied. 'Sorry, I'm confused. I was nowhere near the fight when it broke out. Why do you think that?'

'We have heard a different story from a number of your colleagues up in Dublin. They name you as the trainee who started the fight,' he replied.

'That makes no sense. Someone is trying to frame me,' I argued. 'I bet it's because I'm Brian Stack's son. I bet they think if they can blame me that the Service will be lenient on me and we will all be saved. I didn't start the fight. I was nowhere near it.'

I could see that the POA officials had bought into the false narrative and I got quite angry with them. I knew that they were going from Portlaoise to meet another group of officers in Limerick, and I told them to question those lads on what happened and see if they mentioned me. In the days before mobile phones and social media, I was fairly sure that there would have been no contact between the two groups and the POA would find a different story when they went to Limerick.

Several days later I took another call from the POA requesting another meeting. When I asked if the group they met in Limerick had backed my version of events, they refused to answer. By now I was beginning to get worried that the POA were going along with this fabrication in order to get everybody off the hook, so I refused to meet with them and told the vice-president, 'I don't see any point in meeting you if you won't believe me. I'm going rogue on this and will look after myself.' There was no way I was meeting them unless believing me was the starting point for that meeting.

Eventually, a few days later, a meeting was brokered by the chairman of the local Fianna Fáil Cumann, Tom Colgan, whom I trusted. At the start of the meeting I looked at the two POA officials and asked, 'Well, did the lads in Limerick tell you I didn't start that row?' Yet again they refused to tell me what the group in Limerick had told them and I shouted, 'I'm done with you lot, I'm going home' and left the meeting. I was quickly followed out of the meeting by Tom Colgan, who asked me to return. I outlined my position to Tom: 'I can't go back in there if those people want to blame me for everything, Tom. You know I wouldn't do something like this.' He said to me, 'Look, I'm trying to save your job so just stay here for a minute' and he went back inside to them. After a few minutes, Tom returned and told me that the POA officials had told him that the Limerick group had indeed given a completely different version of events to them. I wanted to hear this for myself, so I returned to the meeting and eyeballed the vice-president and said, 'So?' as I made a hand gesture for him to tell me everything.

'We know you weren't involved and we know you didn't start the fight. The Limerick lads never even mentioned you and we questioned them about everything.' I glanced over at Tom saying, 'How difficult was that? Now you see what I'm up against.' I was then told that the POA were organising a big meeting for all 15 of us in their headquarters in Dublin a few days later and I was expected to attend.

When we all arrived in the POA headquarters in Millmount House on Dublin's northside, we were put into a room and each asked to write down our version of events. When the POA officials saw that my colleague Tom backed my version of events in his statement, they called me into a side room and the general secretary commented to me, 'Why couldn't everybody tell the truth at the start?' and I just smirked and replied, 'Well I did but you didn't believe me.' He then apologised and reassured me that they now believed that I had nothing to do with the fight.

After two weeks our suspensions were lifted as the Garda investigation found nothing. The Prison Service decided to issue us with a small fine and we had our probation periods extended by two months for leaving the training centre without permission.

After that I was assigned to Saint Patrick's Institution for young offenders in Dublin to start my career properly, but I knew that the mud from what had happened would stick for some considerable time.

My whole experience from the interview and training to what happened on the night out showed me that I was never going to be treated just like any other prison officer, by colleagues or by management. This was really difficult for me and I was more wary in my dealings with colleagues and always went out of my way to make sure I was never going to leave myself open to being set up or blamed for something. Being Brian Stack's son meant that there was the potential for some colleagues to try blame me if things went wrong in the hope that they would get away with it. Some of the managers might think I was trying to pull rank because of who I was, and then there were those who kept suggesting that I was going to be promoted up the ranks very quickly due to my name. So, I went from being the reluctant prison officer to being the cautious and wary prison officer.

Chapter 12

With all the drama that unfolded at the end of my training, I was glad to be finally assigned to a prison. On Monday, September 2nd, 1991, I walked through the gates of Saint Patrick's Institution with my new friend Eddie Mullins. We were the only two officers from the group who had attended the ill-fated night out who were assigned there, and we decided to arrive together as moral support for each other.

That morning we got our first taste of the infamous 'jail banter' as the other prison officers made us feel welcome in the unique way that only they can. They held us between the main gate and the inner gate as all the staff came out of the canteen to chant and jeer at us in a typical jail welcome.

Comments like 'Close that window or Stack will jump out through it', 'You'll never be let near that training college again' and 'You let a bunch of kids beat you up' were all too common in those early days. But it was all good natured and the staff in Saint Patrick's Institution were a great bunch of people who went out of their way to help us fit in.

I spent the first four years of my career there and, to my surprise, I found myself working with several officers who had worked with Dad in the early 1980s in Portlaoise. When talking to these officers, the respect that they had for Dad shone through and they all spoke in glowing terms about him and the way he managed things. In what would become a recurring theme when talking to former colleagues of Dad's, they never wanted to talk about what happened to him.

Likewise, my mother wasn't too inclined to talk about what had happened either. She had been through a very tough time after Dad's shooting and death, and she had concentrated on raising the three of us. In the first few weeks after the shooting, she had some initial contact with the Gardaí leading the investigation, but she had never received any update on the progress of the case. She just assumed that the Gardaí were doing their job and we would be notified if there was a breakthrough. She hadn't made any contact with the Gardaí either in those first five or six years after the shooting, and I think she regrets now not putting more pressure on them in those early days, but she was in a vulnerable state and all her energy went into taking care of us and trying to ensure we turned out OK. The other problem in relation to this period was that neither my mother nor the rest of us had information to go to the Gardaí with, and so it would have been easy for them to just keep saying that the case was open. It just seemed to us that the case was in limbo and the Gardaí were waiting for a breakthrough, and we trusted them.

When I had received notification to attend my medical examination for the Prison Service, it seemed to prompt my mother into action and she wrote a letter on December 13th, 1990 to Detective Inspector Michael Connolly in Kevin Street Garda Station, who was in charge of the investigation. This was the first time that she had sought a formal update on the case and, after receiving no reply, she wrote again on January 9th, 1991. This time she received a very short reply in a letter dated January 14th, 1991 from Detective Inspector Connolly: 'In answer to your letter of 9/1/91, the present position regarding the shooting of your late husband is that the investigation is ongoing. There have been no developments. When there is, you will be notified without delay.'

Since Dad had died, I had often thought about what had happened and why it happened. I used to lie awake at night trying to process everything, and different scenarios about what happened would be going through my mind. It was frustrating for me as a teenager and that is when the sleepless nights started.

For about 20 years after the shooting, I had two sleep patterns: the first was lying awake until two or three in the morning thinking about everything; the second was waking up in the middle of the night and not being able to get back to sleep. My mind would be racing and I had no way of stopping it. I needed answers but I had no information and very little chance of getting any.

I even remember going to Manchester for a football match early in the 1995/6 season and the crime reporter Veronica Guerin was sitting opposite me on the plane from Dublin and in front of me at the match. I was so tempted to approach her and ask her to take an interest in the case. I just knew that there was something not right about it but nobody was talking. There seemed to be no interest in it, and we were completely in the dark. However, that was all about to change. I got my first little bit of information in the autumn of 1996.

PART 3:
HELL

Chapter 13

Ater spending four years working in Saint Patrick's Institution, the Prison Service attempted to upgrade service-wide catering facilities and had built a new state-of-the-art kitchen in Mountjoy Prison. They were looking for staff to work in this kitchen, which would have a training emphasis as well as producing the daily meals. Having some cheffing experience and training, I applied for one of the jobs and was successful, so I transferred to Mountjoy in December 1995.

As Mountjoy Prison is such a large complex, there was also a satellite kitchen located in the Medical Unit, which at the time mostly housed prisoners who had been diagnosed with the AIDS virus. As part of my role in the kitchen, I was sometimes assigned to work in this satellite kitchen.

It was while working in Mountjoy that I got the first real piece of information about what possibly happened to Dad and what was going on in Portlaoise Prison at the time. It was sometime during the autumn of 1996 that I met a former colleague of Dad's, whom I shall call 'John' (not his real name). He was somebody I was very familiar with as he had worked in Portlaoise Prison when he was a young officer during the early 1980s.

After the early-morning duties were complete and the officer who was assisting me had gone to deliver some food items, John came into the kitchen for a cup of coffee. I could immediately sense that he wanted to talk to me. After I made the coffee and we were sitting at a table in the corner of the kitchen, he began to open up.

'Austin, do you know what happened to your dad?' he asked. 'Has anybody ever told you what was going on in Portlaoise at the time?'

'No, our family doesn't know anything about what was happening in Portlaoise Prison at the time,' I replied. 'Dad never shared his work life with us. The Gardaí have told us very little and everything we know we've learned from news reports. Some of them suggested a splinter republican group or a Dublin criminal gang may have been responsible, 'cause the IRA and INLA denied responsibility. But I'd really appreciate hearing anything you can tell me.'

'Well, in the weeks prior to your dad's attack, he had learned that guns were being smuggled into the prison,' John revealed. 'Rumour had it that this was done with the assistance of some prison staff and that separate component parts were being smuggled in by different people.'

I hung on every word.

'People believed that the gun components were smuggled past the security search. Apparently, an officer could bring in the gun component and hide it in their lunch box, which was then placed into a plastic bag. They would then simply hand the plastic bag containing a lunch box to the officer on the staff searches, then they would be checked with the hand-held metal detector and the other officer would hand them back their plastic bag. It was that simple!'

According to him, when my father became aware that there was a gun in the prison, he notified Governor Bill Reilly. He said that normally, if the Governor became aware of such information, there would be a large-scale search, but this time nothing happened.

'Your dad was constantly ahead of the IRA prisoners in their attempts to get replica keys and smuggle in guns or explosives. He was so obsessed with the security of the prison that he would regularly change the lock on one particular gate that only senior managers had the key for. Your dad was suspicious that a senior manager was making copies of that key.' He told me that this lock in particular was critical to any potential escape attempt and 'that's why Brian kept changing it, at least once a month'.

'That senior manager had also been involved in the smuggling of guns and ammunition into the prison. I believe, because your dad was so meticulous in his approach to security, the IRA needed to get rid of him.'

He then went on to talk about the IRA's attempted escape from Portlaoise Prison on November 24th, 1985. He said that while the staff and prisoners were in Mass that Sunday morning, 12 IRA prisoners attempted their escape, which they had been planning for a number of years. The IRA had staff uniforms that were allegedly smuggled into the prison. He told me that the escape was led by the man commanding the IRA prisoners, Thomas McMahon, who was doing life for the murder Lord Louis Mountbatten in August 1979, along with the murder of three other people who had been on his boat.

The prisoners had two guns, but he said the information doing the rounds in the prison was that Thomas McMahon was allegedly not happy with the individual who had been given one of the guns after the prisoners drew lots. The prisoners had agreed not to shoot any prison officers and McMahon was allegedly afraid that one of the prisoners who had a gun might do so.

'One of the bullets seems to have been interfered with to ensure that the gun wouldn't fire,' John continued.

He then explained that this was very lucky for one particular officer, Assistant Chief Officer Paddy Powell, as during the escape attempt, Powell had closed a gate going from E3 landing to E2 landing and the prisoner with the gun was left behind. This prisoner ordered Powell to open the gate and, when he refused, he pointed the gun at him and fired. As the bullets had been allegedly tampered with, it misfired.

When the gun misfired, the other prisoners continued with the plan; using smuggled uniforms and replica keys, they made their way to the gate that my dad had been very concerned about. With my dad out of the picture, they had their replica key for this important gate. Indeed, according to a newspaper published by Sinn Féin, *An Phoblacht*, in an article commemorating the escape: 'Using duplicate keys, the escape team opened six further steel gates.'

However, they became stuck at the next stage of the escape. They placed Semtex on the lock of the prison's large main gate in order to blow it open, but when the Semtex exploded it buckled the gate and the prisoners could go no further.

At this point, McMahon ordered them to stand down, and when the Deputy Governor Ned Harkin arrived on the scene, McMahon handed the gun over to him. It is alleged that at this point Deputy Governor Harkin handed the gun back to McMahon saying, 'Can you take the bullets out of that?'

If this is true, it was indeed an extraordinary thing to have happened, but the more I learned about the unusual events in Portlaoise Prison during this period, it really wouldn't surprise me.

I had always been suspicious that my dad's murder was connected with the escape attempt by IRA prisoners on November 24th, 1985. It was just a hunch I had, as I knew how good my dad was at his job. I've always believed that the IRA prisoners were unsure about how unwell Dad was after the attack and were probably aware that he was getting information from somewhere in relation to their escape plans.

They were definitely planning the escape attempt prior to them shooting Dad. Alan Bailey, who was the Detective Sergeant on the Cold Case Unit, which reviewed the case many years later, backed this theory up in an article he wrote on August 17th, 2013. In this article, Bailey, who had access to a lot of the investigation material, said: 'Brian Stack was, I have no doubt, taken out because the masterminds behind a huge plot that was even then being put in place to carry out a mass escape from the prison feared that he would, through his diligence and devotion to duty, disrupt their carefully hatched plans.'

So, when they failed to kill him initially, they couldn't immediately go ahead with the plan as they just didn't know what information Dad may have passed on to the investigating team. They had no idea about his brain damage and memory issues, and they waited until he passed away to carry out their plot.

When I heard all of this new information, I was stunned and didn't know what to say. It shocked me but, for the first time, somebody had given me an insight into what was going on in Portlaoise Prison at the time, and why the IRA might have had a motive for killing Dad. I didn't for one minute believe that John could be making all this up; he had nothing to gain by doing so and the manner in which he approached me was that of a man looking to get something off his chest.

About a year later, John was transferred to another prison and as staff locker space in Mountjoy Prison was at a premium at the time, he gave me his locker. When he opened the locker to clear it out, I was astonished but touched to see that he had my father's memorial card pinned to the inside of the locker door.

Chapter 14

Thirteen years after Dad's attack, I had finally received background regarding why he'd been targeted. This kernel of truth spurred me on and I was hungry to uncover more. And in an amazing twist of fate, a few months after this encounter in the Medical Unit kitchen, another former colleague of Dad's approached my younger brother Oliver.

It was coming up to Christmas 1996 and this particular officer used to drink in my uncle's pub, Donoghue's of Portlaoise. Oliver worked part-time in the pub when he was going through college and would have regularly encountered this man.

On the night in question, as closing time approached and the pub started to empty, the man called Oliver over to a quiet corner. He then proceeded to tell him, nearly word for word, the same story that had been relayed to me in Mountjoy. This particular colleague was very close to my dad; he was a good sportsman and Dad used to mentor and motivate him, making sure he had time off work if competing and he often drove him to events. I was often with them on these occasions and knew that Dad had great time for him.

There was one major difference between the two stories, however, but it was crucial as it was a first-hand account. When telling Oliver his story, my dad's former colleague said, 'I was one of a small, hand-picked group of officers that Brian had selected to stay back late one night in an organised search for a gun.' He explained, 'Brian had an informant on the IRA landings and that's how he knew there was a gun.'

He told Oliver that on the night of the search, which was a few weeks before my father's shooting, my dad told him that he was 'working on something that would rock the State to its foundations'. He said that my dad had reported the information about the gun to Governor Bill Reilly and, when nothing was done about it, Dad organised a search himself. It was in one of these searches, a month prior to the attack on Dad, that explosives were found in a workshop. Dad always thought Governor Reilly was a little too cautious in relation to these things and he feared that this caution would come back to haunt them all.

He also told Oliver about an incident during an escort to the courts with an IRA prisoner, which he was on, where the prisoner wanted to go to the toilet and there was a gun planted for him in the toilet cistern.

I made contact with this former colleague of Dad's and went through these events with him at length. I have no reason to disbelieve the stories of these former colleagues of my dad, and they have made statements to the Gardaí in relation to the disclosures that they made to us. The timeframe that these officers were talking about was the few months immediately prior to Dad being shot. It was also around this time that my mother had become concerned about Dad's mood. 'What's up with you Brian?' she asked him one evening after work, to which he replied, 'It's work, it's not you. I'm working on something but don't ask me any questions about it.'

While myself and my family were naturally very shocked and disturbed by these revelations as they tied in with what my mother remembered about Dad's mood at the time, it was all still pretty much hearsay and there was no real hard evidence to back any of it up. It was very frustrating to have gone from not knowing anything to now knowing something, but not having any way to prove it.

I made a decision there and then to get the answers to my questions: Who murdered my dad? Why did they murder him? Why had there been no convictions for his murder? I had to find the truth, to get justice for my dad and to fight for him like I know he would have done for me.

Chapter 15

It's very hard to describe the frustration that I was feeling in the years that followed these revelations. I had no further information other than the hearsay of two former colleagues of my dad's – I had no hard facts or other information. I thought about contacting the media but felt that they would think I was a crank throwing about wild allegations without any substance or proof. Really, in those years I was hoping that some investigative journalist would take an interest in the case and see what they could find. Eventually this is exactly what happened.

Ten years later, I was working in Limerick Prison in late 2006, having been transferred there on a promotion, when I took a call one evening from Nigel Mallon, who was the National Public Relations Officer of the Prison Officers Association. Nigel gave me the news that I had been waiting years to hear. 'Do you know Barry Cummins? He's a journalist from RTÉ. He has contacted the POA looking for your contact details.' He explained that Barry wanted to talk to me as he was writing a book about unsolved murders and wanted to explore the possibility of writing a chapter on my dad for his book.

I gave Nigel permission to pass my number on to Barry. I was eager to hear what he had to say and I wanted to have all the facts before talking to my mother and brothers about anything that he was proposing. I was conscious that some journalists in looking at this case might tend to sensationalise things rather than go after the hard facts. I also wanted to be sure that Barry was the right person to tell the story and look after our interests when doing so.

Barry was quick to make contact once he had my number and, after a brief chat, we agreed to meet for a coffee where he would tell me in more detail what he was proposing. The initial vibe I got from the phone call was that Barry was a decent guy and that we might be able to work with him, but I still wanted to check him out before meeting him in person.

At the time Barry was working for RTÉ's main evening news programme *Six One*, so I knew that some of my former political friends might know him. Seán Sherwin had been the Fianna Fáil National Organiser for a long time and I trusted his opinion, so I asked if he could talk to the party's press office about Barry and find out what type of person he was. Seán was only too happy to help and he returned my call a few days later, telling me that Barry 'is one of the good guys'. When I got this reassurance about Barry, I made an arrangement to meet with him a few days later.

We had our first meeting in BB's coffee shop in the food court in the Liffey Valley Shopping Centre early one Saturday morning. I was immediately struck by how genuine he came across and I felt that I could trust him right from the start.

After the initial chat about what he wanted to achieve in his book, we got down to business. 'Austin, what information does your family have on the status of the Garda investigation? Have the Gardaí kept in touch with your mother?' I replied, 'My mother got a very short one-liner from the Gardaí in 1991 to say the case was still open. We have heard nothing since. That's been our only contact with them since 1984.'

'I'm not surprised, Austin,' he responded. 'In the preliminary research I've done, I found it hard to find anything in the media archives apart from the initial reports of the shooting and the funeral.'

When I told him the stories that Dad's former colleagues had relayed to us, he began to feel that there might be more to the case than he originally thought.

'I want you to know that I will not write about your dad's case if your family are not happy for me to do so,' he explained. 'That said, my research may help you uncover more of what happened to your father and help answer a lot of lingering questions.'

I nodded; I had been thinking just that. 'I'd like to interview your mother and brothers as part of the work for the book. Do you think that'd be a problem?' he queried.

As my mother would be very nervous about doing something like this, we decided that he would come to Portlaoise for a casual chat with her before any interview, but this was of course contingent on us agreeing to take part.

After the meeting with Barry, I spoke with my brothers and Mam and told them what he was proposing and how it might benefit us in terms of fresh information. My brothers had the same gut feeling as me about the book and thought that the opportunity to get some answers or information was too good, while Mam initially wanted to 'let sleeping dogs lie'.

Mam did, however, agree to meet with Barry, and we all met him together for a casual chat in my mother's house in Portlaoise. After that meeting my mother asked if we wanted to go ahead and cooperate with the book. Without hesitation my brothers and I told her that we were in favour of it. Mam then told us that she would cooperate for us as she felt that we needed answers more than her.

After Barry had done some initial research for the book, he called me sometime in late January 2007 and told me that he needed to meet me as what he had to tell me was too important to disclose over the phone. I knew by the tone of Barry's voice and the way he was speaking to me that he had uncovered something and I was really anxious to meet him as soon as I could.

When we met a few days later, Barry disclosed things that shocked me, leaving me bewildered and angry.

'I was given a few minutes with the original case file for your father's murder and I took some notes from it,' he shared. 'There was a lot of material and forensic evidence gathered from the crime scene and in other locations. This included fingerprints taken from a newspaper discarded by one of the individuals involved in the shooting, fingerprints taken from the car that the motorbike driver was leaning up against prior to the shooting, fingerprints taken from a getaway car that was used to collect the shooters after they had ditched the motorbike in the canal, and the discovery of a helmet belonging to the motorbike driver, which was found on the roof of a factory beside where the bike had been dumped.'

I was aware that a motorbike used in the attack had been dumped in the canal near Portobello as this had been widely reported in the media at the time, but that was the only piece of information that I had in relation to the aftermath of the shooting. So, as all this new information was disclosed by Barry, I was reeling.

But it didn't end there, as Barry then revealed another crucial piece of evidence: an eyewitness testimony from a young lady who had seen the motorbike driver without his helmet a short time before the shooting. Her statement to the Gardaí formed the basis of the photo-fit that was done at the time.

'It appears that five men were arrested under Section 30 of the Offences Against the State Act in the weeks after the shooting,' Barry explained. 'Four of these had Dublin addresses and were originally from Belfast, Armagh and Donegal, while the fifth was from Antrim with a Donegal address.'

By the time Barry had finished telling me everything, I wanted to scream – all this time the Gardaí had this evidence and they did nothing. I was so angry but I also needed Barry to fill in some of the gaps as my mind was working overtime trying to process everything. I had never previously heard about a potential getaway car and wanted to know more about that.

'After the bike was dumped,' he began, 'a car met the shooters and drove at speed away from the area. This car subsequently ran through a red light at a junction and was pursued by a Garda car for the road traffic offence as they had no idea that it was connected to the shooting. The getaway car crashed near Dartmouth Square and the occupants fled on foot. There were fingerprints taken from the rear-view mirror and some of the objects in the back of the car.'

We had never been told about all this fingerprint evidence or the discovery of a helmet, which could today be examined for potential DNA. While I was angry and frustrated, I also knew that if the Gardaí still had all this evidence, there was the potential for a breakthrough in the case.

When I asked Barry about the eyewitness who saw the motorbike driver some time before the shooting, he was able to provide me with her name. However, he told me that there was no mention in the file of this lady being asked to perform an identification parade. This seemed incredible to me considering that the Gardaí had arrested five potential suspects.

Barry also told me that a Garda source had mentioned to him that a top-secret operation had taken place in the late 1980s when several officers from Portlaoise Prison, including Deputy Governor Harkin, were arrested and questioned in Bridewell Garda Station in Dublin. He told Barry that this was in relation to trafficking items into Portlaoise Prison, but there would be no records of this because it was so sensitive.

While I was trying to work through all this in my mind, Barry said, 'From what I could see on the file, there was a lot of work done in the first few weeks after the shooting and then it all just stopped.'

I knew instantly that the investigation team must have discovered something that made them back off or that they were told to back off, and that is why the eyewitness was never asked to perform an identification parade and why the existence of all the material evidence was never disclosed to us or anybody else.

After I left Barry, I called my brothers and explained what Barry had found out. They had the same reactions as I had and we were now faced with having to tell my mother. We agreed that it would be best if we all did this together and then, depending on her reaction, decide what to do next.

When we told Mam, she was in complete shock but also wasn't the least bit surprised, as she knew all along that things just didn't add up. We agreed that the first action we needed to take was to send a letter to the Garda Commissioner, Noel Conroy.

So, on January 30th, 2007, I wrote on behalf of the family and asked if the case was currently being investigated, who the lead investigator was, and what progress had been made on the case. I also asked that if the case wasn't currently being investigated, was there a reason for this and could a new team review the case file. I made the Garda Commissioner aware that there was a book due out shortly which featured the case and that we had become aware of certain matters. I told him that I felt it would be prudent for my family to meet with a Garda representative prior to the release of the book.

The Commissioner's office sent an acknowledgement and nothing more happened. So I wrote again on March 17th and May 30th, again receiving the standard acknowledgement. I didn't know it at the time, but we had probably caused a great deal of panic and the Gardaí were likely wondering what we knew about a case they thought had long since been buried.

We waited months before they agreed to meet with us, but having waited 24 years, a few more months wasn't going to overly frustrate us. It did, though, give us an early indication of how we were going to be treated.

On July 25th, 2007, we had our first meeting with the Gardaí since 1983. Superintendent Thady Muldoon and a Detective Sergeant Doyle from Kevin Street Garda Station travelled to Port-laoise and we all met in Mam's house. Kevin Street Garda Station had taken the lead on the case in 1983 and it was there that the file on the case was stored.

Initially, Superintendent Muldoon appeared to be on a fishing expe-dition and seemed very anxious to find out what we knew. 'So what's in this book?' he asked after we had exchanged pleasantries. I imme-diately answered with a question of my own, 'Are there fingerprints? I know about the fingerprints.' When I mentioned the fingerprint evidence, his face dropped; I could tell that he wasn't expecting us to have that level of knowledge. He tried to find out where the informa-tion had come from but we wouldn't tell him, but I'm sure he guessed that somebody from within the force had given it to Barry.

I pressed him to admit they had the fingerprints: 'Just give us a straight answer, have you got fingerprints?' And he finally did so, saying, 'OK, OK, there are fingerprints.' Straight away I jumped in with, 'And you'll have the helmet as well?' When I said this, he started to shake his head in disbelief and must have been wondering what was coming next. He then dropped a bombshell, 'We had that helmet but it's missing. We have turned Kevin Street Station upside-down looking for it, but it can't be found.'

I couldn't believe my ears and emotions got very high. 'How can you lose such a large and important piece of evidence?' I kept asking them over and over again in disbelief, but they couldn't answer.

This would be our first encounter with the never-ending excuses that the Gardaí would come up with in relation to hard material evidence and interviewing potential suspects or people who might have information. The standard excuse offered would be, 'It was the 1980s, things are done differently today.' The July 25th, 2007 meeting was the first time we heard that excuse and it wouldn't be the last.

We also had questions for them in relation to statements taken from friends of Dad and a very unusual questioning of Oliver which took place in the National Stadium. A few short weeks after Dad was shot, Oliver was about to get into the ring to box in an All-Ireland semi-final. I was with him and the coaches in the dressing room when two men in trench coats appeared and asked to talk with Oliver. They said that they were Gardaí, but didn't show any identification.

Oliver was 12 at the time and I was 14, so we didn't know any better, but I did ask them if they had spoken with my mother, who was outside. They told me that they had and she said it was OK to speak with Oliver. They took Oliver around the corner and questioned him about an incident a few weeks before Dad was shot when a guy who appeared to be following them after he had won the Leinster title fell off a motorbike. Oliver told them that he hadn't seen the incident. This whole experience had a huge impact on Oliver as he got into the ring literally minutes later and totally underperformed. My mother would tell me afterwards when I asked her about the 'detectives' that nobody had approached her. This left us all, especially Oliver, wondering if these guys were actually Gardaí at all.

Mam then found her voice and tackled Muldoon: 'When was the last time somebody looked at the case file?' The reply left us reeling: 'It was put on the shelf about a month after his death.' This was the cold, uncaring answer he gave to a woman who had finally gotten the courage to ask the Gardaí about her husband's murder.

This essentially backed up what Barry Cummins had witnessed when he saw the file, and my suspicions about what happened only began to grow and grow.

It was agreed that Superintendent Muldoon would forward a report to Deputy Commissioner Fachtna Murphy requesting that the case be looked at again with an emphasis on the 1985 attempted breakout, staff trafficking items into the prison, interviewing staff, interviewing informants, tracing suspects and tracing the helmet.

We adopted a tactic from an early stage of summarising important meetings and sending a note of them back to the Gardaí. In this case, Superintendent Muldoon forwarded the notes to Commissioner Conroy, who in turn sent it to the National Bureau of Criminal Investigation (NBCI). The NBCI is essentially the Garda unit that deals with investigations relating to organised crime, terrorism, gangland crime, and other serious crimes on a national level. The unit was formed in 1997 with the amalgamation of a number of national and specialist investigation units, and they perform a strategic role within the Gardaí. This all looked good on paper and meant that after all this time, maybe they were about to finally carry out a proper investigation.

*   *   *

I suggested to the rest of the family that we needed to also work a political route on this to keep the pressure on the Gardaí. Áine Brady, who was a friend of mine, was a junior minister in the

Department of Health and I asked her if she could secure a meeting for us with Brian Lenihan, who had recently been appointed as Minister for Justice. Brian was a young and upcoming politician who was starting to make a big name for himself.

Both Dad and I knew Brian's father, who was also called Brian. Brian Lenihan Snr was a former Tánaiste and Dad would have known him through work, as in those days ministers dealt directly with prison management. I knew Brian Snr from my time in youth politics, when I was a member of the Fianna Fáil National Executive, and he actually had given me lifts in his State car on a few occasions if I was returning to Dublin after meetings. I had been particularly loyal to Brian Snr, especially when he ran for election for President of Ireland, and I was his Deputy Director of Elections in Laois.

Áine told me that Minister Lenihan had agreed to the meeting and that she would be in touch as soon as she had a date. I only found out 15 months later, through a Freedom of Information request, the lengths that officials in the Department of Justice went to to stop the Minister meeting with us. There was a series of emails back and forth between Áine's office and the Minister's office, and in these it becomes obvious that Áine is getting frustrated that the proposed meeting was being pulled. Ultimately, this ended with a hand-written note from Áine's office that was sent to the Minister's office via fax, reading: 'Áine did speak to your Minister and he did agree to this meeting. Thanks.' After this intervention, I could see from further emails that the wheels were put in motion for a meeting.

In September, before that meeting would take place, Barry's book was published. The promotional campaign that went along with the book offered us an opportunity to bring awareness to the wider public of Dad's case for the first time in years. Kieran and I did a few daytime TV programmes with Barry and we could see that it was generating a lot of interest. We really still didn't have a whole lot of information about what happened and were hoping that the media attention might lead to a break in the case.

This publicity led to a call from the RTÉ Radio 1 *Liveline* programme presented by Joe Duffy. *Liveline* is a radio phone-in show which takes place in the early afternoons, and it has one of the highest listenership figures of any radio programme in Ireland. They rang me and asked if Mam would be prepared to go on the programme. As a family, we had decided to keep Mam out of any publicity stuff because she was afraid that she might end up saying the wrong thing. I had done a lot of training on media participation while I was involved in politics, so I was the obvious choice to do something like this.

The few interviews that Kieran and I did on daytime TV were very casual and light entertainment pieces, but this would be a different kettle of fish altogether. I only agreed to take part if I was given at least 15 minutes uninterrupted to tell the story. Phone-in shows have a habit of descending into farce if they aren't moderated properly and I wanted to avoid this.

In fairness, they agreed to my conditions and I went on the show on October 2nd, 2007. I knew this was going to be reaching hundreds of thousands of people, so while I was a little nervous, I made some notes and stuck to the story. For the first time ever, I said publicly that I had a suspicion that somebody on the inside was helping the IRA by arranging for keys to be copied and weapons to be smuggled into the prison. For the first time, I publicly put the IRA in the frame for the attack on Dad, linking the murder to the 1985 escape attempt from Portlaoise Prison.

Several of Dad's friends from the sporting world rang into the show, including Joe Ging who was with Dad on the night, and they gave a really good insight as to the type of man he was. The discussion ran for the whole show, which is unusual, and I got so many calls after telling me how good it was. I got an immediate sense that this was going to really put the case front and centre and it might lead to something. The following day the programme returned to the story and an ex-IRA man came on the show saying he believed they did it, while the former General Secretary of the Prison Officers Association, PJ McEvoy, made some astonishing claims.

First, he claimed that the POA had met with IRA representatives following the shooting and they guaranteed him that the staff working in the prison were safe. Then he said it was his belief that the State had murdered my dad. Both these claims were baffling in the extreme and they just didn't make any sense at all. I have no idea why he made these claims and he didn't provide any evidence to back them up.

What was even more extraordinary was that the day after this I received a phone call from Brian Purcell, the Secretary General of the Irish Prison Service. He said that he was calling in an official capacity as a representative of the State to refute the allegations that PJ McEvoy had made. I asked him would they be making a public statement to that effect and he replied that that would be up to the Gardaí to do.

Then, when I went back to work the following day, an even more extraordinary thing happened. A prisoner approached me and asked to see me privately. We went into a quiet room near where he was working and he told me that he had heard the *Liveline* show. 'I need to tell you that everything you said was true,' he blurted out. 'I can't say any more than that.' I asked him how he knew what I'd said was true and he told me, 'I served time in Portlaoise sometime after your dad was shot. The guy in the cell with me was there at the time and he told me everything that happened.'

Brian Purcell making that call and the information from the prisoner were further triggers that suggested to me and the family that there really was something more to this case than met the eye, and we would have to fight every step of the way to gain even the tiniest amount of information.

During early October, Áine Brady was still trying to secure a meeting with Minister Lenihan. As well as the letter and phone call to him in July, Áine followed this up with a letter on September 28th. The response was the standard acknowledgement letter, but Áine called me a few days later to say that she had spoken with the Minister and she invited me to Dáil Éireann on October 16th to meet with him. I got the impression from Áine that this meeting would be an informal meeting in her office and he was doing it because of the pressure from her.

When I arrived at the security station at the front gate, my old friend from Ógra Fianna Fáil, Gearóid Lohan, was waiting for me. I knew Gearóid for years and he was now working for Áine as an adviser. He brought me up to the office where Áine was waiting for me. 'The Minister will be along in a few minutes,' she said, as she offered coffee. We busied ourselves with some chat about local politics while we waited. It became apparent after about half an hour that something was wrong – there was no sign of the Minister and Áine made several attempts to contact his office without any success.

After waiting about 90 minutes, Áine felt really bad about what happened and said, 'I was only talking to him in Government Buildings an hour before you arrived and I reminded him about this.' She continued by making excuses for him. 'He must have been caught up in something urgent.'

She took me for something to eat in the restaurant in the hope that some of her officials would be able to track the Minister down before I left. I had a good idea what had happened though. I just knew that some of the officials in the Justice Department must have gotten to the Minister after what had happened on the *Liveline* show and they didn't want him meeting me in an uncontrolled environment.

After discussing what had happened with the rest of the family, Kieran suggested writing a letter to the Minister, making reference to his no-show on October 16th, and formally request a meeting. The idea behind this was to create our own record of the attempts to meet with him. I sent this letter on November 4th and received the standard acknowledgement from his office on November 14th.

Meanwhile, my Freedom of Information request showed that Áine was working in the background at the same time trying to secure the meeting. She received a letter in early November after my own request for a meeting was sent to the Minister. In this letter, Minister Lenihan informed Áine that he was refusing to meet with us due to his 'heavy schedule'. It was at this point, on November 20th, that Áine's secretary sent the previously mentioned fax, which appeared to spark a response. I can see from further released documents that by November 26th, the Minister had conceded to the meeting, which would take place on December 18th. Áine never told me of the extent to which the Minister's officials appeared to be blocking a potential meeting; I think she was just happy to have finally succeeded in delivering for a trusted friend. If I had known all of this prior to the eventual meeting, it probably would have changed how we approached it.

Meanwhile, the Gardaí had made contact again. This time Superintendent Christy Mangan called me to say that he had just been appointed to take charge of the Serious Crime Review Team, which had just been set up. This was essentially the Cold Case Unit. Christy let me know that Dad's case would be one of the first cases to be reviewed and he asked for an early meeting with the family.

Chapter 16

That first meeting with the Serious Crime Review Team took place in my mother's house in Portlaoise on October 22nd. Superintendent Mangan was joined by Detective Sergeant Alan Bailey, his second in command on the team. My initial take was that Mangan was going to prove difficult, while Bailey appeared to be the more approachable of the two. We were told that the team would begin work straight away and their primary objective was to review the original investigation and case file. The one piece of significant information that they shared with us that night was the list of five suspects, who they claimed were people of interest at the time. They asked if we had ever heard of any of these named individuals, and at the time the names meant nothing to me, but later I would receive information from several sources that identified one of them as the ringleader of the operation to murder Dad.

They also informed us that *Crimecall*, which was a weekly TV programme on RTÉ used by the Gardaí to seek information on crimes old and new, would feature Dad's case and a reconstruction of the shooting. As it happened, this programme was to air on December 18th, which is a date that I will long remember, as we finally had our meeting with Minister for Justice Brian Lenihan.

My mother was very nervous about the meeting, but she joined me and my brothers in Buswells Hotel opposite Dáil Éireann. 'We'll have some lunch first and a quick chat,' I said, nodding to them to sit in a comfortable but quiet corner. This relaxed everybody and eased some of the obvious stress that my mother in particular was feeling. We then made the two-minute walk across the road to the security office at the front of the Dáil, where again Gearóid Lohan was waiting to escort us to meet with Áine Brady, as she was going to accompany us to the meeting with the Minister.

Once we were in the main building, Áine greeted us with the big smile that she always had. 'Sheila, I'm so pleased to meet you,' she said and started to make a bit of a fuss about my mother, which further put her at ease.

Áine brought us across to Government Buildings through a link corridor, and we were shown into a very large meeting room with a wide boardroom table. We were told by an official to sit on one side of the table and wait, as the Minister would be along shortly. Little did I know but we were about to experience an attempt by justice officials to effectively shut us down and keep a minister in the dark.

Our first surprise came when the Minister walked into the room followed by what can only be described as a platoon of senior civil servants. I immediately recognised Seán Aylward, who was Secretary General of the Department of Justice, and I knew this was not going to go well. I knew Aylward from his time as head of the Irish Prison Service and wasn't expecting to see somebody of his rank at the meeting. In fact, we were expecting that the meeting would be attended by ourselves and the Minister with possibly a personal assistant.

The introductions were brief and Aylward took charge right from the off, placing Minister Lenihan directly opposite me while he sat to the Minister's left. I noticed that the Minister wasn't going to be taking notes and appeared to be there just to listen. Aylward then opened proceedings asking what they could do for us. Not having the knowledge that we subsequently gained much later, our agenda was small but pointed.

'We want to know why the Garda investigation was stopped in 1983,' I said. 'What happened, what was the reason it wasn't fully investigated? We also want to know why the Department of Justice has not issued a public response to the claims made by former POA General Secretary, PJ McEvoy, on the *Liveline* radio programme.' I was still completely baffled by McEvoy's allegations and even more so that no public rebuttal had been made by the Department of Justice. To my mind, these were just throw-away ramblings, but they needed to be formally rebutted. And finally I said, 'We want the State to suitably recognise the role my dad played in serving his country.'

They obviously wanted to get the second and third items off the table quickly and pawned us off with promises to see what could be done about recognising Dad in some way, while suggesting that it would be inappropriate for Justice to respond publicly to the comments made by PJ McEvoy.

Then, like the first meeting with the Gardaí, Aylward went fishing to see what we already knew. I responded to this in a forceful but straight-talking manner: 'We know about the evidence that the Gardaí have, the fingerprints and newspaper. We know they had a helmet but they lost it. We know that the investigation was stopped for some reason. Was the investigation stopped because it was discovered that a member of staff was helping the IRA?'

This triggered an angry reaction from Aylward, who said, 'There was no senior member of staff involved in that.' By this, he was referring to senior prison officers. He had just made a very serious mistake. I took a long breath, looked him in the eye, and said, 'I never mentioned the word "senior", you brought that to the table and you have now just confirmed my suspicions.'

I could see he was annoyed with himself for making such a schoolboy error. It was at this point that Minister Lenihan, who had said nothing and just picked his nails and looked disinterested up to this point, interjected. 'What rank was your dad?' he asked to my disbelief. Not only had the Minister not been properly briefed before the meeting, but it appeared that he had zero interest in being in the room, and I suspected that the officials may have told him that we were trouble and that they would handle things. The meeting couldn't end quick enough, and when it did a short time later, I remonstrated with Áine as we left: 'What the fuck was that all about?'

I could see that Áine wasn't happy with the way things had played out, but as a junior minister she had to be careful about what she said and did. She ushered us to the bar in the Dáil and the second we sat down Kieran rounded on her: 'What was all that about in there? He had no interest in meeting us. Does he not know we are Fianna Fáil people? Does he not know all the work that Austin has done for the party?'

I felt bad for Áine as she had been put in a very awkward position. 'I know, I know, I'll go and try to find him' she offered as she left us in the bar. About five minutes later, she returned with Minister Lenihan in tow. She had clearly explained to the Minister that we were a Fianna Fáil family of long standing, that both my dad and I knew his father Brian Lenihan Snr, and that I had previously been a senior member of the party. He sat down and, looking at us, said, 'I really had no idea who you people were,' referring to what Áine had obviously filled him in about. Again, Kieran took the lead and, pointing towards me, said, 'That man dragged people out to canvass for your father on a horribly wet night during the presidential election after his famous meltdown on the evening news.' He kept going, not letting the Minister get a word in edgeways. 'We are all Fianna Fáil, did you think we were coming here looking for money? We just want to find out what happened to our dad.' The Minister nodded his head and, in a low voice, responded, 'I got this wrong and anything I can do to help I will. Keep in touch with me through Áine.'

Five months later, in May 2008, Bertie Ahern resigned and Brian Cowen became Taoiseach unopposed. Years of financial excess were coming to an end and the country was about to enter one of its severest economic collapses in history. Brian Lenihan became Minister for Finance and we never got to meet with him again. He died three years later from pancreatic cancer.

* * *

Following the *Crimecall* programme and its appeal for information, the Gardaí received a number of calls. People also came directly to us as a family with information. In the first instance, my brother Oliver, who was working in Portarlington at the time, was approached by a man. He told Oliver that he had been at the boxing in the National Stadium the night Dad was shot. He also told Oliver that a garda from Portlaoise was sitting behind him with his young son. On enquiring who the garda was, Oliver was told his name was Louis Harkin. Oliver immediately rang me and blurted out, 'Austin, do you know a Louis Harkin? Is he related to Ned?' I told him to slow down and asked him what this was all about. I had never heard of a Louis Harkin at this point, so I rang my mother. 'Ma, do you know a Louis Harkin?' 'Yes,' she replied, 'he is a son of Ned Harkin and is high up in the Gardaí.' Alarm bells immediately started ringing in my head as Ned Harkin was the previously mentioned Deputy Governor of Portlaoise Prison who several people mentioned as being under suspicion of aiding the IRA prisoners. I decided to log on to the Garda website to see if I could find anything on him there.

I couldn't believe this information and while it might just have been a huge coincidence, we now had a witness placing Louis Harkin at the scene of the crime – the son of a man who Gardaí told us was a person of interest. To make matters even more suspicious to us as a family, this man Louis Harkin was now an Assistant Commissioner in the Gardaí. He passed away in 2017.

The second thing to come out of the *Crimecall* programme was a letter that I received in work from a man who it transpired was using an alias. In his letter, he claimed to have vital information in relation to Dad's murder. The letter included a phone number and when I rang and introduced myself, the individual on the other end of the line became very nervous saying, 'I can't talk over the phone, I have information that I can only deliver in person.' I got some details off this man and arranged to meet him in a pub in an isolated part of west Clare.

Needless to say, I didn't want to make the trip alone to meet an unknown person in a place so isolated, so my brother Kieran came with me. When we got to the pub, there were only two elderly men inside and they both glared at these two strangers who had just invaded their hallowed turf. We ordered drinks and chose a seat where we could monitor the door. After a few minutes, Kieran was getting a bit uneasy, saying, 'Are you sure we have the right place?' I was beginning to wonder myself when a man walked in dressed like something out of a 1950s spy movie. He was wearing a broad-brimmed wax hat and one of those long wax coats that have a half cape on the shoulders. Kieran whispered, 'Seriously, Austin!' as the man nodded to us and we nodded back.

When he came over and sat down, he introduced himself and claimed to have worked with Dad for a short period of time in Limerick Prison. He proceeded to rehash stuff that was already in the media and I could sense Kieran was getting frustrated. By nature, I tend to indulge people like this hoping that by letting them talk they might eventually provide something of relevance. Kieran, on the other hand, is far more direct and eventually just looked at him and said, 'Look, we have come a long way, all you've told us is already out there. You said you had new information; what is this new information?' When confronted with this directness, the man spent a few minutes recanting second- and third-hand information that was jail gossip and hearsay.

This meeting was to serve as a lesson to me and I became far more cautious about meeting people I didn't know after that. When I look back on it now, it was a silly and dangerous thing to do – we could have been walking straight into an ambush and been disappeared like so many others.

We had a further meeting with Superintendent Mangan and Detective Sergeant Bailey on January 15th, 2008 and I emphasised the importance of interviewing Ned Harkin. When I pushed them on the issue, all Mangan would say was that everybody they have spoken with in relation to the investigation up to that point had mentioned Harkin.

It was at this meeting that I sensed a huge reluctance on their behalf to carry out this interview. However, it was in the meeting following this, on April 8th, that we suspected something rotten was going on. At that meeting, they relayed to us that they had a report ready for the Garda Commissioner following their review. They told us that there were almost two hundred recommendations in the report in relation to things that were not done in the original investigation. We obviously asked if we could have sight of the report, but we were told that it was an internal Garda document and it wasn't possible to release it to us. However, in giving us a slight flavour of what was included, Superintendent Mangan told us, 'We managed to identify all those who were at the boxing that night, we have a name on every seat.' I wasn't inclined to believe this and thought it was a bit of bravado, so I asked, 'How did you manage to trace all those people?' 'Well, once we identified one person, they would tell us who was with them and so on. We built up a picture that way,' Mangan said. He then made a statement that changed our relationship with him and the Gardaí: 'We will be interviewing any of those people who are still alive.'

He no sooner had those words out when Oliver spotted the opening: 'Does that mean you will be interviewing the Assistant Commissioner so?' Immediately, Mangan became animated and angry. He went on the defensive and, in a raised voice, said, 'That man was just at the boxing with his son.' I looked him in the eye and said, 'We are not inferring anything but are just asking if he will be interviewed.'

It was amazing how this one nugget of information that Oliver had gotten opened up a pandora's box and led to a breakdown of relations and trust with the Gardaí. We decided that we needed to document this meeting by sending a letter to Superintendent Mangan, which was copied to the Garda Commissioner, Taoiseach, and Minister for Justice. In this letter, we highlighted what we felt were priorities for the investigation: the interviewing of Ned Harkin, the processing of the fingerprints found at the scene of the crime and in the getaway car, the search for the missing motorbike helmet (which still could not be found), interviewing witnesses, and interviewing staff and prisoners from Portlaoise Prison.

The immediate reaction to this letter, which was diplomatic and carefully worded, was that Superintendent Mangan and his team cancelled two meetings with us at the very last minute on June 24th and July 10th, 2008. Following this, we asked for an urgent meeting with the Garda Commissioner, which was on our part an effort to restore relations and build trust. This meeting eventually happened on September 15th in Garda Headquarters in Dublin. Fachtna Murphy was Garda Commissioner at the time and he was accompanied by Deputy Commissioner Martin Callanan, Chief Superintendent Noel White and Superintendent Mangan.

At this meeting, the Commissioner kept emphasising from the outset that the passage of time would be a potential problem in resolving the case. He did, however, commit to re-opening the case and sending the matter for further investigation to the National Bureau of Criminal Investigation (NBCI), which was headed up by Chief Superintendent Noel White. They informed us that NBCI were ready to start the following day and would be in touch with us the following week. Myself and Kieran then prepped them on the potential use of informants from the 1980s; for some reason this made them uneasy, particularly Deputy Commissioner Callanan. I zoned in on this and rehashed a question on informants in a few different ways, leading to Callanan snapping, 'You don't give up, do you?' As I had done previously with Sean Aylward to great effect, I showed him that I wasn't a pushover by eyeballing him and replying, 'No, I don't, and you need to remember that.'

As we were leaving the meeting, Commissioner Murphy gently pulled my mother aside and spoke to her out of earshot of myself and my brothers. He had my mother's hand clasped between both of his hands in a friendly manner. However, when we got outside, Mam looked at me and said, 'He told me with the passage of time, a positive outcome to the investigation would be difficult to achieve.' I couldn't believe that after committing to re-opening the case fully, in the same breath he was basically saying it would be difficult to get results. So, right from the start of this new investigation, we were of the opinion that there was a lot of window-dressing going on to keep us happy.

Within weeks, the new investigation team made contact and told me that they would like to start their investigation by interviewing members of the family, in particular my mother. While I could see the merit of interviewing her, I could see no rational in interviewing Dad's sisters or my mother's siblings. They insisted on interviewing Mam first and would then interview me the following day. As Oliver was living in Portlaoise at the time, I asked him to sit in on the interview with Mam and be there as a support.

Following the interview, Oliver rang me in a very distressed state and just blurted out, 'Austin, they are treating us like the criminals.' When I calmed him down he recounted what had happened and likened the interview to a suspect being interrogated. He told me that Mam had gotten so upset that he told the Gardaí to stop the interview and asked them to leave. I was shocked at this treatment of my mother, and for me it showed not just the complete lack of empathy that they had, but also the lengths that they were prepared to go to in order to find out who was giving us information. They had essentially tried to bully a vulnerable widow in the hope that she would give them some nugget of information before they interviewed me. They seemed to have the misguided belief that we weren't sharing everything with them, and this really annoyed me as I had always been honest and upfront with them.

On October 14th, it was my turn to be 'interrogated'. Detective Sergeant Ian McLoughlin and Detective Garda David Foley arrived at my house and I immediately lay down the ground rules: 'You are not here to treat me like a suspect. I will give you a statement about what I know but the minute you start to question me, this is over. What you did to my mother was a disgrace and it won't be happening tonight.' Having set the tone I then gave them a full account of everything I knew over two separate evenings, which culminated in a 27-page statement.

They interviewed a lot of family members in the following months, and one of the most staggering of those was with my mother's sister Catherine. When they arrived to interview her, she asked them how come it had taken them 25 years to come to her door. She told me that the response was that they didn't have the resources in the 1980s and that they hadn't travelled past Newlands Cross in investigating the case. Newlands Cross was the outer limit of Dublin city at the time. This was just another incredible statement in a long line of them which demonstrated that the original investigation was probably shut down for fear of what it might reveal.

The NBCI investigation ambled along for the next few years and any time I made enquiries, we were told to let the team do their work. I had been continually badgering them to interview Ned Harkin and it got to the point where we were informed that he was too ill to be interviewed and a medical cert had been provided by his family to that effect.

On being told this, I rang Mam to let her know, and she responded, 'Well he wasn't too ill to drink pints because I saw him in the shop last night.' The shop was how my family referred to my grandad's pub, which was now run by my uncle Seamus. I had my suspicions that his son, the Assistant Commissioner in the Gardaí, was protecting him, but this could never be proved. However, the optics weren't good.

The next formal meeting we had with NBCI was on April 14th, 2011 in Kieran's house in Dublin. Detective Inspector Stephen Courage had been appointed as a liaison to the family and had been putting off meeting us for some time. At this meeting, I could see that not much work had been done on the case and I needed to find an angle to get back into the media to highlight what was going on.

* * *

Sinn Féin nominated Martin McGuinness as their candidate for the 2011 Irish presidential election, which was held on October 24th. McGuinness was a former chief of staff of the IRA and was known as a particularly brutal terrorist. Under his command, the IRA had carried out what became known as a 'proxy bombing', in which they kidnapped an innocent man – Patsy Gillespie – brought him to say goodbye to his family, and chained him into a vehicle loaded with explosives. They then ordered him to drive into a British Army checkpoint where they detonated the bomb, killing him and five soldiers. Sinn Féin sought to portray McGuinness as a peace-maker who had gone into government with hard-line unionists in Northern Ireland, but his murky past followed him around Ireland during that campaign like a bad penny.

One of the most iconic images of that whole presidential campaign was the photo of David Kelly, son of Private Paddy Kelly, chal-lenging McGuinness to reveal what he knew about his dad's murder by an IRA kidnap gang in Leitrim in 1983. In the same year that my father was fatally wounded, the Provos shot dead Private Kelly and Recruit Garda Gary Sheehan during the rescue of British busi-nessman Don Tidey, who had been held in Derrada Wood outside Ballinamore for 23 days. In a calm and cold manner, McGuinness effectively told David Kelly to 'move on', and in my mind this showed the true callous nature of the man.

A few days previous to this, McGuinness had appeared on the TV3 presidential debate where the presenter, Vincent Browne, challenged McGuinness on his IRA past. At one point he asked,

'How do you sleep at night?' to which McGuinness replied, 'Very well.' I was sitting at home watching this and I nearly exploded. With all of my sleepless nights since Dad had been shot, I was now listening to Martin McGuinness, a hardened terrorist, tell the world that he had no issues sleeping. If I had been able to drag him through the TV that evening, I would have done so. It was at that point that I decided I had to do something, and the following morning I wrote an opinion piece that I was hoping to get published. I had written the piece in anger and I knew this, so I let it be for a few days before going back to edit it, removing much of the bitterness.

The article was published in the *Irish Independent* on October 13th:

What has remained outside this debate and has only recently been mentioned is how the victims of McGuinness's IRA past feel about the newly reformed peacemaker and candidate for the Áras. These are the people who had loved ones murdered, who have been the victims of punishment beatings or kidnappings or who have been terrorised during bank robberies. I am one such person. My father was Brian Stack, the Chief Prison Officer of Portlaoise Prison, who was murdered by the IRA in 1983. McGuinness had previously been upfront about his IRA membership, but since entering the presidential contest he has tried to water down his involvement and now claims that he left the organisation in 1974. The weight of evidence from former justice ministers, Garda commissioners, intelligence chiefs and respected journalists would seem to suggest that McGuinness is being untruthful about this and was, in fact, on the IRA army council right up to decommissioning. This is the same army council that sanctioned operations that led to 1,800 deaths during the Troubles. You would think, then, in light of his conversion to democratic politics, that

McGuinness would have some feelings of guilt or a troubled conscience. But he tells us that he sleeps very well at night. I'm glad that he sleeps so soundly but I can tell you that many of the victims of his organisation don't have this luxury, as they lie awake at night, crying over their murdered husbands, wives, fathers or mothers. Since coming in from the cold, McGuinness and his friends have never said 'sorry'. They have used words like 'regret' and they still try to justify those 1,800 murders. But if he was a true democrat, McGuinness would realise that no amount of discrimination and gerrymandering can justify even one murder.

My father was walking down a street opposite the National Boxing Stadium in Dublin when a gunman approached him from behind and shot him in the back of the head. This callous and cowardly act against a defenceless man was sanctioned by the IRA army council, of which McGuinness was a member. He will try to justify this brutal assassination and say my father was a casualty of war. Brian Stack was targeted because, as Chief Prison Officer in Portlaoise Prison, he was responsible for security and making sure the IRA prisoners did not escape.

The simple facts of the matter are that my father was just too good at his job and McGuinness and his friends on the army council wanted to get rid of him for good.

Not satisfied with having taken my father from me as a young teenager, the McGuinness PR machine now seeks to assault the Irish republican values that he instilled in me by labelling me a 'West Brit'. His reason for doing this is because people like me choose to remind those not young enough to remember what he and his colleagues did in the name of their bastardised version of republicanism.

This slick PR manipulation has also added insult to the years of hurt by trying to label the families of his victims as being bitter, intransigent and incapable of moving on. It may be easy for somebody who directed terrorism to move on, but McGuinness has no right to tell those of us on the receiving end of his murderous campaign to move on.

That morning, I took a call from an old college friend, Mary. 'Austin, I read your article in the paper this morning. It was very bitter.'

'You should have seen the first draft,' I responded, before she began to lecture me on the virtues of forgiveness.

We had a back-and-forth discussion on this for a few minutes before I finished the call by telling her, 'I don't believe in all that.' As she hung up, she pleaded with me one last time: 'Just think about it, Austin.'

I hadn't had the benefit of counselling about my father's death, I wasn't sleeping, I was bitter, and I had a chip on each shoulder, so what Mary said played on my mind all day. That evening, as I was driving home, it was like I got struck by a bolt of lightning. I can still remember where I was on the road that evening, opposite Allenwood Celtic football ground, when the thought just came to me. If I can forgive them and say to them, 'You did this, you are responsible for this, now you take ownership of this,' I would be forgiving them for *me*, not for them. I thought, 'I'm taking the monkey off my back and giving it to them.' I have done a lot of presentations around this theory and helped many other victims by explaining how 'giving them back their monkey' can help them get some inner peace. Since then I have managed to sleep, I am more content, and I have lost the bitterness that I was carrying. When I explain the concept to other victims, some get it and some don't, but it has worked for me.

After the episode with David Kelly, Sinn Féin tried to protect McGuinness from any further incidents of this nature, but when his campaign came to Portlaoise there was only one question the local journalists wanted to ask him and that was what he knew about the murder of Brian Stack. The local Sinn Féin TD Brian Stanley tried to silence this line of questioning by telling the journalists, 'The IRA had nothing to do with the murder of Brian Stack.'

The following week, the *Laois Nationalist*, a local newspaper, carried this story prominently. McGuinness brazenly told the newspaper that he wasn't on the IRA Army Council when my father was killed: 'I have no idea. How could I? I was up in the north-west.' Sinn Féin TD Brian Stanley said whoever killed my father, it was 'not the IRA'.

* * *

In January 2012, Inspector Courage visited me in Wheatfield Prison where I was working at the time. In what was the singular most deflating meeting I ever had with anybody about Dad's murder, Inspector Courage sat across the desk from me and said, 'I don't think we are going anywhere with this.' I was completely shocked that he was essentially prepared to throw in the towel on the investigation. I was getting frustrated with the whole investigation by this stage and retorted, 'The dogs in the street know the IRA did it.' He then started to shift a bit uneasily in his seat and came back with a statement that will live with me for a long time: 'Austin, I don't believe the IRA did this. I have looked senior members of that organisation in the eye and believed them when they told me they didn't do it.'

The admission by the Gardaí that they no longer believed that the IRA had murdered Dad had left me reeling: I was confused, shocked and didn't know what to do next in my search for justice. As a family, we had always put our faith in the Gardaí and the Irish justice system, and now it felt like they were abandoning us and didn't care about Dad or what had happened to him. I knew that the IRA were the only ones who could have done this, but how was I going to make anybody else believe me if the Gardaí were saying that they didn't think it was the IRA? I still had no solid information and the Gardaí had not shared anything that they had learned with the family. I needed information and I had spent most of 2012 trying to figure out how I was going to get it.

From that moment on, I knew that I had to push the case myself as the Gardaí obviously weren't going to. I needed to get Sinn Féin and the IRA to admit responsibility for Dad's murder as they had always denied it, and in doing so they left a cloud over Dad's reputation. I knew that 2013 was going to present plenty of opportunities to publicise the case as the 30th anniversary of the shooting would be in March, so I had to put a plan together to pressurise the leadership of Sinn Féin and the IRA.

I was well aware that Sinn Féin had begun to make inroads politically in the Republic of Ireland and that they had started to promote new young candidates who had no obvious connection with the Troubles or the IRA. However, many of these new young candidates came from families who were always supportive of the IRA's campaign, and there were still many of the old guard holding elected positions within that party.

The one thing Sinn Féin didn't want was people like me coming forward to challenge their new supposedly clean politicians by connecting them to the past. I knew that if I was able to do this then Sinn Féin would have to make some effort to stop me for the sake of their political operation. I was hoping that if I started talking about their local Portlaoise TD Brian Stanley in the same breath as

Gerry Adams, Martin Ferris (who served time for gunrunning) and Dessie Ellis (who served time for explosives offences), that it would frighten them into getting the IRA to finally admit what they had done in order to shut me up. It was a high-risk strategy but one I felt would work if I was prepared to be patient and wait for the anniversary to arrive, especially as I had an ace up my sleeve. That ace centred on the statement Brian Stanley had made in defending McGuinness when he came to Portlaoise during the presidential election. I drew up a plan to entrap Stanley on the 30th anniversary of the attack on Dad using the article that had appeared in the *Laois Nationalist*.

Chapter 17

Following the murder of Garda Adrian Donohoe on January 25th, 2013 at a Credit Union robbery near Dundalk by criminals who had loose links to former IRA terrorists, Gerry Adams made a contribution to a debate on the murder in Dáil Éireann on January 29th. Adams suddenly went off topic and said that the murder had 'provoked memories of the killing of Jerry McCabe' and then, out of the blue, he made a startling statement that caught everybody off guard. Adams told the Dáil: 'I want to apologise to Mrs McCabe and the McCabe family, and to Garda Ben O'Sullivan and to the families of other members of State forces who were killed by republicans in the course of the conflict. I am very sorry for the pain and loss inflicted upon those families.'

In the days that followed this statement, many politicians and commentators aired their views on it, but I felt that all had missed some important points about what I would call a 'cynical attempt to read into the record of the Dáil an apology' when I wrote an opinion piece for the *Irish Independent* a week later on February 6th.

The first thing I pointed out in my article was that Adams had in an under-handed manner used a debate on Garda Donohoe's murder to make his statement. This meant that there was no pre-warning to other politicians of what he was about to do and no questions could be put to him about his statement.

The second point I drew attention to was that he had said Garda McCabe and others in State service were 'killed', going out of his way to steer away from using the term 'murder', and that this deliberate use of language was very hurtful to victims. By doing this, he showed that Sinn Féin and the IRA were trying to soften their image with the public at the expense of victims' feelings.

The third point I made in that article was probably the most important one, and it was something completely missed by the media up to then. Who was Adams actually apologising to when he said 'State forces', as the IRA had always denied having played any role in those murders? I continued:

> Many of these unanswered questions can be resolved by Sinn Féin agreeing to do three things. Firstly, it must realise that victims are not expecting or wanting any form of apology. What victims want is a genuine acceptance of responsibility. This means the IRA finally admitting to murders it has tried to defend as being part of a 'war'. Let's call them what they really are. This means the IRA admitting to murders it carried out and for whatever reason has failed to claim. This means no more acts of triumphalism at Sinn Féin conferences where these murderers are feted as heroes.

It was at this point that I decided that I needed to do more than get an admission of responsibility for Dad's murder from Sinn Féin and the IRA; I needed to make Gerry Adams and his people know how we felt, how his actions were impacting us, and I needed him to be the one to take responsibility. As I said in the opinion piece, 'We are long gone past the time where victims can be ignored and their hurt trivialised and glossed over as it was by Gerry Adams.'

I finished off the by asking Adams if he was brave enough to meet me, but I wasn't surprised when this invitation was ignored. What I did know, however, was that Adams' cynical attempted apology had backfired, and there was now more media scrutiny of him, Sinn Féin and the murder of Irish State forces by the IRA than there ever had been in the past.

A few weeks after my opinion piece was published, my brother Oliver phoned me to ask if I knew Jim (not his real name), who was a crime reporter for a major newspaper. I knew Jim to be a very reputable crime journalist and I had previously given him an interview. Oliver told me that he had met Jim on the periphery of a meeting that we were both attending and Jim had inquired if Oliver was my brother. When the connection was made, he told Oliver that he might be able to help and that I should give him a call. I waited until the next day to make contact with Jim and when I did he said that he needed to meet me in person, so we met later that day for a coffee.

I had previously disclosed to Jim my theory on what had happened to my dad and the name of a suspect that had a good likeness to the photo-fit the Gardaí had drawn up back in 1983. While we drank our coffees, Jim told me that he had come into possession of some information in relation to Dad's case and he thought that the information I had previously told him wasn't entirely accurate.

'Austin, I was told that Mr A [identity withheld for legal reasons], who was the Officer Commanding of the Southern Brigade of the IRA at the time, had sanctioned the attack on your dad,' he claimed.

I knew Mr A was a senior Sinn Féin politician in Northern Ireland and was also aware that he had a close relative who had served a long sentence in the UK for IRA crimes. Even though Mr A was known to many people as being a member of the IRA Army

Council, up to that point I had never heard of him being involved in the IRA. Because of this I was reluctant to believe what Jim was telling me. Jim tried to reassure me that his information was good and told me that Mr A had organised the IRA Army Convention prior to the ceasefire.

Jim then told me that he would do a little more digging and see if he could come up with any more information. Naturally, I was a little suspicious, but I knew that Jim was probably after a scoop if things turned out well, so I told him that anything he could find out would be welcomed. To be honest, I wasn't expecting to hear back from Jim as I knew how difficult it was to get people within the IRA to talk and I thought I wouldn't hear from him again.

*　　*　　*

As the 30th anniversary on March 25th drew closer, I put my plan into full swing by drafting a press release. The anniversary was on a Monday and if my plan was to work, I knew I had to get the press release out on the Friday. Once I sent the press release to various media outlets, I called Sinéad Hubble, who worked as a producer with the *Midlands Today* radio programme on Midlands 103 FM. The station covers counties Laois, Offaly and Westmeath, and the programme was hosted by Will Faulkner. I asked Sinéad if she had seen my press release in her emails and, if so, would there be a possibility of Will having me on the programme on the Monday to talk about Dad's case.

She called me back an hour later to confirm that I would be on the show and it was at that point that I put my plan into operation by telling her to source a copy of the *Laois Nationalist* from the week after Martin McGuinness canvassed in Portlaoise during the presidential election. All I told her was that I would be making reference to the main article on the front page and that Will needed to be prepared.

When Monday came around, I had prepared myself for the radio interview as I always do by jotting down three or four key points that I wanted to get across. I've learned many tricks over the years of campaigning and always found radio to be a great way of promoting a cause, but it's essential to understand how it works. If I do an interview, I always prefer to do a live one so that it can't be edited, but I also know that a small segment of the interview can feature on news bulletins throughout the day so it is important to get your key points across. The way to manage this is to stick to three or four main points and keep rehashing them throughout the interview, so when it is edited for news bulletins the points that I want to get across cannot be edited out.

When I took the call from Midlands 103 FM, I was ready for what I knew was going to be the most important interview in my fight for Dad. I wasn't in any way nervous because while Will Faulkner is a tough and skilled interviewer and will probe your answers to questions with some tricky follow-ups, he is always fair. The interview went as it normally would – I tried to engage the listener early by talking about the effects Dad's murder had on me personally, and then Will asked me about the progress of the case and who did I feel was responsible. I explained to him that in my view, the IRA were the only possible suspects as they had the motive, which was that my dad kept thwarting escape attempts, and they had the organisational ability.

'Will, I would like to sit down with Gerry Adams to discuss these things with him,' I affirmed. 'I feel that Sinn Féin need to accept responsibility for the murders committed by the IRA against security forces in Ireland.' By this I meant in the Republic of Ireland, as they had always denied these murders in order to keep themselves within their own Rule Book.

I then delivered the line that I had been waiting over a year to say, and I told Will that during the presidential election, Brian Stanley had stated that the IRA had not murdered my dad.

'I now want to know what information Stanley had, as to make such a definite statement he must be in possession of some information. I'd encourage Stanley to talk to me about this and believe he has a duty as a public representative to go to the Gardaí with the information that he has.'

I knew that Stanley would have somebody monitoring the local radio programmes and that he would instantly react to my statement. Now I sat back and waited to see if he would take the bait.

True to form, Stanley couldn't wait to get a right of reply and by doing so fell straight into the trap that I had carefully laid for him. Exactly an hour later, Stanley went on the same radio programme and, in what can only be described as a car-crash interview, he started off by trying to water down what was a very definite statement by claiming that it was 'opinion' and his 'belief' that the IRA hadn't murdered Dad as 'they had always accepted responsibility' for their attacks.

During the course of the interview, Stanley kept trying to shift the focus onto other paramilitary groups who were incarcerated in Portlaoise Prison at the time, while Faulkner kept probing him and asking if Gerry Adams would meet with me. Finally, Stanley said that he had spoken to Adams before he had come on the show and that if I sent a request to Adams for a meeting, it would be facilitated. I couldn't believe that my plan had worked and that by shining a spotlight on Stanley I had got to Adams.

Like other times when I've been in the media about Dad's case, it seems to create a domino effect with several outcomes. The first thing that I was made aware of was that some internal discussions took place within Sinn Féin about making a statement of admission for Dad's murder. I was told by a well-placed journalist that these discussions had taken place while Adams was on a short trip to the USA and that his opinion would be sought on his return.

The second thing to happen was that I was made aware of the date for an RTÉ *Prime Time* TV discussion with Gerry Adams in relation to several murders carried out by the IRA, one of which was my dad's. I had recorded an interview for this programme with my brother Oliver some time ago, and I knew that the programme was waiting for Adams to agree a date to do it. Adams had now agreed to do the interview on April 8th and he was probably hoping to be able to go on the programme and say that he had met us, and in doing so claim the high moral ground.

I didn't want that RTÉ programme to be used by him to deflect from the importance of any potential meeting, so I delayed sending the request for a meeting to Adams until Friday March 29th. This tactic clearly worked as Adams responded to me on Thursday, April 4th, stating that he would be happy to meet with me but that 'it would be remiss of me to raise your expectations that I or the Sinn Féin leadership can resolve these particular matters for you'.

There would be no meeting before the *Prime Time* programme and I would now have the advantage of seeing how Adams addressed the issues around Dad's case before I went to meet him. After some further contact with Adams' office in Dáil Éireann, the meeting was arranged for Thursday, May 9th.

When Adams turned up to RTÉ, he was expecting to be inter-viewed for about 10 minutes in relation to the cynical apology he had made in the Dáil. He had no idea what was being lined up by the *Prime Time* team and that he would be subjected to a grilling on several IRA murders, which would go on for more than 30 minutes. That night we saw the real Gerry Adams. He initially tried to make himself out to be a victim and then, as the interview progressed and the questions got tougher, he got very annoyed and snapped at the interviewer, Miriam O'Callaghan, on more than one occasion.

When asked directly about Dad's murder, he tried the old trick which the Gardaí had fed the media back in 1983, and which Stanley had used on Midlands 103 FM, and tried to blame other paramilitary groups, such as the INLA, or Dublin crime gangs, who had members locked up in Portlaoise Prison at the time. On two occasions he spoke about what he called 'the cruel regime' in Portlaoise Prison and both times mentioned that IRA prisoner Tom Smith had been killed there. What he deliberately left out of his false narrative was that Smith had been among a group of armed prisoners who had blown a hole in the prison wall and attempted to escape, and he was killed by a ricochet when the Irish Army fired warning shots to stop the prisoners. I was getting very frustrated and angry watching this charade as he was practically trying to justify Dad's murder.

Eventually, when cornered by very persistent questioning from Miriam O'Callaghan, he lost his composure and angrily told her, 'No, I don't know who murdered him.' There was no way I believed him and I knew that his credibility was much damaged after that interview. I also suspected that there would be more internal discussions and soul-searching within Sinn Féin and the IRA about how to prevent stories like Dad's becoming a liability for them, and, indeed, some were probably beginning to view Adams as a liability also.

* * *

The domino effect was in full swing now and a few weeks after the Adams interview on *Prime Time*, Jim, the crime journalist, contacted me again. On Thursday, April 25th, he sent me an email saying that he had made progress and had some concrete information for me. I immediately phoned him and he told me that he had spoken to two individuals who were IRA men and both had given him the same information about the identities of those who had carried out the attack on Dad. He told me that neither man knew he had spoken to the other and, because of this, he found the information reliable. He then said that he wasn't prepared to say any more over the phone and that we needed to meet.

I met Jim at 6.30 p.m. that evening in the Costa Coffee shop in Liffey Valley, after spending an anxious day of waiting for what would likely be ground-breaking news. 'Austin, let's go over to that corner there,' he suggested when I walked in, and he was already heading to the quietest corner in the coffee shop so that he could talk privately. After we had ordered our coffees and had a brief catch-up, Jim got to the point and told me that after our last meeting he had discreetly asked two contacts that he had within the IRA what they knew about Dad's murder and that they had only come back to him in the last few days. He explained, 'Both of these people are well placed within the IRA organisation and the information I'm about to give you is very credible.'

After years of searching for answers, you begin to get a bit sceptical every time somebody tells you that they have information for you, as generally it is third- or fourth-hand hearsay. What I found was that most people who come forward with information are usually well-meaning and trying to be helpful, but at the end of the day their information would never pass any critical analysis. But I had a good feeling about what I was going to hear as I knew Jim was held in high esteem among his colleagues and within the wider media circles. He had my full attention by the time he started to relay what he had been told, and I was trying to grab onto every word that he was saying.

'Have you ever heard of an IRA man called Mr B [name with-held]?' he asked. Immediately I thought that I recognised the name as being one that the Garda Serious Crime Review Team had shared at our very first meeting with them nearly five years previous.

'I'll need to double check my notes, but I think the name had been mentioned to us by the Gardaí,' I replied.

'Well, my informant revealed that Mr B was the ringleader of the operation to murder your dad and that he was very well connected to the IRA leadership through his friendship with Mr A, who was a senior IRA Army Council member. As I said before, Mr A was the Officer Commanding of the Southern Brigade of the IRA during the 1980s and Mr B was his Adjutant. I was told that Mr B had put together a plan to murder Brian and had gone to Mr A looking for permission to proceed, but initially Mr A had refused to sanction the attack. Not satisfied with the refusal to sanction the operation, apparently Mr B went back to Mr A on a few occasions, badgering him until he finally caved in and agreed to sanction the attack. Once Mr B got the go-ahead, he needed to put together a team for the operation and the most important part of that team would be the gunman. On the night of the attack, Mr B had been the motorbike driver and he had chosen a close friend to be the gunman. My source said that the name of this gunman was Mr C [name with-held], at least I think it is. It's definitely Mr C [used his second name only] anyway. Does that name ring a bell?'

'No, I've never heard of a Mr C before,' I replied.

'I'll double check with my source on the name again,' Jim continued. 'My source told me that those involved in the attack on your dad had also three months later been involved in the attempt to kidnap Galen Weston, the Canadian millionaire.' Galen had lived just outside Dublin in Roundwood, Co. Wicklow. Jim continued: 'This information can be verified as both Mr B and Mr C had been injured in the shootout after Gardaí received a tip-off about the kidnap attempt. Both Mr B and Mr C were arrested at the scene.'

Galen Weston was a wealthy Canadian businessman whose wife, Hilary, was Irish. He had purchased Roundwood House and its 350-acre estate in the late 1960s as an Irish base for the family. On August 7th, 1983 a heavily armed IRA unit of seven men broke into Roundwood House in the hope of kidnapping its owner. What they didn't know was that the Gardaí would be waiting for them, having received a tip-off from an informant. When Gardaí told the Westons what they knew, they said that they would not be there as they had plans in the UK. As the Gardaí lay in wait, five members of the IRA gang entered the yard where they were confronted. The gang refused to surrender and a fire fight ensued, which left four of the IRA men injured. The Gardaí had been courageous against the much better armed gang and managed to arrest five of them, who all received sentences in the Special Criminal Court. Interestingly, Gerry Adams attended the court for their sentencing and waved to the gang as they were taken down to begin their sentences.

By the time Jim had finished, I just sat there trying to take it all in. I had been given information before which mentioned names of people suspected of being involved and not all of it stood up when I did any sort of double check. But this was different – Jim was very reliable and he told me that his sources were impeccable, and sometimes you just have to trust your gut instinct. I knew that once I got home and checked my notes from that first meeting with the Serious Crime Review Team that the name of Mr B would be there. I couldn't wait to get home and, as soon as I did, I went straight to the book that I used to document our meetings with the Gardaí. There in blue ink looking back up at me was the name Mr B. I emailed Jim straight away to confirm that Mr B's name had, indeed, been given to us by the Gardaí a few years previous as a person of interest at the time of the shooting. Jim then a few days later confirmed to me what Mr C's first name was.

This was the moment that I knew I had finally found out the names of those who murdered my dad. While this information was only coming from one source for me, he had gotten it from two separate sources. I knew that Jim's sources were probably very credible, and I would subsequently receive the exact same information from two other unconnected sources in the near future. But, more importantly, I now had solid information connecting Sinn Féin and the IRA to Dad's murder before I went to meet Gerry Adams.

*　　*　　*

During this time, I was jumping from one thing to another as the dominos kept falling. I don't know how I kept going and managed to juggle everything without dropping the ball. Sandwiched in the week between my meeting with Jim and the upcoming meeting with Gerry Adams was a very important event on Friday, May 3rd. The Irish Prison Service had, after 30 years, finally decided to recognise Dad's sacrifice and create a lasting memorial to him. The Prison Service College was going to be renamed as Brian Stack House, there would be a bronze bust of Dad unveiled, and the Prison Service gold bravery award would now be called the Stack Medal and my mother would receive the first one of these on Dad's behalf.

This event had been in the planning since the previous November when the then Governor of Wheatfield Prison, Colm Barclay, had attended the annual Remembrance Day in Northern Ireland for prison officers who were murdered during the Troubles. The day after he returned from Northern Ireland, Colm came into my office in Wheatfield and said to me, 'Austin, is there even a plaque anywhere in the prison estate remembering your Dad?' I had to tell him that there wasn't and that it was something that annoyed me when I thought about it. Colm told me that he felt this wasn't right and if it was OK with me, he would raise the matter with the Director General of the Prison Service. He came back to me a few days later and said that he had brought it up and that I should expect a call from Director General Michael Donnellan.

Later that morning, I took a call from Donnellan and he invited me to meet him that afternoon in the Prison Service Dublin office. He hadn't given me much time to gather my thoughts, but I had a good idea what I wanted if he was going to ask my opinion on what they could do to remember Dad. I had always thought that renaming the Prison Service College in Dad's honour would be a fitting tribute to him and, as it was on the main Dublin Road beside the prison, my thinking was that this was very visible and everybody passing the busiest road in the town would see it. Future generations and young people would ask who Brian Stack is and his story would live on. I also wanted those visiting the paramilitary prisoners to see it and let them know that they hadn't won and Dad's memory would live on.

On my way across Dublin city to the meeting, I knew that the senior civil servants in Headquarters had obviously tossed various ideas around among themselves before reaching out to me, so I decided that the best course of action was to see what was being proposed.

When I got to the Dublin office, which was based in Phibsborough, the Director General greeted me and we went into a small office where he got straight to the point. He told me that the Service wanted to do something to recognise Dad and he asked, 'Have you any thoughts on what your family might like us to do?' I wanted to stick with my plan of seeing what their thought process was on it, so I responded: 'Michael, you asked me here to discuss this so I'm sure you have some proposals. If you tell me what they are I will discuss them with my family and see if we can agree on something.' He was slightly taken aback by my approach but disclosed that they were thinking of building a memorial garden on the site of the old D block in Portlaoise Prison. He said that they would name it in honour of Dad and that it 'would be a nice quiet place of reflection inside the walls of the prison'.

I was absolutely flabbergasted and a little angry, but I needed to stay calm. I was thinking that they wanted to do this just so they can say that they did it, but at the same time they wanted to hide it. Michael looked at me and asked, 'What's wrong, Austin? Do you not like that idea?' I remained as calm as I could and said, 'That's a really nice idea, Michael, but as you said yourself, it's in behind the wall of the prison, nobody will see it. My mother could never go and sit in it and young people growing up in Portlaoise will never know it's there.'

I knew that I now had to tell him what I thought would be an appropriate memorial, so I explained my rationale for wanting the Prison Service College renamed after Dad. Michael did everything possible to persuade me that this was not a good option, saying that name changes never catch on, or the training college could be moved sometime in the future. But I had an answer for that: 'Michael, the name of the Mountjoy Female Prison has been success-fully rebranded as the Dóchas Centre and it took about three years for that name change to catch on.' Eventually, he agreed that they would rename the college and also told me that they were proposing renaming the Prison Service Gold Bravery medal in Dad's honour as well, which I agreed to.

On my way back to Wheatfield Prison, I rang my mother and brothers to tell them the news. All were of the view that it was 30 years too late, but we would accept the proposals that I had agreed with Michael as we wanted a lasting memorial to Dad.

If I thought that this was the end of the matter, I was mistaken. When I got back to work Colm Barclay asked how the meeting had gone and I told him. He was impressed with how I had handled it and that I came away with what I wanted. Then the next morning, while we were having coffee, he told me that he had been put on a committee to organise the memorial to Dad and they were having their initial meeting later that morning. Things were moving at pace and I was happy with that, but when Colm returned from his meeting I could see that his mood was different.

He made a beeline for me and asked me what exactly I had agreed to with Donnellan the previous day. When I told him, he said I needed to be careful: 'They are trying to pull the wool over your eyes. What they proposed at the meeting today was renaming one of the buildings in the college after your dad.' I was annoyed and straight away started to type an email. Colm tried to stop me and said, 'Don't send an angry email.' He needn't have worried – I wasn't going the angry route; I was going the cold, calculated route. I sent an email to Michael Donnellan which said, 'I just wish to confirm this is what was agreed between us yesterday' and I went on to outline the agreed proposals. Colm was still standing beside me when a reply came back from Donnellan with just one word in it: 'Agreed.' Colm just looked at me and said, 'Fair play to you, they are committed to it now.'

In fairness, when they committed to it, the Prison Service did a fantastic job. On Friday, May 3rd the Minister for Justice, Alan Shatter, presided over a lovely ceremony to rename the college. They had also commissioned a bronze bust of Dad, which my mother unveiled, and they presented her with the first Stack Medal. It was a really special day and we had secured part of Dad's legacy and made sure that future generations would know who he was and how he had defended the State.

We also took the opportunity to have a private meeting with the Minister for Justice to outline our concerns around the Garda investigation, and we let him know that relations had broken down with the Gardaí. I told him that we had sent a letter to the Garda Commissioner, Martin Callinan, on January 6th outlining our concerns around the conduct of the investigation team and requested a meeting, but we had no response to this request.

In fairness to Minister Shatter, he came into that meeting with just one aide, he listened to us and committed to seeing what he could do regarding a meeting with the Commissioner. As a family, we had decided to make no media comment about this ceremony as the Irish Prison Service press team were looking after all the media on the day and we didn't want to take away from Dad's special day by commenting on the investigation. I knew that we were going to get all the media attention that we required the following Thursday.

My brother Kieran, who had flown in from Chicago for the ceremony in the college, had gone home, and Oliver and I spent the week preparing for our meeting with Gerry Adams. Initially, Adams' secretary, Máire Grogan, had tried to persuade us to have a private meeting in a quiet hotel away from the media glare, but I was having none of that. I told her that the first meeting had to be done publicly and in his office in Dáil Éireann. After they agreed to this, I let the media know what was happening so that there would be as much coverage of it as possible. This was important, as I needed the media to help with my strategy to put pressure on Adams to deliver admissions of responsibility for us.

During the week, I took soundings from several journalists who had interviewed Adams and they told me that he would talk very slowly and veer off the point in a deliberate mechanism to run down the clock. I also prepared myself by watching the recording I had of his *Prime Time* interview. I went back over the recording several times to get a sense of how he would answer questions, and while I was doing this a funny thing happened. My son, Freddie, who was nine years old at the time and was sitting beside me as I was studying the interview, looked up at me and said, 'Dad, that man says he knows nothing about Grandad Brian's murder, why don't you believe him?' For me that summed up exactly what Adams' strategy was: if you tell a lie often enough then it becomes the accepted truth. Here was my son being influenced by that strategy.

From that moment on, I knew what I was up against, and I was determined not to allow Adams to dictate the narrative of our engagements. The other thing that I noticed from his *Prime Time* interview was that Adams was fond of playing the victim and trying to equate his own perceived victimhood with that of the people his movement had murdered. I let Oliver know that I wasn't going to stand for that and told him how I would approach this if it occurred. Oliver said to me, 'You do all the talking and I'll listen and if you miss something I will pick up on it.' We were actually a good team and instinctively knew what the other was thinking, and we would definitely need that going into this meeting.

That week went very quickly and on Thursday, May 9th, 2013, I went to work as normal as the meeting with Adams wasn't until 5 p.m. I decided that I would do my usual morning's work and finish up at lunch time before driving into Dublin city centre. I could then meet up with Oliver and my mother in Buswells Hotel where we would have coffee and go through some last-minute preparations. Originally, I had wanted my mother to take part in the meeting with Adams, but she told me that there was no way she could bring herself to be in the same room as him and I accepted that, but she did want to be in Dublin with us as a support and also to hear first-hand how the meeting went.

While we were having a coffee and generally trying to keep ourselves relaxed, Oliver said to me, 'Austin, I can't shake his hand when we go in here.' I knew how he was feeling and shaking the hand of somebody who was the leader of a movement that murdered 1,800 people is not something that you do lightly. When dealing with people from the Provisional Sinn Féin/IRA movement, I had long since realised that I was not dealing with ordinary political people. This movement was not content with having murdered, bombed, robbed and disappeared people, but its political arm, headed up by Adams, tried to justify these horrible deeds at every turn. They have no moral compass. I had seen how Adams and Sinn Féin had tried to take the high moral ground for years with unionists when they wouldn't shake his hand, and I had made a decision that I wouldn't be allowing him to do this with me. I told Oliver, 'We can't afford to allow these people to view us as bitter or stubborn as they will use that against us.' I continued, 'Ollie, it's only a handshake, it means nothing but we need to do it.' There would come a time when we would both refuse to shake the hand of Gerry Adams, but this was not that day.

When it was time to cross the street and take the short walk to Dáil Éireann, I could see that my press release had had the desired effect and there was a large media presence waiting for us. I think this took Oliver by surprise, especially when they started to film us as we crossed the street. When we got to the gates of the Dáil, we were swamped and the questions were coming from every angle. So, I just held my hand up for them to pause and sought out the RTÉ TV camera and reporter – if I was going to say anything, I had to direct my comments towards the number one media outlet in the country.

Helen Donohue, the reporter for RTÉ *Six One News*, had called me earlier to say that she would be covering the meeting so, once

I had their attention, I just looked at Helen and pointed, offering her the chance to ask the first question. It's funny, but when you do that the other media outlets tend to back off and wait their turn; it's like they have an unofficial pecking order. Helen asked me an easy, straightforward question: 'What are you hoping to gain from today's meeting?' I responded that we wanted the IRA to admit responsibility for Dad's murder as they had been denying it for 30 years, but I knew they did it and, as a family, we needed them to accept responsibility for their actions.

Helen then asked, 'How can Gerry Adams help with that?'

'I'd like him to talk to people within his own movement, as they may have some answers,' I replied. 'I'm talking about people sitting around the table at parliamentary party meetings, such as Dessie Ellis and Martin Ferris, who both served time in Portlaoise Prison around the time of my dad's shooting, and they may be able to provide some answers.'

Again, I deliberately threw in the names of two TDs who had an IRA past and had served time as I knew that this might focus Adams in his dealings with me. Both Ferris and Ellis had serious IRA pasts and, while neither at that time had come onto my radar in relation to Dad's murder, they were still people who might have heard things or might be in the know. I knew that the *Six One News* programme would probably go out while we were still meeting with Adams, so at that point I didn't think it would affect how the meeting went.

Once we had said our few words to the media, we went into the security waiting area and told the Dáil usher on duty who we were and which TD we were there to see. I imagine he knew quite well who we were, having witnessed the media attention outside, but you still have to go through all the security formalities.

Within a few minutes, Máire Grogan appeared and introduced herself to us. She escorted us across to the main building where we were given visitor passes and then brought to the part of the building that housed the TDs' offices. Máire was very friendly and chatted to us as we made our way along the corridors passing all the offices. Finally, she stopped outside an office and we could see the name 'Gerry Adams' on the wall beside the door. I didn't know what to expect once she opened the door, but I was ready for whatever was going to happen.

The room behind the door was actually a small outer office with a connecting door to the left to a bigger office. Once we entered the room, Máire went and sat behind the desk, her job done. It was then that we saw him standing in the doorway leading to the bigger office. Gerry Adams was actually a lot more of an insignificant figure than I had imagined, and he had what I would describe as a menacing type of grin on his face as he looked us up and down before welcoming us with an outstretched hand.

As much as it pained me, I took his hand – after all, I was there to get something from him, so there was a game that had to be played, and Oliver followed me and also shook Adams' hand. He led us towards a meeting table in the office and directed us to two seats, which is when I first noticed that we weren't alone. I had been so fixated on Adams that I hadn't seen Richard McAuley, who was his assistant.

After we were introduced to McAuley, Adams took a seat, but he sat at the side of the table, turning his chair towards us. Then, in a very casual way, he sat back in the chair and threw his arm over the back of it before fixing us with a stare and saying in a calm voice, 'You are two very brave men to come and see me.' While I was ready for anything and the adrenaline was definitely flowing, I couldn't believe what I had just heard. Here we were in the centre of our democracy and the leader of a large political party was trying to intimidate us. I was shocked but, nevertheless, not one bit surprised.

I don't know if Adams was expecting a response, but he got one – I was not about to let this man intimidate me and had to set the tone of the meeting right from the start. I have always believed the old story that if you confront the bully then they will back down. So, I took a breath, sat up in the chair, making myself as tall as possible, and looked him in the eye. Then, in a strong but calm voice, I said, 'Deputy, there is nothing brave about coming to see you in your workplace. I have been in here a thousand and one times and this place holds no fear for me.'

Having lost the first battle, Adams decided to change tactics and went down the anticipated route of playing the victim. Still adopting a very casual pose he said, 'Look, we are all victims here, I had two members of my family who were shot.' I couldn't believe that having lost the opening skirmish he allowed himself to be placed firmly on the back foot by resorting to playing a card which he had often played in the past. Anybody else would have known that I would be ready for this, but I genuinely think that he underestimated me.

I had been planning for this all week and, buoyed by my initial success, I just went for it. I adopted a fake rage approach and started to shout at him while banging the desk and jabbing my finger in his direction. 'You are not the victim here, I'm the victim, my brother is the victim, and my mother sitting in the hotel across the road is the victim. I'll tell you what a victim is: a victim is somebody who has to get up at 2 a.m. in the morning to scratch her husband's nose as he cannot do it himself after being left paralysed; a victim is somebody who watches his father cry as he shaves him because he cannot shave himself. That's what a victim is, so don't you play the victim with me.'

I then completely changed my tone and, in a calm and soft voice, said to him, 'All we want is your help. We want you to get us some answers, we want you to help us get an admission of responsibility. I am prepared to work with you and to trust you in order to get that.'

When I finished, I knew I now had his attention. He was sitting upright in his chair and shifting a little uneasily, and I think he didn't know where to take the meeting next, so he said to me, 'You've said that you know who killed your dad, do you want to tell me?' I replied, 'I'm not here to give you names, but I have good information on what happened. I know that the person who organised it tried to get it sanctioned a few times, they kept going back to a certain individual who was on the Army Council, and on the third or fourth occasion it was sanctioned by him.' Adams just smiled at me and said, 'Austin, that's not how the IRA did business.'

At this stage, Adams decided that he needed to have a private discussion with McAuley and possibly others who were in a nearby room. They told us that they wanted to gather their thoughts and would be back in a few minutes. In the meantime, they sent in sandwiches and coffee while we sat waiting for them. It was at this stage that Oliver noticed an Apple iPhone had been left on the table face down. He motioned to me by pointing to the phone and then making a zip sign across his mouth to indicate that he thought we were being recorded. With that in mind, we didn't speak about the meeting while we waited and we just ate some of the sandwiches they had provided and watched the TV in the office as the RTÉ *Six One News* came on. Of course, the first item on the news was my statement to the media outside the gates of the Dáil. I had been hoping that we would have finished the meeting before that was aired as I knew it would possibly annoy Adams. I knew that he would see it wherever they had gone and was expecting him to bring it up on his return.

When Adams and McAuley returned, the mood seemed to have shifted. They no longer seemed to take the situation for granted and had decided that we were no pushovers. Adams sat down and got straight to the point: 'We can do business with you, but there will be a process and I cannot guarantee you anything.' He stressed that our meetings must be confidential and that what was said at this meeting and any further ones must be kept between us. We agreed as we had expected this.

He then addressed the statement that I had given to the media before the meeting and he said, 'Austin, please don't mention those people that you mentioned on the news again. Those are some of the people that I need to talk to.' I knew he was referring to Dessie Ellis and Martin Ferris. I assured him that I wouldn't mention them again as I didn't want to jeopardise any discussions that he may have to undertake.

He then suggested that we make a joint press statement on the outcome of the meeting, but that was not something that we were ever going to agree to. We wanted to retain control over our own media briefings and were not going to allow Adams to censor us. We did agree with him around the language that we would use, and that both sides would say that we wanted to 'reflect' on the meeting as an outcome.

With our business concluded, Adams told us that he would get back to us in due course. He got Máire to bring us back to the front gate of the Dáil where some of the media were still waiting for us. I gave a brief statement to them, saying that the meeting had been productive and that both sides needed some time to reflect on it. After doing this, we started to walk down the street towards the hotel where we were to meet with Mam, but we hadn't gone far when my phone rang. I immediately answered it thinking that it was a journalist looking for a comment on the meeting, so I was surprised to find Gerry Adams on the other end of the line. He told me that he needed me to keep off the airwaves and not do any media for a period of one month. He guaranteed me that if I did that, he would get back to me before the month was up with an update on his progress.

While it was easy to agree to this in one respect, as I knew that he would be possibly having discussions with people about making a statement of admission, I also knew that the media would be pestering me for a comment. From the reports that I had heard the previous month, I fully expected the IRA, after internal discussions, to issue some sort of statement claiming responsibility for Dad's murder, but I wasn't expecting what happened next.

* * *

In the days after our meeting with Adams, I was wondering what the Gardaí had made of it all. I knew they had to be curious about what had been discussed or promised and what information we might get access to. We had basically been on a solo run and had no contact with the Gardaí after our attempts to secure a meeting the previous December had failed. I had a fair idea that Garda HQ could not let this situation develop and, sure enough, on May 14th, almost a week after our meeting with Adams, I received phone call from a man who identified himself as Detective Superintendent George Kyne.

Kyne told me that he was now heading up the investigation into Dad's murder and that both he and I were going down a similar road with what we were doing. I asked what he meant by this, and he told me that the Gardaí were doing a piece of work on the case that would mean them making contact with Gerry Adams. George asked me not to have any more meetings with Adams as it might hinder their work and harm the case. To say that I was furious was an understatement. For years the Gardaí had done nothing and achieved very little, and now, just as we might be about to get some answers, they were trying to head us off at the pass. I had never met George before this conversation and I don't know if he had been properly briefed about me, but there was no way I was going to let him talk me out of finding the truth, even if that meant talking to Adams.

I reminded George, 'You have had since 1983 to interview Adams and never did so. Now that I have met him, you suddenly want to do so too.' I was angry and frustrated by the naked attempt of this call to rein us in, and it appeared to me that just as we were about to make some progress, all they wanted was to save face. I let him know with some strong language that I wasn't interested in anything he had to say and we would not be meeting with him until after we had a meeting with the Garda Commissioner Martin Callinan. Our attempts to get the Commissioner to engage with us still hadn't paid off and our relationship with the Gardaí was now at an all-time low.

While I knew I had done the right thing in dismissing the advances of the Gardaí, I still wasn't sure that our meeting with Adams was going to bring real results. There were still a few anxious weeks to wait until Adams was due to make contact and, like the rest of the family, I was counting down the days waiting for the call to come.

Both Oliver and I had a positive feeling about the initial meeting and, as a family, we all felt that we were close to finally getting some sort of admission of responsibility from the IRA and we couldn't wait to see where it was all going to lead. I had also been nervous in case they might attempt to string us along and, in doing so, the media might lose interest. It had taken a lot to convince the rest of the family that this was the right road to go down, so I really wanted Adams to come back to me when he said that he would.

*   *   *

When the call eventually came through just before the month was up, I was one very relieved man and knew that we could potentially get results from whatever process lay ahead. When we were making arrangements for that second meeting, Adams told me that there would be at least one further meeting and that he wanted to make these meetings informal, that they be as discreet as possible, and that the media could not know.

Adams or those close to him had probably guessed that I would have had a difficult time fending off questions from journalists and that I was likely to start getting requests for an update once we reached June 9th, 2013. So, it was quite a clever move for them to make contact just before the month was up, and by suggesting June 5th for our second meeting, they knew that it would be done and dusted long before the media started asking questions.

The Davenport Hotel, just off Merrion Square in Dublin, is one of a number of hotels that are near Dáil Éireann, and it was here that Oliver and I had our second encounter with Gerry Adams. Right from the off, there was a different atmosphere to this meeting. Adams was sitting in a discreet bay window on the right when we entered and, as we approached him, he greeted us the way anybody would greet a friend. He had already ordered sandwiches for himself and asked us what we wanted. After we settled for scones and coffee, he called the waiter over to make the order and in typical Sinn Féin fashion, he managed to get in one or two words of Irish while dealing with the waiter. It was something that I noticed he did regularly when we were in his company in a public setting and it had all the hallmarks of a publicity stunt. I don't know how much Irish he has, but I have always felt that making a kind of political statement by using the odd Irish word here and there is very condescending to the language.

We engaged in some small talk as we waited for the scones to arrive, but he also seemed to be distracted by something as he kept taking calls and checking text messages. However, once the waiter had left after bringing our food, he got down to business. He told us that he had been in contact with a person who had agreed to help us and they would see what information could be found. We were told that this person was a former IRA man who, because of his position within the organisation, would be able to help. Adams said that this may take a few weeks but he also reminded us that it might be difficult to get information as the IRA were no longer in existence and some people may not cooperate.

I told Adams that as an incentive, if the IRA delivered us the whole truth, then we would be prepared to release a statement saying that we did not want charges brought against the perpetrators of the attack. He thought that this was a very big gesture from us and said that he would relay that to the person that he was dealing with. We then agreed to meet again once this person had reverted to Adams.

As we were getting ready to leave, Adams took another phone call. This time when he finished, he told us what it was about. The government had just brought forward a Bill to hold a referendum on the abolition of the Seanad (the upper house of the Irish Parliament), and Sinn Féin were trying to establish a position on it. As a keen follower of politics, I knew that they had two conflicting policies on the issue, so I asked him which side they were going to take on the referendum. Adams looked at me and replied, 'That's what all the calls are about, we just don't know what to do on this one.' As it turned out, they thought they had adopted the populist stance and backed abolition, but in the referendum the public backed retention of the Seanad.

After this, things started to move fairly quickly and, on June 14th, I received an email from Máire Grogan with a request to put another meeting together with Adams. This third meeting took place at the same venue, the Davenport Hotel, on June 25th. Prior to the meeting, my brother Kieran had suggested that if there was an offer to meet the IRA, he would like to come home for that meeting.

Oliver and I discussed this at length before we went to the meeting and we were both of the view that as a family member he had a right to be there, but Gerry Adams might take a different view having never met Kieran. I was also concerned that the dynamic might be different with Kieran present as he hadn't seen the way things had gone up to then. So, I thought the simplest thing to do was to put the question to Adams when he suggested a meeting.

From the outset of this meeting, Adams told us that the former IRA man he had asked to help was able to get some information for us and that there would be a meeting with him. I immediately asked if they would allow Kieran to take part and Adams ruled it out, saying, 'I don't know that man.' I knew this wouldn't be what Kieran would like to hear, but I didn't want to pick a fight with Adams at this stage.

As somebody who is passionate about restorative justice, I asked Adams, 'Is there any chance it's going to be possible to meet with the people who carried out the attack?' I had first come across the concept of restorative justice while I was studying criminology and I was very impressed with how the process works and its outcomes. Usually, the process involves the offender and the victim having a meeting, which is facilitated by a trained facilitator. At the meeting, the victim will outline the harms and effects that the actions of the offender had on their life. The offender will also speak and explain what happened from their perspective. This is important as it allows the victims to get answers and some truth. Over the course of the meeting, the two sides may come to an agreement on how to move forward. I had eventually trained as a facilitator and mediated many restorative meetings, especially in work, so I was anxious to propose a meeting with those who were involved in the attack on Dad.

I outlined how such a meeting might benefit both those who carried out the attack and us. Adams was very quick to shut down any suggestions that this might happen, saying, 'Former IRA Volunteers could never put themselves in such a position as they would always be then looking over their shoulders for years in fear of arrest.'

We then had a discussion around the idea of a truth commission, as it is something that I believe is required in the context of the Troubles. Adams told me that their movement was very much open to that idea, but there would have to be amnesties issued before former IRA Volunteers would be prepared to talk to such a commission. I explained to him that I felt any truth commission that issued amnesties prior to engagement would be flawed from the outset, as the perpetrators of crimes would then have no incentive to be truthful. Whereas if a family felt they had been dealt with truthfully, then they could recommend an amnesty at the end of the process. I also explained that my view was that the IRA had nothing to fear from a process like that as anything disclosed to a truth commission could not be used in a court of law. Adams seemed to be eager to explore these ideas with me but was holding firm on his belief that amnesties must come before engagement.

We then got back to talking about a potential meeting with the individual who Adams had asked to help us. He suggested that it would be helpful if we would write out a list of questions that we would like to be addressed at a meeting. I didn't have any difficulty doing that, but I explained that we may need to ask follow-up questions depending on any answers given to us, and it was agreed that this would be allowed. Adams said that the IRA man was concerned that if there was a meeting, we might be wired. In order to reassure them, I suggested that we could be searched if there was a meeting, but Adams said that there would be no need for that. He said that he felt he could trust us. He then asked if we would be prepared to travel into Northern Ireland for any potential meeting. Straight away Oliver said, 'I'm not prepared to do that.' Sensing that this might be a problem, I asked Adams to give us a few minutes alone.

When Adams left the table, I told Oliver, 'This is our one and only chance at getting information and if it means going into the North then we have to do it.' I continued by reassuring him that we would be safe. 'If anything happens to us then it is on Adams' head as people will know he arranged everything.' Oliver came around to my way of thinking on this and when Adams came back, we told him that we would be prepared to cross the border.

He then informed us that if this meeting could be arranged, it would mean taking part of the journey in a blacked-out van. To be perfectly honest, I had assumed that if we were going to be taken to a meeting then something like this was bound to happen, and neither Oliver nor I baulked at the idea when it was put to us. We were then told that there would be one final meeting to confirm the details and firm up arrangements, and we were again warned about the confidentiality of the process.

We spent the next week or so drafting up a list of possible questions for the IRA. With my brother Kieran living in America and my mother not being an email user at the time, this proved time consuming as we needed to make sure all the family members were happy with the questions and had sufficient input to them. When I called down to Mam in relation to this, she was adamant about two questions that she wanted asked. She wanted to know if the intention of the gunman was to kill Dad or was the attack meant to be a warning, and she wanted to know why he was specifically targeted. Between my brothers and I, we came up with a list of questions that we felt would best get the information and admissions that we were looking for. When we had agreed on the questions, I printed them off and was ready and waiting for the next call from Adams.

When that call came through, Adams said that he wanted to meet on Friday, July 26th. I said that I would get back to him about the suggested date as I would have to confirm with Oliver. As it turned out, Oliver couldn't make that date, but Adams seemed anxious to proceed and told me that it would be a very brief encounter and it was really just to relay details of the meeting with the IRA person.

After a discussion with Oliver, we agreed that I would go to the meeting on my own. This is not something that we would have normally done but we decided to take a chance that nothing unusual would come up as most of the groundwork had already been done. I was prepared, however, to adjourn that meeting if anything came up that needed a wider family view, so in that context I agreed to go alone to the final meeting in the Davenport Hotel.

When I turned up at the hotel, Adams was again waiting for me at a table in the bay window. After we ordered some coffee, he told me that the meeting with the IRA man was confirmed and that we should free up the weekend and all the following week. He said that we would only be told the evening before the meeting and that once we got this call, we should go to the Regency Hotel in Drumcondra the following morning for 11 a.m. I knew these dates would possibly cause a problem for Oliver as he had a foreign holiday booked from Wednesday, July 31st until Thursday, August 8th. When I put this to Adams, he agreed to see what he could do and suggested that the following day, Saturday, July 27th, was an outside possibility, but he would try and see if it could be arranged for Monday, July 29th or Tuesday, July 30th. I was told that we should not bring any mobile phones with us and that the meeting would definitely be held on the southern side of the border.

When Adams then asked if we had been able to draw up a list of questions for them, I handed over a copy of the questions we had prepared. The meeting was over as quickly as it had started, and I immediately rang Oliver to tell him what had happened and to make sure to cancel any plans he had for the next few days. My guess was that the Saturday was a non-runner as it was too close, so it was all going to go down on either the Monday or Tuesday.

The next few days were nervous ones for all of us, but particularly my mother, who was worried sick that something terrible was going to happen to us.

Earlier that week, I also finally received a proper response from the Garda Commissioner's Office to a letter I sent on January 2nd and a follow-up letter I sent on July 8th. In the letter of January 2nd, we had specifically requested a meeting with the Commissioner to outline our concerns about the direction that the investigation was taking. In response, the Commissioner said that he would forward our correspondence to the operations section and they would be in contact with us. We were specifically seeking a meeting with the Commissioner and we felt that we were being fobbed off. I made those points to Detective Superintendent Kyne in our phone conversation on May 14th, and we had also relayed the same message to Minister for Justice Alan Shatter on May 3rd when we met him in Portlaoise.

What was incredible about this latest letter was that the Commissioner was holding firm and refusing to meet with us, saying that we first must meet Detective Superintendent Kyne. This letter really annoyed me and it just reinforced my opinion that we were doing the right thing in going down the road that we had chosen to go. I felt that we had no other choice, and my determination to find the truth got me through those next few days.

Chapter 18

All weekend I tried to keep myself busy to take my mind off things. Each evening I did something different: one day I went to the cinema, the next the gym, and the next the swimming pool. It was my way of dealing with the enormity of what was about to happen.

Friday and Saturday nights both passed without any contact from Adams. All day Sunday I never left the phone from my hand as I waited for the call. Finally, at about 8 p.m. on Sunday night, the call I had been waiting for came, and I was told that Gerry Adams and Richard McAuley would meet us the following morning in the lobby of the Regency Hotel in Dublin at 11 a.m. We were again warned that there was to be no mobile phones, that we should be alone, and nobody could know what was happening.

I rang Mam and Kieran as they deserved to know what was going on, not least for our security. I knew that Mam would be going up the walls from the time I told her until she heard from us after the whole thing was finished.

I was actually very calm myself the night before. Again I tried to distract myself by watching a movie and then going to bed early. I was wondering how the whole thing was going to work, and both Oliver and I were of the opinion that the initial meeting would probably be moved from the Regency Hotel.

Monday, July 29th, 2013 was a lovely summer's day: the sun was shining and there wasn't a cloud in the sky. I got up at my normal time and decided to go into work early as I usually would. I was living in County Kildare at the time and the drive to work in Wheatfield Prison was about 45 minutes. I remember gliding along the road as the adrenaline had started to kick in. Once I got to work, I had my coffee and breakfast and went through my emails, just another way of keeping busy until it was time to go to the Regency. Then, at 10 a.m., I left work for the 30-minute drive across the city.

When I got to the hotel, which was on the north side of the city, I parked in the large carpark at the rear of the hotel and I sat in my car waiting for Oliver to arrive. We had agreed to arrive there a half an hour before Adams and McAuley were to show up, as we wanted to get our bearings and have a quick scout around the place for anything unusual. I was only in the carpark five minutes or so when Oliver arrived and he pulled his car in beside mine. We got out and had a look around the carpark, which only had a handful of cars in it. We didn't notice anything unusual and there were no Northern Ireland registered cars visible, so we went into the lobby of the hotel. We again had a good look around and commandeered a table and two chairs that had a good view of the door.

As 11 a.m. came and went without any sign of Adams, I said to Oliver, 'I hope we have the right place and there isn't another Regency Hotel.' We waited and waited and then at about 11.20 a.m., Richard McAuley arrived and came over to us. Richard was dressed for the good weather, wearing a short-sleeved shirt, chinos and 'Jesus' sandals without socks. After a little small talk about the fine weather, he told us, 'Take one car and follow me, we are going to another location. I'll be driving a green Citroen car with Northern Ireland registration plates, which is parked at the front of the hotel.' Oliver and I gave each other a knowing look as we had expected this.

We went back to the carpark, got into my car, and when we drove around to the front of the hotel we saw the green Citroen. McAuley's car was old and it looked like it had seen better days. I commented to Oliver, 'Well one thing is for sure, we will have no problem keeping up with him' and we both laughed as we were pulling out onto the main road behind him. Anything to lighten the mood!

We turned right as we exited the hotel and drove in the direction of Dublin Airport, and when we got to the motorway we merged onto the M1 heading towards Belfast. McAuley drove slowly on the inside lane of the motorway and we were beginning to wonder where we were going.

Finally, as we approached the CityNorth Hotel, which is just outside Drogheda, McAuley indicated that he was turning off and taking the slip road. The hotel is located on the edge of the motorway and it is a favourite stop for people from Northern Ireland on their way back home from football matches or concerts in Dublin.

As we got into the carpark, McAuley drove towards the right side of it and, down at the bottom of one of the lanes, we could see Gerry Adams standing beside a car. Like McAuley, he was dressed in a short-sleeved shirt and was also sockless in a pair of 'Jesus' sandals. I tried to lighten the mood a little again and commented to Oliver, 'It looks like we haven't come properly attired.'

McAuley pulled into the empty space beside Adams and we pulled into the one beside that. When we got out, Adams came over and shook our hands and said that we would be going the rest of the way in his car. He gave McAuley the keys and told him to drive, then got into the passenger seat while Oliver and I got into the back. Adams' car was an Opel saloon that was about six or seven years old, and it looked like it wasn't the first time McAuley had driven it.

As we left the hotel, McAuley drove the car back onto the M1, again in the direction of Belfast. As soon as we got back on the motorway, Adams turned around to us and said, 'Lads, you're going to get an admission today.' I looked over to Oliver and just smiled; this was going to be a good day.

Adams told us that the man we were going to meet was a friend of his and that he had 'asked him to carry out an investigation into what happened'. As we were driving, Adams then engaged us in small talk about my dad. He asked if he was originally a Portlaoise man and I told him that while Dad was a Portlaoise man, his father was raised in Dundalk and had won an All-Ireland Football Championship with County Louth. We then got talking about GAA and, in particular, hurling in Northern Ireland. All this small talk was definitely taking our minds off what was to come and we were all like GAA experts commenting on the various teams and how well or not they were doing.

Then Adams suddenly looked at his watch and said to McAuley that we were ahead of schedule, and directed him to pull off the motorway at the next slip road. I didn't know where we were, but we ended up in a lovely small village and parked outside a pub that hadn't been open long. We got out of the car and myself, Oliver and McAuley sat at a picnic bench at the front of the pub while Adams went in to order some scones and coffee. When Adams was inside the pub, I asked McAuley if he was a coffee man or a tea man, and I was surprised when he said that he loved his coffee and had a Nespresso machine. So, while we were waiting on Adams to come back, we were sitting in the sun discussing the various types of Nespresso coffee that you could get and which ones we preferred. It was a surreal situation considering these guys were going to be putting us in a blacked-out van a little while later.

When we had finished our coffee, we got back on the road again and, as before, we took the M1 motorway in the direction of Belfast. As we approached Dundalk, I began to wonder when we would be leaving the motorway. Dundalk is right at the border with Northern Ireland, so by this stage I knew the meeting was going to be close by and we wouldn't have long to go. There are three exits for Dundalk off the M1 and as we approached the third of these exits, McAuley indicated left to come off the motorway. This is the Dundalk North exit and when you reach the top of the slip road you come to a large roundabout, the Ballymascanlon Roundabout. I knew a little about this part of Dundalk, as my dad had a lot of relations in the area, and we used to visit the Ballymascanlon Hotel as kids to see Dad's cousin, Irene Quinn, who owned the hotel.

However, I wasn't familiar with the road that we took to the left off this roundabout. I decided to spook Adams a little by telling him that I was familiar with the area and letting him know that Dad's people were from here. I wonder what was going through his head when I said to him, 'We used to spend a lot of time in this part of Dundalk as kids. Dad's cousin owns the hotel down the road.' All Adams could muster in response was, 'Oh right, the Ballymascanlon?'

When we turned left off the roundabout, we went under a bridge and proceeded up a hill until we came to an old graveyard, which I later found on Google Maps. They had taken us to the Faughart Old Graveyard, and I didn't know it at the time, but it has historical significance as the resting place of King Edward Bruce, the brother of Robert the Bruce and the last High King of Ireland, who died in 1318.

When we got to the graveyard, McAuley pulled the car into the carpark, which was very well maintained. It was at this point that I saw a blue Ford Transit van parked to the extreme right of the carpark. McAuley drove right up beside the van and, just then, a short overweight man got out of the driver's side of the van and stood beside it. We all got out of the car and as we did, Oliver indicated to me that he had noted the van registration, so I didn't pay much attention to it. I knew that the registration plates were probably false but at the same time it was good that Oliver took note of them.

As we approached the van, the driver became visibly excited. He was in awe of Gerry Adams and did everything except genuflect to him when Adams shook his hand. Adams dutifully played the role of an important person granting a besotted follower 30 seconds of his time and thanked the guy for doing his bit on that fine summer's morning.

The driver then opened the sliding door of the van and Adams motioned for us to get in. As I climbed into the van, I was astonished by what I saw. This was no ordinary van and a lot of work had been done to make it suitable for an operation like this. A bench had been made and fixed onto the van wall opposite the door, and I also noticed that sheets of plywood had been professionally cut to measure and screwed into the van walls covering the windows at the back and sides. They had also placed this wooden sheeting between the back of the van and the driver's cab so there was no view from the front. When Adams and McAuley got into the van and the door was closed, we were in complete darkness – we couldn't see a thing. I remember thinking, 'Who was the last person to sit where I'm sitting and what happened to them? Did they end up on a lonely border road with a bullet in the back of their head?'

This van appeared to be built for such a purpose and Oliver commented to me afterwards, 'This is isn't the first time that van was used to bring people to meet the IRA.' He was right – the work on the van was too professional and it wasn't done just for our meeting. Sitting there made me think what we were doing here. I wasn't scared, but I was definitely aware of my surroundings and what they had possibly been used for before. The other thing that struck me was that Gerry Adams was in this van with us, the leader of a political party that had quite a few seats in our Dáil.

As the van started up, I checked my watch and tried to focus on the direction we were going. We turned right as we left the carpark and I could tell that we were on winding back roads, and we took a few more turns before I could sense that the van had pulled in somewhere. Then the engine stopped and I checked my watch again: it had been 10 minutes since we had left the graveyard. Adams had assured me that at all times we would remain south of the border and while I knew we were very close, as in two or three miles from South Armagh and the infamous Bandit Country, I trusted Adams when he told us we would stay on the southern side of the border.

A few years later, while making a personal statement to the Dáil, Adams admitted that we had in fact been taken into Bandit Country. South Armagh had acquired this label as it had become completely lawless during the Troubles and it was the only part of Northern Ireland that the British security forces dared not enter. This meant that diesel smuggling, cigarette smuggling and drug dealing, among other things, were rife in the area, and all were controlled by the IRA as a way of funding their campaign.

I waited in anticipation to see what was going to happen next and, to my complete astonishment, when the van door was opened, I was literally looking directly at a kitchen table filled with scones and sandwiches! It took me a minute to realise what had happened. The van driver had skilfully brought the sliding door of the van to within an inch of the sliding patio door of a house. Again, this suggested a practised art that had been done before. The patio door in the kitchen had been opened from the inside and then that person opened the van door, so we stepped straight from the van into the kitchen of a house without being able to see our surroundings.

Immediately I could tell that the house was what has become known in Ireland as a 'one-off rural bungalow'. The person who had opened the doors for us was greeted warmly by Adams, who thanked him for his hospitality. This man was in his late fifties, had a thick head of grey hair, an equally thick grey moustache, and was wearing glasses.

We were then ushered into a living room through a set of French doors. Gerry Adams came with us but McAuley, the van driver and the owner of the house stayed in the kitchen. Adams closed the doors and a man who was sitting in an armchair reading the *Irish Times* looked up. This was another man in his late fifties and he looked for all the world like a schoolteacher, wearing one of those sports jackets with leather elbow patches. I began to think, this definitely can't be our guy, he looks nothing like a terrorist.

Then he introduced himself saying, 'My name is John . . . well, for the purposes of this meeting I'm John.' He then said, 'I had a leadership role in the IRA all during the struggle and held a senior leadership role at the time of the ceasefire.' He got straight down to business and told us that he had prepared a statement for us and he would read it out. After this he said that they would leave us alone for a while to digest what was in the statement and they would allow us to transcribe it. I took a deep breath as he began reading:

I want to acknowledge that the IRA was responsible for the death of your father. I regret that it has taken so long to clarify this matter for you. In 2005 the IRA ordered an end to its campaign, put its weapons beyond use and left the stage. This was a secret guerrilla army. It kept no record of its military operations. During the 30 years of war activists were killed, many thousands were imprisoned and leadership at all levels were constantly changing. Reliable information is therefore not readily available and sometimes not available at all. The IRA did have rules and regulations, including a rule which prohibited any military action against Irish State forces. Regrettably at times these rules were breached. Between the 1970s and 1980s there were prison struggles in Britain, the North and the South. The prisoners resisted these harsh regimes. Prison officers were killed by the IRA in the North. These killings were sanctioned by the IRA leadership but none were sanctioned in the South and none was asked for in the case of your father. In Portlaoise a brutal prison regime saw prisoners and their families suffer greatly. This is the context in which IRA Volunteers shot your father. This action was not authorised by the IRA leadership and for this reason the IRA denied any involvement. Some years later, when the Army Council discovered that its volunteers had shot Prison Officer Brian Stack, the volunteer responsible for the instruction was disciplined. Those who carried out the attack were IRA Volunteers acting under orders. The IRA was responsible for your father's death. This operation should not have taken place. While the IRA can no longer comment on this matter let me express sorrow for the pain and hurt your family suffered.

When John had finished reading this, he said to us that he appreciated that it was a lot to take in, so they would leave us alone for at least a half an hour. Adams then left the room with John and the owner of the house came in with coffee and sandwiches and placed them on the coffee table.

When they left the room, before we did anything else, both of us had a good look around. It was a normal living room and had family photos of graduations and other family events on the walls and in the cabinets. I also took the opportunity to go to the toilet and when there I looked out the window, but all I could see was a garden with some very high fern-type trees. Walking from the living room to the toilet also confirmed my belief that we were in a bungalow.

While John had been reading out the statement and, in particular, the first line of it, all I could think about was Dad and how we finally got them to admit what they did to him. It was a proud moment for us. I was also angry that we had to do this ourselves with no help from the Gardaí, who still believed that the IRA weren't responsible. I knew the Gardaí were going to be red-faced once we announced what had happened and they would probably be hounding us to meet with them to find out more.

Oliver and I then decided that we would both transcribe the statement to be sure that we made no mistakes. It was while we were doing this that we both saw all the flaws in what was clearly a half admission. When I was listening to John, I probably only heard what I wanted to hear and the statement was read so quickly that it needed us to go through it line by line. Transcribing it let us give it that critical analysis.

I couldn't believe that they were admitting to murdering Dad but at the same time they were trying not to take responsibility as they claimed it hadn't been sanctioned. To make matters worse, they were trying to justify it by saying the context of the murder was the 'brutal regime' in Portlaoise. I hadn't come this far and gone to all these lengths not to challenge these things, and I told Oliver that once they returned, I had far more questions for them than the ones that we had provided.

What I also noticed when transcribing the statement was that it was designed to answer most of the questions that we had provided to Gerry Adams before the meeting. We had a list of 28 questions that we wanted to ask and while most were covered by the statement, they had shied away from addressing some very specific questions in their statement. We had asked questions such as, 'Were any current senior leaders of Sinn Féin or current elected Sinn Féin representatives responsible for and/or aware of the decision to murder Chief Officer Brian Stack?' Another question in a similar vein was: 'Were any associates known to any current senior leaders of Sinn Féin or current elected Sinn Féin representatives responsible for and/or aware of the decision to murder Chief Officer Brian Stack?' These questions were designed to see what they would say in relation to Mr A, who was at the time an elected representative and held a leading role in Sinn Féin.

Once Adams and John returned, I went through all the questions with them. When there was a question that had been answered in the statement, I skipped it, but the answer to most other questions, including the two already mentioned, was a straight 'No'. Once again, they were lying to us, but if they had to say 'Yes' to these two questions, they would be going down a road that would create a lot more problems for them.

I then proceeded to ask some follow-on questions and I first tried to pick holes in their half admission by asking if the operation wasn't sanctioned and if they had disciplined a Volunteer, would he be prepared to say that the murder of Dad was a criminal act. At that stage John lost his composure and started to waffle before settling for, 'It was wrong and shouldn't have happened.'

I challenged both John and Adams on the fact that they were claiming that the operation wasn't sanctioned: 'This was too well planned, the organisation that went into this shooting was very detailed, this was an attack on the State, the IRA were the only ones with a clear motive.' Adams answered by using the standard line that they had successfully fed the media in 1983 and that he had used in the *Prime Time* interview in April: 'Austin, it could have been anybody: Dublin criminals, INLA or other republicans. We only found out about three years later.'

I countered by saying, 'Are you telling me that you were sitting in Sinn Féin HQ the following morning after the attack and you didn't think it could be your guys? Your people were the only ones with the organisational ability to pull off something like this, the INLA were a rag-tag setup.'

In response to this, Adams said, 'Sure, the INLA carried out the attack on Airey Neave.' He just would not budge on this issue. I purposely didn't ask him about how they disciplined the IRA officer who organised the attack, but what did jump out at me was that Adams said they knew three years later that they had done it, so my question was, why not admit it then? Why not tell the family who they knew were seeking answers? Adams just responded that he personally didn't know.

I then challenged John about what he called the 'context' of my dad's murder and the fact that he seemed to be justifying it by saying there was a brutal regime in Portlaoise Prison at the time, and that prisoners and their families suffered.

I asked him to explain that statement and his answer showed how the IRA and Sinn Féin tried to make political capital out of everyday, normal procedures in a prison. John claimed that the regime was brutal because prisoners were being strip-searched and the families suffered because their visits were behind screens. I told John that these practices were not unique to Portlaoise Prison and that as a standard operating procedure in every prison in the country, two prisoners on each prison landing have to be strip-searched each day. I also explained to him that a prisoner is never completely naked in these searches, as the top half of clothing is removed and searched before being returned, then the bottom half of the clothing is removed once he puts back on the top half. Sinn Féin and IRA propaganda would have you believe that the prisoners were completely naked and the searches were intrusive, which they never were. I also explained to John that, at the time of our meeting, two prisons in Ireland had no open visits and all visit areas were screened. I also explained that all prisons have some screened visit areas, which are routinely used when required. I told John that these issues could not be seen as 'brutal' and if the IRA prisoners had not been involved in smuggling guns and Semtex into the prison, there would not have been a need for those measures.

John was completely bemused by my retort and look blankly at Adams for help, but all Adams could say in response was, 'You do know Austin is a high-ranking prison officer? So he knows what he is talking about.'

At several points throughout the meeting, John had clearly indicated to us that he had spoken with those who were involved in the attack on Dad. So, near the end of the meeting, with my restorative justice hat on, I asked John a direct question: 'Are you aware how those who carried out the attack feel about it now?' John said that he wasn't aware how they felt about it now, so I asked him if he felt that they would be prepared to meet with us so that we could talk to them about what happened. John replied saying, 'That's unlikely.' I then asked him if those involved were still alive and if he had met them, and he responded, 'I'm not getting into that.'

As the meeting was drawing to a close, I asked John if he had anything else that he wanted to add and he responded by saying, 'This should not have happened and on a personal level, I'm sorry that it did.'

Adams then called time on the meeting saying that he needed to get back to Dublin. At this point, John shook our hands and said, 'It was a pleasure to meet you both, I just wish that it was under better circumstances.'

We went back into the kitchen where the van driver, McAuley, and the owner of the house were sitting at the kitchen table. We thanked the owner of the house for the coffee and sandwiches, and we were then escorted back through the patio door into the van. I timed the journey back to Faughart Old Graveyard and this time the journey was shorter, taking seven minutes. We also entered the carpark of the graveyard from the opposite side, so clearly there was a loop involved and they had come back by a different route to try to confuse us.

The journey back to the CityNorth Hotel was uneventful and we agreed with Adams that we would wait until Oliver came back from his holidays before any statements would be released. He again tried to get us to do either a joint statement or for us to include a line in a statement saying that we wanted no charges brought in relation to the case. I told him that we had been very clear that we would be releasing our own statement and said that we would decide as a family if they had gone far enough for us to include the line about no charges.

By the time we got back to the CityNorth Hotel, I was mentally drained and I think we both knew that it would take some time for the enormity of what had happened to sink in. On the way home, we rang my mother to let her know that we were safe and sound and we filled her in on what had happened. She couldn't believe what we had achieved and I think she had a sense of pride mixed with anger, just like I had felt. My brother Kieran, on the other hand, had a hundred and one questions, and we did our best to answer them, but it's always difficult straight after the event to remember everything. But we had taken notes and I told him that we'd do a proper debrief the next day.

We now needed to prepare a statement for the media and with Oliver going to Egypt on holiday and Kieran being in the USA, this was going to take time. So, we decided that I would do an initial draft and send it to the others and also talk to Mam. They would then make additions and alterations as required until we reached an agreed statement.

Oliver was very firm in the car on the way home that in his opinion they hadn't reached the threshold in their admission that would allow us to put the line about no charges being brought into our statement. I agreed with him. They hadn't given us a full and complete admission, and while they had taken a limited form of corporate responsibility, they still tried to evade full responsibility by saying the operation hadn't been sanctioned.

Over the following week, we managed to put together what I have always considered our best statement. We worked hard on it as a family and when it was finished, I knew that I would be so proud delivering it on behalf of the family. After a few phone calls with Gerry Adams, it was decided that we would both release our statements on Friday, August 9th. Adams told us that they would release their statement about an hour after our one went out, but he would require a copy of our statement the day before. I was happy enough with those arrangements.

Once Adams got our statement on the evening of August 8th, he rang me in a last effort to get us to include the line about no charges being brought. I told him very clearly that they hadn't gone far enough and I was disappointed that I couldn't put that line in, but I assured him that if things developed and a restorative meeting could be arranged with the perpetrators then this might change in the future.

Once I had the statement put together, I drafted a press release and attached the statement from the family and sent it to all the major Irish, UK and local news media on the evening of August 8th. I knew how the game worked regarding press releases: in order to get the press to show up, you have to show them that something significant is happening, that's why I attached the statement. However, you also don't want them jumping the gun and releasing your statement before you do, so I placed an embargo on the press release and statement until 3 p.m. on August 9th. When you do this, the media will respect the embargo and it gives them a chance to also have some of their story prepared, which helps with deadlines. The stage was set; all I had to do now was show up.

Chapter 19

On that Friday morning on August 9th, I got up nice and early. I was very calm and not a bit nervous. I decided that I would have to look my best and so went for a classic navy pinstripe suit with a red tie. I then drove to Dublin to meet Oliver, who had come back from Egypt the day before.

We had told the media that we would be doing a press conference outside the gates of Dáil Éireann at 3 p.m. and had gone into Buswells Hotel for lunch. When we left Buswells at 2.55 p.m. and looked across the road, I nearly died – the place was saturated with media and TV cameras. I don't usually get nervous speaking in public, but I can tell you, I was shaking crossing that road as the media started to take photos and surround us.

When we managed to wade through the crowd and took our place, ensuring the national parliament was our backdrop, I nervously turned to face the media. With Oliver standing to my left, I took our statement from my pocket and was ready to deliver it. At that moment, a man from deep in the middle of the media throng shouted, 'Austin, Austin, over here.' When I looked over, the guy was behind a TV camera and he said to me, 'I need you to look into this camera when you do this, this is the camera that is going to deliver this worldwide.' When he said this, the media people in front of the camera parted and made a little space for him to get an unobstructed view of me. If I was nervous before this, I was now planking it. Then all of a sudden I returned to a calm state – it was like Dad was guiding me and telling me it was all going to be OK. I then did something that I wouldn't normally do: I looked up to the heavens and, while trying to hold back the emotion, I said in a whisper, 'Dad, this is for you.' I took a deep breath, looked directly at the 'worldwide camera', and delivered the following statement in a measured tone:

On the 25th of March, 1983, the Chief Officer of Portlaoise Prison, Brian Stack, was shot in an attack outside the National Boxing Stadium in Dublin. He subsequently died from his injuries. Brian Stack was a proud and loyal servant of this State, a role model in his community and a dedicated family man. Despite three separate Garda investigations, no individual or organisation has been found responsible for his murder. The case review conducted by the Serious Crime Review Team between 2007 and 2008 uncovered many unsettling aspects and major flaws in the original investigation. As a consequence, now-retired Garda Commissioner Fachtna Murphy in July 2008 instructed that the case be passed to the National Bureau of Criminal Investigation [NBCI].

It appears to the Stack Family that the original investigation was seriously compromised from the outset – a damning indictment for what was at the time a capital murder charge case, the most serious criminal charge in the State. The Garda authorities have never provided our family with an adequate explanation for these shortcomings. To add insult to injury, as a family we have become frustrated at what we can only describe as the uncooperative nature on the part of the current

NBCI investigation team. It is our view that the distinct lack of cooperation our family has experienced with the current NBCI team is directly linked to the unsettling aspects and major flaws uncovered in the original Garda investigation. We have communicated our concerns to Garda Commissioner Callinan and Minister for Justice Shatter and made a request last January to directly meet with Commissioner Callinan. We still await a positive response to this request.

It is in this context that we, as a family, were forced to explore other avenues in order to find answers and seek closure. On May 9th, 2013, family representatives met with Sinn Féin leader Gerry Adams. At that meeting we requested that Deputy Adams use his contacts and influence to help us gain answers and some measure of closure. Following that meeting, a process evolved and several more meetings with Deputy Adams took place. This process reached a conclusion early last week when family representatives, accompanied by Deputy Adams, met with a former senior IRA leader. At the outset of this meeting, a statement was issued to the family. This statement acknowledged that the IRA was responsible for the death of Chief Officer Brian Stack and that IRA members, acting under orders, carried out this attack. We were further informed that the IRA leadership had not sanctioned the attack and, upon becoming aware that its members, acting under orders, carried out the attack, the IRA disciplined the member responsible for issuing the instruction.

The statement also expressed regret that it had taken so long to clarify this matter and acknowledged that the attack should not have taken place. An expression of sorrow for the pain and hurt suffered by our family was also included. This process has brought an element of closure to our family and it has provided us with some answers that three separate Garda investigations failed to deliver. We would like to thank Deputy Adams for the role he has played in facilitating this outcome.

We are, however, unfortunately still left with unanswered questions. In particular, who are the individual IRA members responsible for the murder of Chief Officer Brian Stack and why does it appear the original Garda investigation was compromised from the outset? We today again call for Garda Commissioner Callinan to meet with us directly to provide us with an update on the current investigation and an explanation for the failures in the original investigation.

The Stack family is very supportive of the peace process and we are fully aware of the terms of the Good Friday Agreement. As a result, we appreciate and have come to terms with the fact that if any individual or individuals were identified as part of the investigation, they would come under the terms of this agreement. As a family, we believe that closure for victims of Ireland's troubled past is a vital part of the peace process. Families should not privately have to take the actions our family has taken over the past number of months to seek answers. We are today asking the governments in Ireland and the UK to look at establishing a formal mechanism through which victims can pursue this. In the absence of any formal process, if any other family feels that they could gain some closure in a similar way to what we have done, we would be happy to help, support and advise them in that.

I really didn't understand the significance or historic nature of what we had achieved, as I had at all times been too focused on getting answers for Dad. But as I waited in RTÉ later that evening to do a

TV interview, Barry Cummins rang me. Barry had been there from the start and had always been a huge help to us, and all he said to me was, 'Austin, you have no idea what you have achieved, these people just don't admit to murder 30 years later. This is enormous!' It was definitely at that point that I realised what we had managed to do.

In the media questioning after I read the statement, I had made it clear that while I was thankful to Gerry Adams for what he had done, I felt that we had only gotten about 70 per cent closure. I alluded to the fact that the IRA shirked taking full responsibility for the attack and I also needed the media to focus on the inadequate police investigations.

Naturally, the media only went for one part of the story as they zoned in on the IRA statement, and the focus on that side of things went even further later that evening when Adams spoke to the media. While at the time I did genuinely believe that Adams wanted to help us, I wasn't blind to him having a political agenda. I knew that he saw this whole thing as a vehicle to show the Irish public that Sinn Féin were in the reconciliation business. But, likewise, I had my own agenda, which was to prove the Gardaí wrong and to finally get the IRA to admit what they did. In thinking that Adams was genuine, I also knew that he had to protect 'project Sinn Féin' and, therefore, was never going to throw senior Sinn Féin figures under the bus as this would be political suicide. In that respect, I thought that we had gotten as much from him as he could deliver.

Chapter 20

About a week after we had released our statements to the world, Gerry Adams contacted me by phone to ask how I was and, in particular, how was my mother. He suggested that in time maybe he could meet her. I still thought at this stage that he might be genuine and was prepared to give him the benefit of the doubt in relation to that, but I also knew he was playing a political game and there was no way I was going to expose Mam to that.

By this time, relations with the Gardaí had improved a little. Following our meeting with the IRA, Detective Superintendent George Kyne reached out to me again. This time he suggested an informal meeting. He told me that he was aware of our previous difficulties with those managing the case, but said that he was now in charge and that things would be different. This sounded plausible and I had a gut feeling that George was a good guy, so I agreed to meet with him and Detective Robbie Comerford in September.

When we met, the first thing George did was to acknowledge on behalf of the Gardaí our achievement in obtaining the IRA statement of admission. He told me things would be different going forward and that he would give me monthly updates on the case progress. In fairness to George, he was the first person who was in charge of the case that attempted to form a relationship with us and, over the next few years, while there were challenges and I had to have strong words with him, I found him to be a decent and honest guy.

As a result of this meeting, I agreed to give the Gardaí a statement about the information I had received from the journalist, Jim, who named Mr A, Mr B and Mr C. They pushed me when giving this statement to divulge details of our meeting with Gerry Adams and the IRA leader, but I refused as there was an agreement on confidentiality in relation to the process. For me, my word is my bond and I wasn't about to go back on a promise that I had made. However, as I was later to realise, others didn't have the same moral compass.

I had another brief meeting with George in January 2014, where he told me that Garda HQ wanted to give the family a full overview of the case and we were invited to the National Bureau of Criminal Investigation Headquarters in Harcourt Terrace in February for this. The meeting in Harcourt Terrace was led by Assistant Commissioner Derek Byrne and they began by giving us an outline of the original investigation. This was followed by a presentation by Superintendent Christy Mangan on the work done by the Serious Crime Review Team. When Christy was finished, I again questioned him as to their reluctance to question former Portlaoise Prison Deputy Governor Ned Harkin and stated that, the whole time we were asking for this to be done, Harkin's son was a Garda Assistant Commissioner. At this point, Assistant Commissioner Derek Byrne denied that this had played a role in Harkin not being interviewed. I responded by saying, 'If you were in our shoes, how do you think it would look? I'm just stating facts.' Christy Mangan at this stage brought up the famous sick cert as an excuse for them not interviewing Harkin, which made me quite angry as we had already been over this several times with them. But I again put it on record that, on the day they originally told us about the sick cert, my mother witnessed him in my uncle's pub having a pint. While the following day, February 24th, 2009, a journalist door-stepped him and he told her that it may have been one of his family members who had sent the sick cert. He told her that his short-term memory was poor but he could remember things from 30 years ago. He also stated that he would have no problem meeting Gardaí from NBCI.

I then asked them, as we had done before, to share the findings of the Serious Crime Review Team's 198 recommendations with us but, as before, this was refused. They held the line saying that it was an internal Garda document. We have never been given a copy of this document.

Finally, George Kyne gave an overview of the current NBCI investigation and told us that they were still actively working on it. I felt like the whole meeting was a stunt so they could say to the media that they had given us a complete briefing on the case. The bottom line was that they told us nothing new and all the real leads in the case had been developed by us.

My brother Kieran was home from the USA in August 2014 and, in order to keep him in the picture, I arranged another meeting with Assistant Commissioner Derek Byrne, George and Robbie. At this meeting, George told us that they were pursuing some fresh lines of inquiry following interviews in April and June with what they called 'sensitive sources'. He did tell us, though, that they believed Mr B was in Canada, as an alias he used came up on a police checkpoint there in the early 2000s.

At this meeting, I also brought up the comments made in July 2014 by former Tánaiste and Minister for Justice Michael McDowell. During the negotiations that led to the Good Friday Agreement and brought peace to Northern Ireland, the British Attorney General gave a commitment that they would issue letters of pardon to those who were known as 'on the runs'. These letters would give an immunity from prosecution to any IRA members who had fled Northern Ireland after committing a crime. Many of these were living in the USA, Canada and Australia and were now free to return. According to Michael McDowell, who at the time was the Irish Attorney General, the British side asked what would Ireland be doing in relation to this. He claimed that there was a 'consensus' going back to at least 2000 that Gardaí would no longer be looking to prosecute historical cases from the Troubles. I asked if this was a factor in the lack of progress in Dad's case and I was told by Assistant Commissioner Byrne that he had seen no such directive and there was nothing of this nature 'written down'.

The fact remains that while the Gardaí state that they have no written instruction in relation to this, in an article he wrote for the *Irish Times* on July 21st, 2021, Michael McDowell again spoke of this matter and claimed: 'Since 1998, nobody has been investigated or prosecuted in the Republic for the murders, bombings, mutilations, tortures, robberies and extortion they are suspected of perpetrating in the Troubles up to the Belfast Agreement of that year. A de facto amnesty has existed in those cases.'

*   *   *

Back in early November 2013, BBC's *Spotlight* asked me to do an interview in relation to a programme they were doing on Gerry Adams. I agreed and I gave what I thought was a balanced interview – I gave him credit for meeting us and told them that I felt maybe he was trying to do some good before he left the stage and retired. I balanced that by criticising him for not giving us the full truth at our meeting. When the programme went out, the edited version only showed my critical points. But my view of Adams was to change anyway.

Sometime towards the end of November 2013, I received a phone call from Adams and this was to be our last civil engagement. When I answered, he enquired how I had been and how my mother was doing since we had last spoken in August. He apologised for not being in touch and said that this was due to 'the little family matter'. The 'little family matter' he was referring to was the trial of his brother Liam Adams for the rape of his daughter. This trial had concluded in early October with Liam Adams being found guilty; he was subsequently sentenced to 16 years in prison on November 27th.

In the period leading up to the trial, Gerry Adams had been the subject of much scrutiny in the media over what he allegedly knew or didn't know, and what he had reported to the police and when he reported it. It's fair to say he would have been totally preoccupied during this period. However, I was completely gobsmacked when he referred to it as the 'little family matter'. Maybe he didn't mean it to come across the way it did or maybe he just phrased it very badly, but the meaning I took from what he said was that he was totally fed up and frustrated with the barrage of media intrusion around his brother's case, and in doing so he intentionally or unintentionally demeaned a very serious matter.

A year later, more cracks appeared in my already fragile opinion of the man and his party. In October 2014, BBC *Spotlight* aired a programme in which former Sinn Féin member Máiría Cahill waived her anonymity and disclosed how as a 16-year-old she had been raped by an IRA man. She told the programme how she reported the matter to Sinn Féin and that they had organised a kangaroo court in which they subjected her to facing her rapist. Máiría managed very successfully to ask serious questions about how Sinn Féin dealt with matters of sexual abuse. Then, in March 2015, the same programme exposed another case, that of Paudie

McGahon, who had also been subjected to sexual abuse by an 'on the run' IRA man.

Like Máiría, Paudie had reported what happened to Sinn Féin and a kangaroo court was held at his home and the IRA man was exiled from Ireland.

A few weeks after the *Spotlight* programme on the Paudie McGahon case, while visiting Belfast, I was contacted by Jennifer O'Leary from BBC *Spotlight*. She had interviewed me a few times and suggested the next time I was in Belfast to call her and we'd go for a coffee. When we met, she naturally asked about Dad's case and inquired who the individuals were who took part in the attack. As she was Belfast-based, I felt that she might be able to do some digging in relation to Mr B and Mr C, and she may be able to get a line on their whereabouts.

The moment I mentioned Mr B's name, her face froze and she just went silent. After a few moments, she said to me that I needed to keep this information to myself and told me that she was going to arrange a meeting for the following morning with somebody who had information on Mr B.

Later that evening, while I was settling into my hotel room, Jennifer contacted me to say that a meeting had been arranged for 10 a.m. the following morning in the lobby of my hotel. I hadn't much time to think about things as it all happened so quickly, but shortly after breakfast the following morning, Jennifer's contact arrived at my hotel.

The hotel was quiet and we were able to sit in the restaurant. Over a coffee, this woman told me that Mr B had sexually abused a young girl in Belfast in the early 1970s and the IRA had exiled him to France. She told me that he was very close to Mr A and that he had been brought home from exile around 1980 by Mr A to reorganise the IRA in Munster. She went on to tell me that, while she was visiting a safe house in Dundalk in the company of her father, Mr B had also abused her. She then gave me information that she had received on Mr B's location. She believed that he was living with a police sergeant in Texas, USA. I was absolutely rocked when I heard all this and it really made my blood boil. I felt physically sick.

Later that day, while still in Belfast, I gave an interview to Máiría Cahill, who was now working for the *Sunday Independent*, and I told her that it appeared to me that Sinn Féin and the IRA were moving sex abusers around in a manner similar to the Catholic Church. I couldn't stop thinking about it all day and it really disturbed me that the chief suspect in Dad's murder was also linked with possible child sex abuse, and it appeared that he was being protected by the wider movement.

Armed with this information, I just couldn't stand idly by and say nothing. I knew that various media outlets would contact me for a comment in relation to the Sinn Féin/IRA sex abuse scandal and I decided that I had to support Máiría and Paudie and all those who were too afraid to tell their stories. I remember one particular radio interview that I did and the host said to me, 'But you thanked Gerry Adams for helping you. Why are you turning on him now?' The simple answer was that I felt morally obliged as somebody who had a voice and who the media respected to let the world know what these people were really like. Adams' comment about the 'little family matter', while not sitting right with me at the time, definitely didn't sit right now.

Following this show of support for Máiría and Paudie, I began to get my first experiences of the social media 'pile on' that supporters of Sinn Féin and the IRA engage in. Twitter was the worst experience of the lot. I joined it in 2012 to help engage the public and the media about Dad's case and to also point out the hypocrisy of Sinn Féin and how they have tried to manipulate the unsuspecting newer voters into thinking they are the answer to all that they perceive is wrong in Ireland. On Twitter they came at me in the hundreds, all new anonymous accounts that you cannot verify. The way they work is that five or six will attack you together using horrible language, attacking Dad's good name or just spewing personal abuse at me. For me, the old adage 'sticks and stones may hurt my bones but words will never hurt me' comes into play here, so I would just ignore and block them. When I did that, within seconds, another five or six accounts similar in nature would swamp my timeline in the same manner. This all appeared to be well organised and very targeted.

Examples of some of the abuse on Twitter include:

@Jim_Moor: Wanker. Son of a SADIST. My dad wasn't afraid of your sadistic bullying dad & I ain't afraid of you.

@jk20142014: @adstack Sadist scumbag, cry on you fucking prick, nobody gives a Fuck about your alcoholic, bullying bastard dad. Scum

@BondTuckerbond: I heard he was a boxer, he offered a fair go to any republican, he was well handy, but he couldn't out run a bullet. Screws need to learn that they can't be knocking people around and think they can brag about it down the gaa club.

I'm not sure if they were bots or actual people, but the whole thing appeared to be very orchestrated.

George Kyne and his team appeared to be busy following leads and he kept in contact with me by phone. Finally we had another proper meeting with him, Robbie Comerford and Assistant Commissioner

Byrne in my mother's house on June 18th, 2015. Kieran was home from the United States and I had arranged the meeting to work around his trip. At this meeting, the Gardaí gave us far more information than they had ever previously given us.

They first told us that they had been to Spain to interview Mr D (name withheld). Mr D was a Belfast man who ended up living in Dublin during the 1970s, and at the time of Dad's shooting he was the Officer Commanding of the Dublin Brigade of the IRA. I had never heard his name in connection with the attack on Dad, but I knew of him and his rank within the IRA. I always just assumed that he would have known that the attack was being planned as it was happening on his beat so to speak, but what the Gardaí revealed was extraordinary.

Mr D was also wanted in relation to another serious matter in Ireland, and he had questions to answer in relation to the murder of Garda Jerry McCabe as well. He had initially gone on the run following the McCabe murder and the Gardaí had renewed a warrant for his arrest, but they eventually let it lapse. At the time, there was a lot of suspicion as to why this was allowed to happen, but it wouldn't be the only piece of 'luck' Mr D was to have when dealing with the Irish authorities.

George Kyne told us that they had gone to interview Mr D in Spain, which took place in front of a magistrate, as is required there. Apparently, Mr D didn't say too much while in the formal setting, but afterwards he had a cup of coffee with the gardaí and told them that he had been in the National Stadium on the night that Dad was shot. He also told them that he was in the company of two well-known IRA activists from the Short Strand area of Belfast whom he named.

I couldn't believe what I was hearing. Not only was the Officer Commanding of the Dublin IRA placing himself at the scene of the crime, he was placing two other IRA activists there too, one of whom later confirmed this story to the Gardaí. Considering that the Serious Crime Review Team had told us that they had mapped the seating of the National Stadium from the night of the attack and had managed to put a name on every seat, this meant that they had either lied to us about it or had deliberately withheld this information.

I asked the Gardaí when they would be applying for an extradition warrant for Mr D, but they told me that they would need evidence to do so. I found this incredible seeing as he was the Officer Commanding of the Dublin Brigade and had placed himself at the scene of a crime that the IRA had now admitted to. To add insult to injury, Mr D would subsequently be extradited to face another very serious charge in Dublin and, even though he had questions to answer in relation to two capital murders, he was granted bail, which of course he failed to honour and has since vanished. The Gardaí assured us that they had opposed bail and blamed the court but, as I said, Mr D seems to be either very lucky or something else entirely is going on regarding him.

The second thing of importance that the Gardaí told us at this meeting was that my information on Mr B appeared to be correct. They had asked Interpol to follow up and check flight records against the alias he was using. This check revealed a pattern of flights from Ontario to Texas from 2000 to 2008. These appear to stop in Texas at that point, so it was safe to assume that he might still be located there, as my information suggested. The Gardaí agreed to fully explore this lead.

The third thing to come from this meeting was again something that backed up information I had given to the Gardaí. They told us that they had spoken to a person who was in the witness protection programme in the UK. They said that it took 18 months to locate this person and another six months to get him to agree to an interview

with them. They told us that he had given them the same information in relation to the shooting that I had received from the journalist
Jim – the same names of those involved and the same theory about
how it was sanctioned. He also told the Gardaí that the operation had
been planned in a house located in a townland just outside Portlaoise
called The Heath. He said that he had been in the house with Mr A
and Mr B when this happened.

I asked the Gardaí if the person they had spoken to was Sean
O'Callaghan. O'Callaghan shot dead a Catholic police officer,
Peter Flanagan, in Omagh, County Tyrone, on August 23rd, 1974,
but he wouldn't be convicted for it until 1988 after handing himself
in to a police station in England. At one stage, he had been Officer
Commanding of the Southern Brigade of the IRA, but he was
also a high-level Garda informant. He had written a book called
The Informer and I suspected that he was living in the UK. George
Kyne looked at the Assistant Commissioner and then back to me
and shrugged his shoulders in a gesture that told me I was on the
right track.

After the meeting, when we were having a cup of coffee, Oliver
asked me how I knew that they were talking about O'Callaghan,
and I told him that it was an educated guess. He then said that he
had been looking over the Assistant Commissioner's shoulder and
had seen his notes, which had the initials 'SO'C' written in several
places.

I knew at this point that I had to get confirmation from O'Callaghan himself about what the Gardaí told us, because if he knew all
this and was in the house while the operation was being planned,
then surely he would have told his Garda handler. I explained
this to Mam and my brothers, but Kieran just looked at me in a
quizzical way and asked how I was going to do that. With that
I pulled out my phone and sent a text message to the journalist

Ruth Dudley Edwards. I knew Ruth had been friendly with O'Callaghan after he came out of jail and had given him a place to stay at one stage. I asked Ruth if she was still in contact with O'Callaghan and, if so, would she seek his permission to pass on his contact details as I wanted to talk to him in relation to Dad's case. We were still at the kitchen table in Mam's an hour later when Ruth came back to me with a message saying Sean would talk to me and to send him an email at an address he forwarded on to her. To say my brothers were flabbergasted would be an understatement.

Within four days, after a few emails back and forth, I agreed to travel to London to meet Sean O'Callaghan on July 14th, 2015. I wanted to keep this mission as secret as possible as I didn't want the Gardaí trying to sabotage what I was doing. My dad had two brothers who settled in London and, as a result, I had a large extended family over there. My brothers and I had always been very close to my cousin Martin, who lived in the East End of London, and I knew I could trust him if I brought him into the loop on what I was doing. I was going to meet a man who had confessed to coolly walking up to a policeman in a pub and shooting him dead. I wasn't going to take any chances, so I needed somebody to watch my back. I swore Martin to secrecy and we agreed that I would stay with him while I was in London.

Martin picked me up from my early morning flight to Stansted Airport, and we went back to his house before then catching the Central Line Tube into the city centre.

O'Callaghan had insisted that I come alone and that our discussion remain private for the time being. He gave me details of and directions to an open-air café in Covent Garden, a location I assume he chose so that he could case it out beforehand to ensure I was alone. Martin and I arrived a good hour before the meeting time and, as we approached the café, Martin went to one end of it and I to the other. I told Martin that I was expecting O'Callaghan to move the meeting to another location and that he needed to keep eyes on me at all times.

It was a lovely summer's day and, while I waited, I was pretending to people watch, but I was, in fact, watching for anything unusual. O'Callaghan arrived bang on time and straight away said that we needed to go to another café as 'this place is far too open'. With that, he brought me on a tour of the back streets of London's Theatre district and we meandered at pace around various alleys. I knew that he was being cautious and trying to shake off any potential tail. If I had trust issues with him, it appeared that he also had trust issues with me – I was just hoping that Martin could keep up.

Finally, we arrived at another open-air café, but this one was small, dingy and very secluded. The first thing he did when we sat down was look me up and down as he lit the first of what would be at least 20 cigarettes that he smoked in the four hours we spent together. When the coffee arrived, I thanked him for meeting me and he asked me how I thought he could help.

I mentioned that I was aware he had spoken with the Gardaí and that they had filled us in on the conversation. I said that I wanted to confirm with him personally what he had told them as most of it matched what I had been previously told by another source. At that point, he started talking and I couldn't stop him. He told me all the same details about how the operation was sanctioned and those who were involved; the story matched exactly what Jim had gotten from his two sources. He did, however, add one other element: he said that the second in command of the Dublin Brigade of the IRA, Mr E, was involved on the night as a spotter outside the National Stadium. He said that the shooter, Mr C, didn't know Dad and that the spotter's job was to point Dad out to him.

As he was speaking, he kept going on and on about different IRA missions that he was on and he talked about different people within the movement. He then got into how he felt he had been radicalised as a young teenager and described how he had shot the policeman in the pub. He seemed genuine when he explained how his conscience got the better of him, and how he felt dreadful about all the hurt he had caused. I got the impression that he was talking nonstop to prevent me asking any probing questions, so, when he stopped to light another cigarette, I asked him about the meeting in the house near Portlaoise, which he told the Gardaí was the planning meeting.

All of a sudden, his demeanour changed and he was lost for words for about 30 seconds. As he took a long drag on his cigarette, I could see that he was trying to formulate a response and then it came: 'Austin, that was a very long time ago and my memory is a bit hazy. I'm not sure if that was the planning meeting or a debrief meeting.' I had spent nearly four hours with him at this stage and up to that point his memory of events back in 1983 had been crystal clear. He even went on to give me details about the meeting. He claimed that he was in the house with Mr B and another IRA man, whom I will call Mr F, and when Mr A arrived, he asked O'Callaghan to leave the room.

Basically, he was telling me that he didn't know what was said at that meeting, yet he had told the Gardaí a different story. What I do know from reading O'Callaghan's book is that at the time of Dad's murder, he claims that he was trusted by the Officer Commanding of the Southern Brigade and was his Deputy Officer Commanding, so why would he have been asked to leave that meeting? It didn't add up. I felt he was deliberately trying to play down his part in the meeting to me.

O'Callaghan was a very intelligent man and that was the only part of what he told me that he fudged or tried to avoid talking about.

He probably assumed rightly that if he told me it was a planned meeting, then my next questions to him would have been, 'Did you not tell your Garda handler?' and 'If you didn't tell him, why not?' It would have played out that either he was playing God with Dad's life or somebody in Garda intelligence was, and he wanted to avoid those awkward questions.

After that he decided that he had to go. He wished me the best of luck with getting justice and headed off in the opposite direction to which we had come. I stood up from the table and started to walk back in the other direction, and I had only gone a few yards when Martin appeared at the door of a pub. He looked at me and in his typical London accent said, 'Bloody hell, I thought he'd never go.' Martin had managed to keep up with us and was sitting in the widow of a pub across the street the whole time, so I felt I owed him a beer.

At the end of the day, I now had a second unrelated source confirm the details of what happened on the night Dad was shot. But, more alarmingly, I was now aware that there were at least six hardened IRA men, three of whom were high ranking, either in the National Stadium or just outside it that night. Gerry Adams claims that they didn't know about it and that it wasn't sanctioned were starting to ring very hollow indeed.

* * *

In the days after I returned home from London, the family was shocked by more unsettling news when Kieran's Freedom of Information request for the Coroner's inquest file arrived at the house. As we were reading through the report, we realised that when Dr Harbison referred to his inspection of Dad's brain and cervical spine, he revealed that he completed this exam on November 28th, 1984. This was nearly two months after Dad had been buried. Not only had we not been made aware that Dad's organs had been removed from his body, but we had never been informed of what happened to them after this inspection. The news sank in: Dad had been buried without his brain and his spine. Instantly, the memory of not being able to kiss Dad's head at the removal flashed into my mind.

I had the unenviable task of telling my mother about this discovery and asking her if she was aware of what had happened and if any request had been made to inter these body parts with the rest of Dad's remains. When she confirmed to me that she hadn't been aware that this had happened and that the brain and spine had not been returned to the family for burial, it left us all completely shocked, angry and disbelieving that the State could do this.

After we made this terrible discovery, I wrote to the then State Pathologist, Dr Marie Cassidy, on July 27th, 2015 asking for her support 'in helping provide an explanation regarding the inade-quacies in the post-mortem examination of my father's body and clarification on where and how my father's brain and cervical spine were disposed of'.

In response, Dr Cassidy replied to my letter on September 3rd, 2015 apologising on behalf of Dr Harbison for unwittingly adding to our grief and said, 'At the time of your father's sudden violent death, the practices were very different from today.' That phrase had come back to haunt us, yet again. Dr Cassidy went on to say:

In deaths where the pathologist was of the opinion that further examination of an organ was essential, as the findings would be of medico-legal importance regarding the circumstances and causes of a death, it was standard, and best practice to do so. The consent of the family or coroner was not required to do so in homicide cases. In homicide cases, any material retained is regarded as evidence and often is retained indefinitely until the trial, and often appeals, are conducted. That has never been the case in this jurisdiction and organs were only ever retained until their examination was complete . . . Unfortunately, the records in the Office of the State Pathologist regarding retained tissues and organs only go back as far as my commencing in Ireland in 1998. Records from then regarding tissues or organs still present within the laboratory do not contain reference to any material relating to your father's death . . . Any material retained at post-mortem is required to be disposed of in a legal and ethical manner and, although I have no proof, I would be confident that Professor Harbison would have followed all the formal procedures as he was a meticulous and highly ethical pathologist.

It's hard for me to put into words the hurt, disbelief, and anger that this episode caused when we discovered it in 2015, and I would hate any other family to go through this.

*　　*　　*

As I recovered from the shock, my drive for the truth was strengthened by what felt like the continued injustice of the end of my father's life. A few months later, I attended an event at the Glencree Centre for Peace and Reconciliation in County Wicklow. I had worked with the group on a few occasions since first attending a workshop in May 2015. When they needed a victim's voice from the Republic to participate in their peace-building workshops, I was more than happy to oblige. I had always felt that if I could do anything at all to bring the people on this island together I would, and taking part in these workshops also helped me in a therapeutic sort of way.

This time, I was invited to an event taking place on November 20th and 21st, 2015 in which a large group of unionist victims from Northern Ireland were attending along with people such as a former Irish Minister for Justice and former Gardaí. The theme of the workshop was to allow the unionist victims to explain how they felt the Irish State had let them down by not doing more to counter the IRA terrorist threat against them.

These workshops only work if everybody agrees to adhere to certain codes and, with that in mind, meetings are held under what is known as the 'Chatham House Rules'. This essentially means that people can use the information provided at the meeting but they cannot disclose who relayed the information.

During the course of the meeting, it was disclosed to me that the Gardaí had definite information about who was responsible for Dad's murder since 1990. I was also told that a phone call had been made and a message was given, which was to be delivered to the current investigation team. This message was that all the information that the investigation team required was already on file. Naturally, I was shocked at not just the information I was receiving but also at the source of this information. I just couldn't believe what I was hearing and I couldn't concentrate on what was going on at the workshop for the rest of the day.

When we broke for a coffee some of the others there came over to comfort me, as they knew what I had been told was earth shattering. Then, as we finished up the meeting and everybody was saying their goodbyes, a retired very senior Garda approached me and beckoned me into a quiet corner of the room. He had all the appearances of a tough cop who had seen it all, and he certainly had – during the Troubles he had been involved in Garda Counter Terrorism and the Special Detective Branch. If I ever wanted a guy to give me some information, this was the guy I would have picked. He didn't engage in any pleasantries and asked me straight up, 'Do you know what happened to your dad and who did it?' I responded, 'I do, but I feel you want to tell me something, so tell me what you know and I'll see if our stories match.' Without missing a beat, he recounted the same tale that Jim, the journalist, and Sean O'Callaghan had told me, except for the spotter part of O'Callaghan's story. He told me that he had been given this information by a high-level informant in the south of the country in 1990. I couldn't believe that I was hearing the same story from a third unrelated source and this one was by far the most credible of them all.

When I left the meeting, I phoned Oliver and explained what I had been told, but I couldn't tell him who had told me. I wasn't prepared to break the Chatham House Rules, so in January 2016 at a meeting with George Kyne and Robbie Comerford, I told them the information that I had received in Glencree without naming the person or his former occupation. All I said was that he was some-body who would be 'very close to home'. They completely denied having any knowledge of the information supplied in 1990 and of the phone call alerting them to it. They tried several times to get me to reveal my source, but I was duty bound to keep my word. I know they were disappointed that I couldn't reveal the former Garda's identity, but I undertook to meet with him and ask his permission to give his name to the investigation team.

This left me in a dilemma, as I needed to be able to use the information but I knew that unless I could name him, the Gardaí wouldn't be interested. I needed to find a way. This information was too important to let it go.

Chapter 21

A General Election was called in Ireland for Friday, February 26th, 2016, and Dad's case became a high-profile election issue in the last two weeks of the campaign. Early in the campaign, Niall O'Connor, the political correspondent for the *Irish Independent*, asked me for an interview. During the course of this interview, which was published on February 16th, he asked if I thought that Sinn Féin were fit for government. I responded by saying that two senior members of the party, both public representatives, had questions to answer in relation to Dad's murder and I suspected one of those was the person who sanctioned the murder. I told O'Connor that it was my belief that Adams and Sinn Féin had covered this up to protect those who were now in a political role.

In a briefing to journalists at a Sinn Féin press conference on Sunday, February 21st, Adams made an astonishing claim, saying that he was aware of the identities of the two politicians to whom I was referring in that interview, and he said that he had been given their names by me. I don't know why Adams said this, but all I can guess is that he was somehow trying to discredit me to deflect from the story.

I responded with a press release on February 22nd to set the record straight, but by the end of the week Adams was now claiming that I had given him four names. He also went from saying that it wasn't his job to speak with those allegedly named to saying that he had spoken to them. His story changed so much during the course of the week that it was laughable, and his creditability was seriously damaged.

What I didn't know at this stage was that, in order to cover himself after making these allegations, Adams sent an email to the Garda Commissioner outlining the information that he claimed I gave him. This whole issue would turn into a major political row later in the year when I found out about the email to the Commissioner.

* * *

When the dust settled after the General Election, I decided that I needed to make contact with the retired senior Garda and ask if I could share his identity and the information he gave me with those currently investigating Dad's case. I sent him a few text messages before he responded. When he did respond, he agreed to meet me but had to push the meeting back due to some work business – he was now successfully working in the private sector in Dublin.

We were both in the vicinity of the Four Courts and agreed to meet in one of those private alcoves just off the Round Hall, which facilitate consultations between barristers and their clients. I told him about my dilemma and asked if he would be prepared to stand over what he said if I named him. He seemed to think that all we wanted to do was take a legal action against the State and said that the State would grind us down. He then said, 'I will never again speak of those things that I spoke about in Glencree.'

I knew that there was no point in pursuing this, so we parted company and I continued wondering how I was going to use his information properly. Some weeks later, I was discussing the situation with my brother Oliver. Oliver still did not know the retired Garda's name at this stage and he asked me to again go over how this official had given me the information and when he gave it to me. When I went back over everything, Oliver said, 'So he gave you the information after the meeting was finished?' and when I said yes, he then asked, 'When he spoke to you after the meeting, did he talk about the stuff he mentioned during the meeting?' Again I said yes. By now I was beginning to see where Oliver was going with this. He said, 'Austin, Chatham House Rules only applied to the meeting, not any private discussion that he engaged you in afterwards.' I said, 'Wow, why didn't I think of that?' I now had enough cover to give the Gardaí their former colleague's name.

So, at a meeting in October 2016 with George and Robbie, I first asked them if they had managed to locate the file that the retired Garda spoke of. When George replied that they hadn't, he also said that it would be really helpful if I gave him the name of my source. I half expected Oliver to do a drumroll as I took a breath and decided to tease them for a few seconds by saying, 'Well, it was one of your own.' I could see from the look on their faces that the comment hadn't gone down well, so I quickly added, 'It was XX. Do you know him?' Now their faces really dropped as they realised that my information had come from within the Garda tent. It would now be up to them to convince him to talk and I didn't envy them going on that mission.

At a short follow-up meeting with George in November 2016, he dropped a bombshell on me. We were nearly finished the meeting when he produced a copy of an email that Gerry Adams' secretary, Máire Grogan, had sent on his behalf to the Garda Commissioner. This email was sent in the last few days of the election campaign and it stated that I had given Adams the names of four people whom I suspected of being involved in Dad's murder. Adams named these four people in the email.

First of all, I was annoyed that the Gardaí had waited 10 months to tell me this. Then my anger shifted to Adams. He had gotten himself in a bind by making this claim during the election and now he needed to cover himself by reporting it to the Gardaí, but why hadn't he reported this to the Gardaí three years earlier if he claims that is when I gave him this information? The answer to that is very simple: he didn't report it as I never gave him any names three years previous. During the General Election campaign, he sought to tell a lie about me, but in putting that lie on paper and sending it to the Garda Commissioner, he reached a new low.

Adams had clearly breached the confidentiality of our meetings, even if what he said was untrue. We had agreed from day one that anything said during our meetings would never be repeated outside of those meetings. I had kept my word on that and had not given the Gardaí or journalists any details of matters discussed at those meetings. I now decided that the gloves were off and that I owed Adams nothing. He had double-crossed me and now he was going to have to pay for it.

I had my good name to defend in relation to this and so I leaked a story to the media and asked them to concentrate on Adams' role in the meeting we had with the IRA. I wanted them to focus on the fact that Adams was a friend of the IRA man we met, that this man had information crucial to the investigation into Dad's murder, and that Adams needed to give whatever information he had on this individual to the Gardaí.

Of course, Adams tried to deflect from this and wanted to keep the 'he said, she said' story of the naming names going, but in doing so he made another blunder. His people released to the media what they described as their notes from our first meeting. As I have said before, there were no notes taken at that first meeting, but we did suspect that we were being recorded. However, the notes released by Adams, while sparse and not a full reflection of the meeting, backed up my story. The notes clearly say that when Adams asked me if I wanted to give him names, I told him that I was not there to name names. It should also be noted that in an interview with Máiría Cahill for the *Sunday Independent* on March 22nd, 2015, well before the February 2016 General Election, I told her that when asked by Adams to name those I thought were responsible, I had refused.

Adams had scored a major own goal and several opinion pieces in the media were very supportive of me, including one by Noel Whelan in the *Irish Times* on December 9th when he asked, 'Should we believe Gerry Adams or Brian Stack's son?' In the article, he went through Sinn Féin and the IRA's pattern of denial over many different events, then he focused on how they attempted to blacken the names of their victims, including Dad's. He said:

> [I]n weighing up any conflict of evidence, one must assess the general credibility of those making the competing claims. Gerry Adams's credibility is shot to pieces. The precedents that illustrate his loose relationship with the truth are stacked very high . . . On the other side of the scale we have the word of Austin Stack, a man who, like his father before him, has given a life's service to the State and is now a senior prison officer. He is a son motivated by his family's need to find answers about his father's death. Given their respective motives and track records, the choice on who to believe in this recent controversy is a no-brainer.

Seeing that he was on the back foot, Adams decided to pull a rabbit out of a hat and sought to make a personal statement to Dáil Éireann. He was granted permission and it took place on

December 7th, 2016. I knew that Adams would try to shape the narrative of the story in his 15-minute address to parliament, but what caught me unawares was that after making a personal statement, a TD cannot be asked any questions. Essentially, he would get to make a statement, put it on the record of the Dáil, and be able to walk away without scrutiny. It was a very clever move and I was raging. So, all week when I was doing media interviews, I tried to get the focus back to Adams and his IRA friend, and how I believed he needed to cooperate with the Gardaí. This worked very well, and I knew whatever Adams said, the media were going to ask him the important questions because the other TDs couldn't.

On December 7th, Fianna Fáil leader Micheál Martin, who had been a constant support to us, brought me and Oliver into the Dáil visitors' gallery to listen to what Adams was going to say. When Adams rose to his feet to speak, I leaned forward in my seat with a pen at the ready to take notes. I knew, as Noel Whelan had said, that he had a 'loose relationship with the truth', but I wasn't expecting it to be this loose. I couldn't believe what he was saying and I wanted to run down onto the floor of the Dáil to challenge his untruths. In his statement, he said that I gave him four names of people who might have information; that the names I gave him came from journalistic and Garda sources; that I asked him to contact the names I gave him; that he told me that after contacting those named, they had no information; and that we were driven to the North for the meeting with the IRA man. All of these statements were untrue, unless Adams didn't keep his word when he told us that we would be staying on the south side of the border for the IRA meeting.

If I thought that things were going badly, they were about to get a lot worse. As Adams sat down after making his statement, Fine Gael TD Alan Farrell rose to his feet and caused uproar in the chamber by naming, under parliamentary privilege, Martin Ferris TD and Dessie Ellis TD as being two of the names supplied by Adams to the Garda Commissioner. As I watched the shouting match develop between the TDs in question, I knew what the following morning's headlines would be. It was all going to be about Ferris and Ellis, and there would be no scrutiny of Adams' statement and its untruths.

I suspected a particular journalist as having set the whole thing up and I glared at him in the press gallery. He knew I was gunning for him but, in fairness, he made his way across to me and apologised. I told him that I had to take back control of the story and he owed me one. When he asked what I had in mind, I suggested that I needed to doorstep Adams at a media event and quickly. He promised to see what he could do.

After things in the Dáil settled down, Micheál Martin came around to the visitors' gallery and suggested we go back to his office so that Oliver and I could write a statement for the media. This seemed like a good idea as we would have some time and space to get the statement right. What happened next, though, was unbelievable. As Oliver and I, accompanied by Micheál Martin and some of his staff, were waiting at a lift to bring us up to his office, Gerry Adams and some of his people arrived. As he approached us, he was talking with somebody on his mobile phone. Then he told the person on the phone, 'Oh, there's Austin Stack.' He said this in a really friendly and excited tone and started to wave at me like I was his best friend.

As he proceeded to walk towards me, he had to pass Oliver first and, as he drew level with Oliver, he offered him his hand. Oliver deliberately put both hands in his pockets and turned away from Adams, blanking him. Not getting the message, Adams stayed on track and when he arrived to me, he stuck out his hand. Refusing to take his hand, I looked him straight in the eye and said, 'Deputy, you are a liar.' With that he took the phone down from his ear and said, 'I'm on the phone to my wife,' to which I responded, 'Well, you tell your wife that you are a liar.'

Poor Micheál Martin must have thought it was all going to kick off and he was trying to get the lift door to open. When the lift eventually arrived and Adams got into it, Micheál looked at us and said, 'I think we'll take the stairs.'

The following morning, Thursday, December 8th, I was having a much-needed lie-in after all the drama of the day before. I hadn't set my alarm and was nice and snug under the duvet when my phone rang at 08.30 a.m. It was the journalist who owed me one. He said, 'Austin, if you want your doorstep, get down to the Davenport Hotel for 10 a.m. Adams is doing a Brexit press conference and all the Irish and UK media will be there.'

I jumped out of bed and, after the quickest shower I ever had, I threw on the first set of clothes that came to hand and ran out the door. As I was on my way to Dublin, I made a few calls to get advice on how I should handle what was about to happen. The one piece of advice I got, which was crucial, was to keep naming him in every sentence and not let him answer me. I was told, 'Say what you have to say and leave.' As I was getting closer to the city, the traffic got worse and it looked like I wouldn't get to the Davenport Hotel on time. After I reached Heuston Station, I looked down the city quays and saw that they were like a big carpark, so I ditched the car and jumped into a taxi as I knew it could use the bus lanes, which was the only way I would get there on time. When the taxi pulled up outside the hotel, I could see through a large window that the press conference was beginning. Racing up the hotel steps, I asked the receptionist to point me in the direction of the room they were in and she indicated in the direction of a library-type room.

As I got there, I could see that the room had been divided by one of those sliding partitions that move along a track in the floor.

The doors on those things are notoriously difficult to open, if you can find it. When I located the door, I pushed it inwards and it opened a few inches before I felt it hit somebody. Martin Kenny, Sinn Féin TD for Sligo–Leitrim, was standing with his back to the door. Kenny knew me as he had been the Sinn Féin representative at several workshops we both attended in the Glencree Centre for Peace and Reconciliation. When he saw that it was me, he half-heartedly attempted to close the door. I was having none of that and I gave the door one almighty push that knocked him a few feet across the floor, and then I was in.

After landing in the room, the first thing I noticed was that this was no ordinary press conference: most of the major TV stations from the UK, Ireland and, indeed, Europe were there, as were all their print and radio colleagues. Then I noticed that they were all looking at me after I had made my dramatic entrance. The silence was broken when Gerry Adams tried to yet again play the old pals act: 'Eh, I'd like to welcome Austin Stack to the press conference.'

'This is your moment now, Austin,' I said to myself, 'don't mess this up and make sure you nail it.' It was time to set the record straight and give the bully his bloody nose.

I took a few steps forward so I was closer to Adams. I wanted to eyeball him; I wanted him to be as uncomfortable as possible. I could sense that some people in the room were wondering what was going to happen next. I took a deep breath and started: 'Gerry Adams, you have information that is crucial to the investigation of my father's murder. Gerry Adams, you took myself and my brother Oliver in a blacked-out van to meet with a senior IRA figure, a man you said you trusted. Gerry Adams, I want you to give that information to An Garda Síochána. You, as a public representative, are an absolute disgrace if you don't do that, Gerry Adams.'

Then Adams attempted to interrupt me. He held his hand up to signal me to stop so he could respond. I was never going to let that happen – he had held his pantomime the day before. I held my hand up in a firm stop motion, like I was a Garda stopping traffic. Again, I fixed my eyes to his and said: 'I have no more interest in hearing anything else that you have to say. You told your lies and untruths in Dáil Éireann yesterday. I am now putting the ball firmly in your court. Take the name of the individual that you know to An Garda Síochána.'

I then turned on my heels and walked out, not giving him a chance to respond. When I walked out the front door of the hotel, I looked back and could see all the media following me. I stopped on the footpath and allowed them to form a circle around me and then I gave a brief impromptu press conference. Now everybody got to hear the truth and the focus was back where it should be.

Now that I was finished with Adams, we still had fish to fry with the Gardaí and, while relations had improved, we weren't about to let them off the hook.

* * *

As a result of the attention Dad's case had gotten before Christmas 2016, I reached out to the Taoiseach Enda Kenny and requested a meeting. I had a feeling that Kenny would want to do the good PR thing and meet us, and he readily agreed to do so, along with Minister for Justice Frances Fitzgerald, on January 13th, 2017.

The meeting took place in Government Buildings, and with Oliver, Mam and I present. The Taoiseach and Minister for Justice were joined by a legal representative from the Minister's department. As he opened the meeting, Kenny, who is an affable man, started to engage Mam in a lot of small talk around how she felt the day that Oliver and I went to meet the IRA. I don't believe he was deliberately trying to run down the clock, but I was well aware that when you meet the Taoiseach you are slotted into a time schedule and you can't waste a moment of your audience with him.

I gently kicked Mam under the table in order to get her to stop the small talk and I interjected to ask if we could get down to business. At that point, he handed the meeting over to the Minister. In fairness to her, the Minister listened to what we had to say as we outlined our concerns.

We began with the inadequate nature of the original investigation, which included mislaying of fingerprints and material evidence, not interviewing suspects, not mapping the crime scene and not carrying out identification parades. The family asked to be told the truth if there was a reason for the shutting down of the original investigation. We then moved on to the Serious Crime Review Team's failure to interview Ned Harkin, the former Deputy Governor of Portlaoise Prison. We mentioned how the family had not had sight of the Serious Crime Review Team's report, which had made nearly two hundred recommendations.

We told the Taoiseach about the uncooperative nature of the NBCI investigation and about the January 2012 meeting with NBCI Inspector Courage, when the family were told that the IRA did not carry out the attack on Brian Stack.

We told him about the July 2013 letters to the Garda Commissioner requesting a meeting, which still had not happened. We shared the information received in November 2015 from a former high-ranking Garda who outlined to me that the Gardaí have known who murdered Brian Stack since 1990, and that he also told me this information was on the case file. We explained how individuals involved were outside the State and needed to be pursued.

We finally mentioned the perceived reluctance to interview Gerry Adams and possible political interference in the investigation. It was agreed that the Minister would see what she could do in relation to our concerns and revert in due course. I knew that it was probably only window-dressing, but it was important for us to put the issues to them at a formal meeting.

Shortly after this meeting, in March, we had another meeting with the Gardaí. This time George and Robbie were accompanied by a new Assistant Commissioner, John O'Driscoll. Kieran was home from the States and it was good to get his input as he had missed out on the meeting with the Taoiseach. At the outset of the meeting, the Assistant Commissioner told us that they had met with the retired senior Garda and he had cooperated with them. He told us that they were now in a position to confirm the information that I had provided and that the file did exist. They said that this information was not previously known to the investigation team because of the way it was stored and they would be looking to meet with the informant. They then went further and said that the information on the file was very significant. We agreed to give George and his team some time to work on this and were hopeful that something would come of it.

When the next meeting with George took place on November 30th, 2017, he told us that the information that the retired garda had passed on was with Garda Intelligence in the crime and security division. George appeared to be a little frustrated that he couldn't get sight of the file himself, and I agreed to give him a few weeks of space to see if he could get anything, otherwise I told him I would go to the media. A follow-up meeting then took place on December 19th and, yet again, George appeared frustrated, but a little less so than at the previous meeting. George had spoken with the Assistant Commissioner in charge of crime and security in an attempt to gain access to the file and said that a compromise had been reached. He told us that a garda from that division was, as we were speaking, en route to meet with the informant to see if he would be prepared to cooperate with the investigation. I told George in no uncertain terms that I wasn't happy that crime and security appeared to be protecting an informant who could be useful to the case. George responded, saying, 'We have a duty of care to the informant.'

At this stage, Oliver lost it: 'Do you not think that the Gardaí had a duty of care to Brian Stack?' George dropped his head.

As we finished the meeting, I gave George until the middle of January to come back to me confirming that he had seen the file and had access to the informant, otherwise I would be going to the media.

Unfortunately, my deadline passed without George being able to confirm these things and I felt I had no other option than to go to the media.

However the Gardaí closed ranks and even our local TD, Charlie Flannagan, who was now Minister for Justice, backed up the Gardaí and insisted that all sections were cooperating with each other. The way they closed this down suggested to me that this informant was a big cheese and they weren't going to risk exposing him.

On March 28th, we got another update, and my suspicions were confirmed at this meeting when we were told that the informant was elderly, in his eighties, was ill and would be of no use to the investigation. I couldn't help feeling if they had known about this informant a few years earlier, the Gardaí may have been able get him to provide more information, but we will never know. The bottom line is one section of the Gardaí had information since 1990 that could have broken the case and, even though there have been various investigations since 2007, they never handed that over and it only came to light when I found out.

We were also told at this meeting that a team had gone to the USA to try interview Mr B, but in their words, 'He is gone again', and his current location is unknown. Maybe like Mr D, Mr B is either just plain lucky or something else is going on. I'm inclined to suspect the latter in both cases. I do believe that the last investigation team headed up by George were doing their utmost to progress the case, but they obviously met the brick wall that is the murky world of State intelligence, informants and political considerations.

George and his team prepared a file for the Director of Public Prosecutions in relation to Mr B. 'I've done the best I could do, Austin,' George told me the last time we met in 2017. 'I hope you and your family know that. I tried my best to get you justice.'

'We know, George,' I replied. 'Unfortunately, it just wasn't enough. The odds have been stacked against you from the start.'

I didn't hear anything further from the Gardaí about the file and, in 2018 and 2019, I tried following up on this with letters to the Taoiseach, Minister for Justice and Garda Commissioner. I wanted nothing less than an official State apology for the shortcomings of the investigations into Dad's murder. Finally, I secured a meeting with Garda Commissioner Drew Harris on July 10th, 2019. Drew Harris had been recruited to change the culture within the Gardaí and had been a high-ranking member of the Police Service of Northern Ireland (PSNI). In 1989, his father, Deputy Chief Constable Alwyn Harris, had also been murdered by the IRA, so I was hopeful that a meeting with him would prove positive.

Prior to the meeting, we met as a family to discuss our tactics. I had seen how Harris had apologised to individuals in the months previous and I suggested that we concentrate on gaining an apology. However, Kieran felt that we would have to give a guarantee that we would not sue the State to get this. I was very forthright and told him, 'I will not be accepting an apology that comes with conditions attached.' Mam and Oliver backed this position.

Commissioner Harris was accompanied to the meeting by other high-ranking Gardaí and, at the outset, told us that the file had not come back from the Director of Public Prosecutions. He then proceeded to do an overview of the case and mentioned all the various issues that we had with the investigation, while trying to deflect responsibility by pointing out that things are done differently now. I wasn't going to let this pass and stopped him in his tracks: 'If things are done differently now, why don't the investigation team know the name of the informant who passed information to you in 1990?' I continued, 'I didn't come in here to hear all the same excuses over again, will you at least apologise to us?'

In a really calm manner, Harris looked at me and said, 'I will think about that.' With this the red mist descended and I let my anger get the better of me. I can't remember what I was saying but he held his hand up to stop me and said, 'OK, what kind of an apology do you want?' No conditions were put on the table for us to consider, just a straight-forward apology. In a subsequent press release, Harris said, 'I offered the Stack family an apology for the failings and shortcomings in the investigation.'

We accepted this apology but reminded him that many issues still remained around the mishandling of the case. The apology was significant as it was an admission from official Ireland that it had let Dad down, it had let Mam down, and it had let me and my brothers down.

It took the Director of Public Prosecutions some time to respond to the file that had been sent and, on March 27th, 2023 we attended a meeting with senior Gardaí where we were told that the file had been returned to them with a request for more information. Mr B's name, aliases and fingerprints are on a watch list and hopefully he can be apprehended at some point.

However, 40 years after my dad, Brian Stack, was murdered, all the main suspects who have been identified to me by three separate and unconnected sources are still free. Mr B, from what I can gather, is living in the USA and was involved in a relationship with a police sergeant, while Mr C is living openly in the northeast of the Republic of Ireland.

Chapter 22

It's a common assumption that since the end of the Troubles and the acceptance of the Good Friday Agreement that Ireland has been a better place for many people. Just because fighting has ended and the bullets have stopped doesn't mean the conflict has ended for the victims. They have to deal with the daily reminders of the harrowing experience – the missing limb or the loved one missing from the dinner table. For these people, the conflict rages on.

The politicians, policy-makers and civil servants will never understand this, as they have not walked in our shoes. They have one concern, and that is to keep the guns silent, everything else is secondary. Certainly, any decisions in relation to the Irish peace process were taken with many of the stakeholders consulted, but with one glaring exception: the victims. We became collateral damage for what was deemed 'the greater good'.

In the aftermath of the process, the nation was on a high and there was a feel-good mood. US President Clinton visited and praised political leaders, while the various international organisations bestowed awards on those who had put the agreement together.

For me, the real heroes were the ones who were never considered for an award. Women like my mother who stayed silent during this time for 'the greater good'. Nobody cared to ask her about her feelings, how she felt about the prisoner releases, or how this was affecting her. I still remember the day in 1998 that the IRA prisoners were released from the HM Prison Maze in Northern Ireland. I had a day off work and, while eating my breakfast, my stomach started to turn as I was watching the news on TV. It showed the scenes from outside the Maze as groups of jubilant terrorists were released to cheers, singing, flag-waving and beeping car horns.

Brian Stack never got to meet his eight grandchildren, and 1,800 others never got to go home, all thanks to the IRA. And here we were, forced to endure these images of celebrating terrorists going home to their families. This was very hard to take.

If it was tough for me, I knew that if Mam was watching this, she would be distraught. I was living in County Kildare at the time and immediately made the hour-long journey home to Portlaoise. When I got there, I parked my car at the side of the house and walked around the back as I would usually do. The house had a small TV room beside the back door and, as I passed it, I could see Mam inside, sitting alone, crying while watching these grotesque scenes unfold. I went in and stayed with her for the day, but the damage was done. The insensitive manner in which prisoner releases were managed was indicative of how victims as a whole were treated. Nobody thought of our feelings or figured that low-key releases of prisoners, one or two at a time, would be better.

Mam was 39 when she was effectively widowed, and she had three sons, the oldest being 14. She is now in her eighties and has lived half her life with the consequences of an act that was visited on her and our family by IRA terrorists. She had to deal with that 18-month period after the shooting when Dad was still alive. Every day she travelled up to Dublin while he was in a coma, and when he came home for the last six months of his life, she had to adapt our home and deal with caring for a grown man who was paraplegic and very badly brain damaged. She also had to deal with three teenage sons who were at a critical stage of life and who were trying to manage the fallout from their own worlds collapsing around them.

Mam got no help, she got no assistance from anybody, she didn't even get a medical card for Dad – she was just left to her own devices. Life is cruel sometimes, but even more so for people like Mam. People like Mam don't get Nobel Peace Awards but they should; never have so few given so much for the sake of peace on the island of Ireland.

I have had to live with the ongoing impact of the IRA murdering my dad every single day of my life since. It's not something that consumes every minute of every day, but the reality is that it has played a significant role in how my life has panned out. I had poor education outcomes as a result of playing the joker in school. I didn't have to be the class clown but this was my way of creating another identity; I wanted to be somebody other than the lad whose Dad was murdered. I did my Leaving Certificate 18 months after Dad was buried. My results weren't great and the only third-level course I was offered was Business Studies in the regional college in Athlone, which I had no interest in. I spent a year there partying and having a good time. Again, I was trying to create an alternative personality; I wanted to show the world that what happened wasn't affecting me. Not getting back to Athlone for a second year led to working in London, then to my time as a chef and then working in a clothes shop. Finally, with no other options left, I joined the Prison Service, which was the last place in the world I wanted to be. But this was the hand I was dealt and everything that happened in my life was directly influenced by the IRA man who shot my dad.

I never got to have a pint with my dad or get to seek his wise counsel at crucial times in life. I never got to do the things that you do with a dad as a young adult and then as a parent yourself. Then there are the effects on my own kids, who never got to meet the man whose murder has had such an impact on their lives. I know my dad would have loved playing the role of grandad. Those IRA prisoners who were released got to have all those things. As well as being cruel, life can also be unfair.

Often, when I express these emotions, I will have families of IRA men who were killed claiming that grief isn't one sided and they are going through the same things. There is one salient difference though: their family member chose to pick up a gun, and they chose to murder, bomb and 'disappear' people. Brian Stack never held a gun in his life, he hated guns.

Now, to add insult to injury, academics seem to have become heavily influenced by the former terrorists. In order to keep many ex-prisoners occupied and give them opportunities that they missed out on because of their own deeds, they have become much sought after on the myriad of 'conflict studies' courses in our universities. Researchers in these universities regularly use terms such as 'combatants' or 'former combatants'. This type of language has become part and parcel of academic discourse and it is nothing short of an attempt to distort the narrative of what really happened.

Brian Stack was not a 'combatant', there was no war in Portlaoise in 1983, and I will always resist any attempt to dilute what happened to my dad by using that type of terminology. The attempt to reframe the story of the Troubles is one of the biggest threats that Ireland faces and many don't even recognise it, yet it seeps through almost daily. The term 'move on' has become the common retort from Sinn Féin public representatives, members and supporters whenever they are challenged about the ill deeds of the IRA.

They will also try to claim that Sinn Féin and the IRA are not linked, and anybody who uses the term 'Sinn Féin/IRA' can be prepared to meet the full pile-on from their supporters. But any sort of critical analysis will show that one is the umbilical cord to the other. Exhibit A in relation to this should always be the 1986 Sinn Féin Ard Fheis (annual conference). When voting to end their policy of abstention, Gerry Adams warned those who might leave the party if the vote went against them that 'to leave Sinn Féin is to leave the IRA'. While Martin McGuinness, addressing the same issue, stated, 'The IRA freedom fighters and the Sinn Féin freedom fighters are one and the same thing.'

Another exhibit would be the standing ovation afforded to Hugh Doherty of the Balcombe Street Gang when he attended the 1998 Ard Fheis. This was a man who was serving 11 life sentences when he was released under the terms of the Good Friday Agreement. At another Ard Fheis in 2003, the murderers of Garda Jerry McCabe got a standing ovation when the then wife of Pearse McAuley, Pauline Tully TD, read out letters from them.

Then, of course, I could use the trip that Oliver and I took in a blacked-out van as an example, arranged by and accompanied by Gerry Adams to meet the IRA. If these are not two sides of the same coin then how was that possible?

I could go on and on, but what is not in dispute is that many former IRA terrorists are members of Sinn Féin and that Sinn Féin regularly hold commemorations for dead IRA members. They will say that it is their right to honour their dead and will do so with colour parties and people dressed in paramilitary attire. But they don't get to tell me to 'move on' while at the same time refusing to 'move on' themselves, as they glorify somebody who destroyed countless lives. They can't have it both ways.

In the attempt to rewrite history, there has been a romantic gloss put on the IRA as being defenders of their community, as being civil rights activists, and the 'we had no alternative' mantra is rehashed and rehashed until it becomes accepted. The hard truth is that while there were many inequalities and sectarian policies in Northern Ireland, the IRA tried to bully and oust the peaceful civil rights movement for their own agenda, which was community control. I heard one former IRA man explain to a small group of foreign students that he saw a man being shot by a plastic bullet outside his front door and this led him to join the IRA. The foreign students were naturally aghast at this and began to feel sorry for his 'no alternative' excuse for becoming a terrorist.

I posed a question to him, if this was a valid excuse for becoming a terrorist, then surely I had more right to become one and seek revenge for my dad? As I said to him, 'We all had choices to make and I chose not to murder anybody as a reprisal.' You will now regularly see commentary in which we are told 'the Brits were shooting us dead in the streets'. This again has become an accepted truth by the younger generation who have become radicalised and buy into the 'no alternative' message. There certainly were atrocities, such as Bloody Sunday and Ballymurphy, and those families have a right to justice the same as the rest of us, but the facts are that the British Security Forces accounted for 10 per cent of all deaths during the Troubles. The IRA were there before Bloody Sunday and Ballymurphy, not because of them.

This has been a clever, long-game tactic to repeat these untruths until they become accepted as the truth. But, when people like me challenge this, we are subjected to the most vile, abusive and disgusting harassment, especially on social media platforms. There appears to be a coordinated attempt to silence critics by making life so unbearable for them on social media that they will delete their accounts, and this has been successful in some cases. But one thing my dad always taught me was to stand up to the bully, so I have no intention of ever letting them get to me.

This harassment on social media usually has three distinct phases. The first phase usually consists of swamping a person's social media timeline with hundreds of abusive and negative comments. The intensive nature of this means that I would end up blocking several hundred accounts in one evening, and most of these would be new and anonymous accounts set up in a coordinated manner to attack me.

The second phase is what I call the 'nasty phase'. This is when a new account will appear and make a particularly vile and vulgar allegation about my dad. An example would be the following: '@jk20142014: @adstack68 Hi, any comment on allegations that your father was a sexual abuser?'

The tactic here is to blacken Dad's name, again hoping that repeating a lie often enough will make it become the accepted truth. They somehow believe that I would be so sickened by this that I would just give up. In one of these encounters, a Twitter user called my dad a 'sadist prison officer', and this was retweeted by Sinn Féin Senator Máire Devine in March 2018. When I became aware of this and challenged her, she dug a deeper hole for herself in a series of follow-up tweets. I was shocked and horrified that a parliamentarian would stoop so low, and that she had no compassion for the victims of a brutal murder. My mother was deeply upset by her actions and felt that the apology issued through the Sinn Féin press office was nothing more than a public relations stunt. As indeed was the six-month suspension that she received from the party, which then welcomed her back with open arms. True to form, shortly after Devine lost her Senate seat in 2020, Sinn Féin coopted her on to South Dublin Council. To me, this had all the appearances of them rewarding her for her actions. Máire Devine, however, was not the first Sinn Féin politician to try blacken dad's name.

In an authorised biography, Martin Ferris, who was at the time a TD for Kerry, made some particularly vengeful comments about Dad in an interview with the book's author. The way he worded the comments was clever as he didn't make reference to any one particular incident, but instead made a wide, generalised accusation. The book's author directly quotes Ferris as saying, 'Stack was a particularly vindictive individual.' He continues, 'He thought nothing of officers holding a prisoner while he struck him with a baton during a strip search.'

In attempting to defame the good name of a dead man, Ferris showed that he was in reality a coward and somebody who had very little regard for the damage his untruthful comments would cause. These comments in the book caused untold harm to my family as they are often repeated by the troll army on social media. What I can say without any hesitation is that I know my dad's character, I know he would never have ill-treated anybody under his care. I also know that Gerry Adams told both Oliver and me, 'I have never heard anybody within our movement say that your father ill-treated prisoners.' While this contradicts what Ferris said, I have also been told privately by several former IRA prisoners that Ferris' bland assertions were rubbish.

Interestingly, in my conversation with Sean O'Callaghan, he told me that this tactic of blackening somebody's good name was also deployed by senior IRA godfathers to convince the younger foot soldiers of a target's unworthy nature. He told me that this happened when he was indoctrinated into believing horrible untruths about RUC Detective Inspector Peter Flanagan prior to gunning him down in a pub. He said that the rationale for this was to ensure that he would not feel bad about what he had done. That name-blackening is still used, except the battlefield is now online.

Due to the nature of the Troubles, many cases have gone unsolved, which has left the families and victims without this justice or truth. Yet we are asked continually to 'move on'. We are asked to be the 'bigger people'. We are asked to 'rise above'. Isn't it funny that only victims of terrorism are asked to do that? As if we haven't endured enough, we must continue to do so for the sake of 'peace'. Unfortunately, I can't, because it is me and not the man who shot my dad in 1983 who is serving the life sentence.

Acknowledgements

Writing this book had been an on and off project for about six years, mainly due to the time involved and my complete lack of knowledge about putting something like this together. It was not until my late friend Kate O'Shea, in her very direct manner, told me that I had to tell this story because it was too important not to, that I decided to start this project. I did not know where to begin, but without that initial encouragement from Kate, you would not be reading this book.

I will be forever grateful to Niall O'Connor formerly of the Irish Independent who instilled a belief in me that I could write, and on hearing that from him, I told myself I could do this. I also owe a huge debt to my great friend Paul Williams for all his help and support. Paul helped me with an outline structure for the book and then, like Niall, was vital in giving me the confidence in my writing ability to put this story on paper. Paul also introduced me to Simon Hess, another person who deserves great credit for opening doors to publishers and for all the practical advice that he gave me.

My publisher Deirdre Nolan, at Eriu in Bonnier Books, stuck with this project and despite many rejections, I knew this is who I wanted to work with as she always left the door open for me. My editor Catherine Gough did a wonderful job on the final manuscript, and I was amazed when I saw all the little tweaks that make such a difference for a reader.

I would not have gotten this book across the line without the help of Ronan McGreevy. Ronan took my work and gave it a very definite structure and advised me on many aspects of putting the final manuscript together. I would also like to acknowledge the work of Elaine O'Neill on the developmental edit.

My agent Faith O'Grady from the Lisa Richards Agency has been brilliant from the outset and was another vital piece of this jigsaw.

I wrote this book over a six-month period while I was recovering from prostate cancer surgery and during this time I focused entirely on writing and researching. My family, especially my mother Sheila and my brothers Kieran and Oliver, were always there during this time to help with their recollections and clarifications around specific events.

About the Author

Photo credit: Derek Ryan

Austin Stack is a retired Irish prison officer and restorative justice advocate with a passionate interest in social justice and social policy issues. He is also a campaigner for a post-conflict commission in Ireland and a regular commentator on Irish media. He lives in Portlaoise with his family.